SQL, PL / SQL

The Programming Language of Oracle

(Second Revised Edition)

by

IVAN BAYROSS

BPB PUBLICATIONS

B-14, CONNAUGHT PLACE, NEW DELHI - 110 001

FIRST EDITION 1998
Distributors:
MICRO BOOK CENTRE
2, City Centre, CG Road,
AHMEDABAD-380009 Phone: 6421611

COMPUTER BOOK CENTRE
12, Shrungar Complex, M. G. Road,
BANGALORE-560001 Phone: 5587923, 5584641

MICRO BOOKS
Shanti Niketan Building, 8, Camac Street,
CALCUTTA-700017
Phone: 2426518, 2426519

BUSINESS PROMOTION BUREAU
8/1, Ritchie Street, Mount Road,
CHENNAI-600002 Phone: 834796, 8550491

BPB BOOK CENTRE
376, Old Lajpat Rai Market,
DELHI-110006 Phone: 2961747

DECCAN AGENCIES
4-3-329, Bank Street,
HYDERABAD-500195 Phone: 512280, 593826

MICRO MEDIA
Shop No. 5, Mahendra Chambers,
150 D.N. Road, FORT, MUMBAI-400001
Phone: 2078296, 2078297, 2002732

INFO TECH
G-2, Sidhartha Building, 96 Nehru Place,
NEW DELHI-110019 Phone: 643825, 6415092, 6234208

INFO TECH
Shop No. 2, F-38, South Extension-1,
NEW DELHI-110049 Phone: 4691288, 4641941

INFO TECH
B-11, Vardhman Plaza, Sector-16, Electronics Nagar,
NOIDA-201301 Phone: 91-512329

COMPUTER BOOK CENTRE
SCF No.-65, Sector-6, PANCHKULA-134109,
CHANDIGARH Phone: 561613, 567538

ISBN 81-7656-072-3

Published by Manish Jain for BPB Publications, B-14, Connaught Place,
New Delhi-110001 and Printed by him at Pressworks, Delhi.

Foreword

Oracle's Workgroup or Enterprise Server, are the world's largest selling RDBMS products. It is estimated that the combined sales of both these Oracle products account for more than 80% of RDBMS engines sold worldwide.

A very large amount of commercial applications are developed around these products. Most ERP software such as SAP R3, Avalon, Marshall, PeopleSoft, Oracle Applications and a host of other such client software work with the Oracle RDBMS engine worldwide.

Whether a corporate entity chooses to use Oracle Work Group or Enterprise Server, the natural programming language of both of these products is ANSI SQL and PL/SQL.

This book has been written to address the need of programmers who wish to have a ready reference book, with examples, which covers ANSI SQL and PL/SQL.

The creation of User Defined Functions, Procedures, Database triggers and other specific data processing PL/SQL code blocks for commercial applications will always require programmers who can code comfortably in ANSI SQL and PL/SQL.

Exception handling, Oracle's default locking and User defined locking has been covered in a fair amount of detail. However these areas are of great interest to commercial application developers.

Programmers with these explicit skills will always find employment in that segment of the software industry, which develops commercial applications.

I have tried to use my extensive commercial application development experience in Oracle using ANSI SQL and PL/SQL to produce a book that has answers to most of the questions that seem to puzzle programmers in ANSI SQL and PL/SQL.

Every single programming question has not been answered, indeed if I tried to actually do that I would fail since I believe that I myself have not encountered every single programming problem. However, I've chosen several key areas in commercial applications and tried to address a set of issues that most commercial application developers require.

Concepts are built using simple language. Examples have easily understood logic. Once this is grasped, the skill gained, must allow any commercial application developer to develop programs in ANSI SQL and PL/SQL very very quickly.

This foreword would not be complete without my thanking the many people who encouraged me and put up with my many revisions and updations of the material with patience and tolerance.

My sincere "THANKS" goes to:

1. My publisher Mr. Manish Jain who has criticized me and made me redo my work sometimes, each time I've improved. Thanks Manish, I'm getting better each day.

2. Ms. Nagalakshmi Iyer who tested each example in this book, then formatted this book to complete my satisfaction. Lakshmi, honestly, this book would have NEVER made it without you and the "TLC" you gave it.

3. Ms. Mita Engineer who criticized the flow of topics in this book and forced Lakshmi and I to rearrange chapters and chapter content several times.

4. The many graduate engineers who study Oracle Developer 2000 at SCT. Each time you found a mistake and suggested a correction you helped me towards perfection. A very big "Thank You".

5. The many programmers who read this book I would welcome your brickbats or bouquets. Without you I would not be an author. You can contact me via my publisher Mr. Manish Jain at BpB New Delhi.

6. Finally to my wife Cynthia who always encouraged me whenever I thought that I'd never get this manuscript ready for publishing. You've always helped keep my feet planted firmly on the ground, with you I am truly blessed.

Ivan N. Bayross.

TABLE OF CONTENTS

Introduction to Managing Data

CHAPTER ONE

IN THIS CHAPTER

> ➤ An introduction to Understanding and Managing Data.

> ➤ Basic Database Concepts

> ➤ The Oracle Product Philosophy

> ➤ Commercial Application Development using Oracle products.

1. INTRODUCTION TO MANAGING DATA

Since you are reading this material, you are already a programmer or have decided to be a programmer. Hence, you will earn your living by managing other people's data for them. To achieve this, the decision to use a computer and a programming environment to manage human data has also been made. The precise programming environment chosen is Oracle using both its Client and Server programming tools.

UNDERSTANDING HUMAN DATA

Let's take a very brief look at human data. Our purpose in doing so is to try and understand whether human data is very complex, if this is so, then by default any system designed to manage this data would in turn be very complex. On the other hand if human data is not complex at all, then any system designed to manage it need not be complex.

If we look hard enough, we should begin to understand that *any kind of human data* we would wish to manage could be expressed either in *Characters* or *Numbers*. *Numbers* may be of two distinct types either *Whole Numbers* or *Floats*, (i.e. numbers with decimal points). Hence, all human data that we will ever manage can be grouped under the two distinct types *Characters* or *Numbers*. This is simple enough, projecting from this, any system used to manage human data cannot be extremely complex.

However, there is a major problem faced when we attempt to manage human data using a computer. Human data is traditionally *Free Form*.

Let's take a very simple example of someone's name. A name can be as small as; four to six characters, e.g. Jane, Jude, Jyoti or *as long as you want it to be* e.g. Venkateshwarlu Velamakanni a very common Telegu name. Thus *names* can be of almost any length. There is nothing pre-determined or rigid about a name. Hence, a name can be conceptualized as *Free Form*.

Hence, we have to get '*Free Form*' human data to appear '*Rigid*' to a computer, so that the computer can manage the data. To achieve this we need to understand the methods humans use to manage other '*Free Form*' materials in day to day life. Then find out if an '*Equivalent Method*' exists using a computer and a '*Programming Environment*'. If such a method does exist, then it should be relatively simple to manage free form human data using a computer.

A simple example of '*Free From*' material is water i.e. a *liquid*. To manage liquids, place the liquid in a container, such as a glass, then manage the glass. This in turn allows the '*Free Form*' material to be managed. Using this as a base, let's see if we can do the same thing or something similar with computers and '*Free Form*' human data.

The idea being to place '*Free Form*' human data into a container of some kind and then get the computer to manage the container. The container being created, maintained and managed via the programming environment we have chosen to work with.

Any programming environment used to create containers, to manage human data, can be conceptualized as a *Data Management System*. Traditionally, the *block* of human data being managed is called a *Database*. Hence, in very simple terms these programming environments can be conceptualized as DataBase Management Systems, in short DBMSystems.

All Database Management Systems (i.e. **Oracle** being one of them) allow users to create containers for data storage and management. These containers are called '*Cells*' The minimum information that has to be given to Oracle for a suitable container to be constructed which can hold free form human data is

- The Cell Name
- The Cell Length
- The type of Data that can be placed into the Cell

Cell Name:

When we wish to view the contents of a cell later, all we need to do is tell the programming environment the cell name. The programming environment is intelligent enough to fetch for us *contents of the cell* rather than the cell itself.

Cell Length:

This is the manner we '*Rigidize*' free form human data. We create a container of a pre-determined length into which we will store '*Free Form*' human data for management. If we map this, to the example on names we were looking at earlier, this automatically puts a limit on the length of a person's '*Name*' that we can hold in the container. We will have to try our best and decide on the longest name we wish to manage and decide on the container length accordingly.

Cell Data Type:

As we had a look earlier, human data is mainly of two types, Character or Numbers, if Numbers then we can have Whole numbers or Floats. We would then have to inform the programming environment, which is creating the cell for us, what kind of data we will store in the cell when it is being used.

Another name that programming environments use for a '*Cell*' is '*Field*' these names can be used interchangeably and generally mean the same thing.

Lets use Oracle to create several '*Fields*' (or '*Cells*') in the same horizontal plane. This will look like:

Name	Age	TelephoneNo
20 Characters	2N	8 Numbers

This really means that we have asked Oracle to create three '*Fields*' for us. The name of the first field is '*Name*', the name of the second field is '*Age*' and the name of the last field is '*TelephoneNo*'. The first field can take a maximum of 20 characters, the second field can take a maximum of 2 numbers, and the third field can take a maximum of 8 numbers.

After we have filled data in the first set of three fields and we have more data to manage, Oracle will oblige us by giving us another set of three fields to fill up. These three fields will be stored exactly below the other set of three fields. This will look like the diagram 1.1 below.

Name	Age	TelephoneNo
20 Characters	2 N	8 Numbers

Diagram 1.1 : Multiple sets of fields placed one below the other

We could imagine that each *field* was an *object* created for us by Oracle. Then the *three fields* created for us in the same horizontal plane would be <u>*another distinct object*</u> created for us by Oracle. Multiple fields placed in the same horizontal plane is an object called a '<u>*Record*</u>'. Several '*Records*', of equal length, placed one below the other to enable users to continue to store data are called a '<u>*Table*</u>'.

Hence a '*Table*' can be visualized as a two dimensional matrix, consisting of '*Rows and Columns*' used for storing data. The '*Table*' therefore becomes the third object after '*Field*' and '*Row*' that Oracle will create for users to help us manage human data.

A **group** of '*Tables*' with '*Related*' data in them is called a '*Database*'

BASIC DATABASE CONCEPTS

What is a database?

It is a coherent collection of data with some inherent meaning, designed, built and populated with data for a specific purpose. A database stores data that is useful to us. This data is only a part of the entire data available in the world around us.

To be able to successfully design and maintain databases we have to do the following:
1) Identify which part of the world's data is of interest to us.
2) Identify what specific objects in that part of the world's data are of interest to us.
3) Identify a relationship between the objects.

Hence, the objects, their attributes and the relationship between them that are of interest to us are stored in the database that is designed, built and populated with data for a specific purpose.

Software houses took up the challenge of designing a system that would help users in managing data in a database. These systems were called <u>Database Management Systems (DBMS)</u>. Some of the DBMS developed by software houses were Oracle, Ingress, Sybase, etc. Let us look at Oracle as a Database Management System (DBMS).

ORACLE 8.XX - THE PRODUCT PHILOSOPHY

Introduction to Oracle and Its Tools:

The Oracle product is primarily divided into
* Oracle Server tools
* Oracle Client tools

<u>Oracle Server:</u>
Oracle is a company that produces the most widely used, Server based, Multi user RDBMS. The Oracle Server is a program installed on the Server's hard disk drive. This program must be loaded in RAM so that it can process user requests.

This Oracle Server product is either called

       Oracle Workgroup Server
           Or
       Oracle Enterprise Server

The functionality of both these products is identical. However, the *Oracle Workgroup Server* restricts the number of concurrent users who can query the Server. *Oracle Enterprise Server* has no such restrictions. Either product must be loaded on a multi-user operating system.

The Oracle Server takes care of the following:

- Updating the database.
- Retrieving information from the database.
- Accepting query language statements.
- Enforcing security specifications.
- Enforcing data integrity specifications.
- Enforcing transaction consistency.
- Managing data sharing.
- Optimizing queries.
- Managing system catalogs.

The Oracle kernel product (*Workgroup or Enterprise Server*) when loaded from the hard disk drive into a computer's memory (RAM) is called the *Oracle DBA, Oracle Engine or Oracle Server or just plain Oracle*. Please refer diagram 1.2

Oracle Engine functionality:
The Oracle Engine can compile and execute SQL sentences issued by a user. If the SQL sentence fails for any reason, Oracle Engine returns an appropriate error message to the user. Very briefly this is shown in diagram 1.2

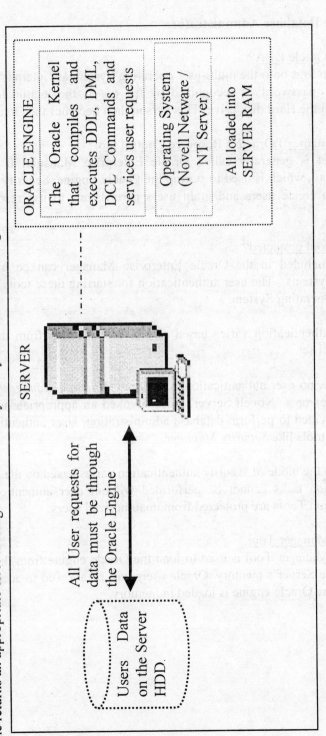

ORACLE ENGINE

The Oracle Kernel that compiles and executes DDL, DML, DCL Commands and services user requests

Operating System (Novell Netware / NT Server)

All loaded into SERVER RAM

SERVER

All User requests for data must be through the Oracle Engine

Users Data on the Server HDD.

Diagram 1.2 : Working with the Oracle Engine.

The Oracle Database Administrator:

Who is the Oracle DBA?
Anyone who logs onto the multi-user operating System as 'internal' or 'system' with the appropriate 'password' is recognized by the o/s as the legitimate owner of 'Oracle' resources on the Hard disk drive. This person then becomes the Oracle DBA.

What is the name of Oracle's Resource Control tool?
The tool set is generally called Oracle Enterprise Manager. It includes the Server Manager Tool, which is used to startup the Oracle Engine, Security Manager that allows the DBA to create users and grant users permissions to use resources of the Oracle database.

How is the tool protected?
The tools included in the Oracle Enterprise Manager can be installed on different Operating Systems. The user authentication for starting these tools vary from Operating System to Operating System.

The user authentication varies based on the tool invoked from the Oracle Enterprise Manager tool set.

For example, no user authentication is required if *Server Manager* is invoked either on an NT Server or a Novell Server. Once invoked an appropriate user-id and password must be provided to perform database administration. User authentication is required to invoke GUI tools like *Security Manager*.

Thus though the mode of security authentication varies based on the tools used, Database Administration tasks cannot be performed without user authentication. All Database Administration Tools are protected from unauthorized users.

The Server Manager Tool
The Server Manager Tool is used to load the Oracle engine from the Server's hard disk drive into the Server's memory. Oracle users will be allowed to access Oracle resources only when the Oracle engine is loaded in memory.

The Security Manager Tool

Once the Oracle engine is running, the Security Manager tool can be used by the DBA to create user accounts and grant permission to the user accounts. Creation of a user account will provide users with:

i). Login identity.

ii). A password.

iii). Permission to use Oracle resources

The login identity and the password will allow a user to connect to the Oracle Database. Once connected to the Oracle database, a user can create or use the Oracle Resources like tables, views etc. depending on the permissions granted by the DBA.

Oracle Client Tools:

Once the Oracle Engine is loaded into a server's memory, users would have to log into the engine to get work done. Oracle Corporation has several client-based tools that facilitate this. The client tool most commonly used for Commercial Application Development is called Oracle Developer 2000.

Interaction between Oracle Engine and Oracle Client tools:

Diagram below illustrates the interaction between an Oracle client and a multi-user Oracle engine and the hard disk of the server.

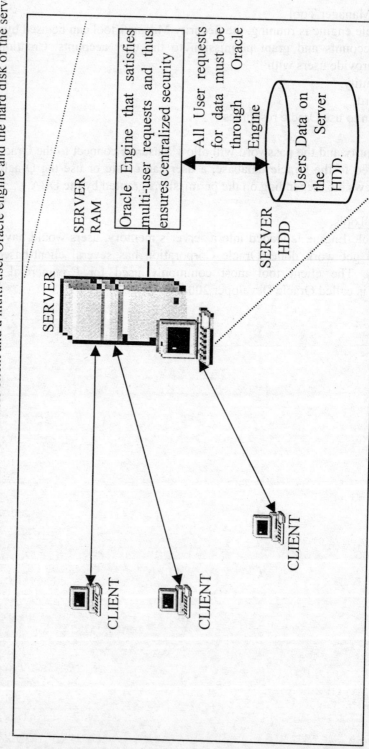

Diagram 1.3 : Interaction between Oracle Clients – Oracle Engine and the Server hard disk drive with data on it.

Commercial Application Development Using Oracle:

Oracle products are tightly connected to commercial application development. Let us identify the components of a commercial application and then link the development of each of these components to a specific Oracle product.

The components of any commercial application when viewed from the *bottom up* are:

<u>A Data Storage System:</u>
All commercial applications manipulate data. Prior the manipulation of data, it has to be stored. Hence logically the lowest layer in any commercial applications is a data storage system. The data storage product, created and marketed by Oracle is either *Oracle Workgroup Server* or *Oracle Enterprise Server*.

<u>A Data Capture And Validation System:</u>
Immediately above the data storage system will be a data capture and validation system.

Business managers will make business decisions based on the data stored in the data storage system. If the data in the storage system lacks integrity then it is likely that the business decision will be erroneous. Hence it is imperative that the data being stored is captured, *validated* and only then stored.

The data capture and validation system, generally **'Forms'** based, will therefore be the layer immediately above the data storage system in a commercial application.

The tool with which a 'Forms' based data capture system is created will have to provide some method, which allows programmers to attach validation code to the data capture objects. This validation code is the means by which 'Business Rules' are applied to the data being captured.

Immediately after data is captured, the 'Business Rule' validation code executes and validates the data captured. If the data captured fails its validation it is rejected and not stored, if it passes its validation the data is permanently stored in the data storage system for further use when required.

The Oracle product that is used for the creation of 'Forms based' data capture and validation objects is called *'Forms Designer'*. Forms Designer is one tool (from among several) inside the Oracle toolbox called *Oracle Developer 2000*.

A Menu System:

It is impossible to create an entire commercial application using a single data capture and validation, form object. This is because a data capture and validation, form object, used to capture 'Financial' data will have a different set of 'Business Rules' to validate the captured data when compared to form object used to capture 'Material Inventory' data.

Hence conceptually there has to be a unique object, a level above the form based data capture and validation objects, that will allow the user of the commercial application to invoke any data capture and validation object, *in any sequence*.

Such an object in commercial applications is traditionally called a 'Menu Object' *i.e. a menu for the commercial application.*

The Oracle product that is used for the creation of a 'Menu' is called *'Oracle Menu'.* Oracle Menu is one tool (from among several) inside the Oracle toolbox called *Oracle Developer 2000.*

A Reports Extraction System:

Generation of textual reports:

Once valid data is stored in the data storage system it needs to be extracted, formatted as required and displayed to users either on a Visual Display Unit or as hardcopy *i.e.* printed on paper.

The Oracle product that is used for the creation of 'Reports' is called *'Oracle Report Designer'.* Oracle Report Designer is one tool (from among several) inside the Oracle toolbox called *Oracle Developer 2000.*

Generation of graphs:

Often users require that a report has a graphic format rather than a character based format (i.e. line graphs, bar graphs, pie charts) to convey meaning to the user. To facilitate this, the Oracle product used is called *'Oracle Graphics Designer'.* Oracle Graphics Designer is one tool (from among several) inside the Oracle toolbox called *Oracle Developer 2000.*

Hence, conceptually, Oracle (*Workgroup or Enterprise Server*) is a *kernel* package that has a number of tools that can be purchased separately and integrated with the kernel as '*Addons*'. These tools allow the user to create database objects, forms, reports, graphs etc. Some of the tools of Oracle are *Oracle Forms, Oracle Reports and Oracle Graphics*.

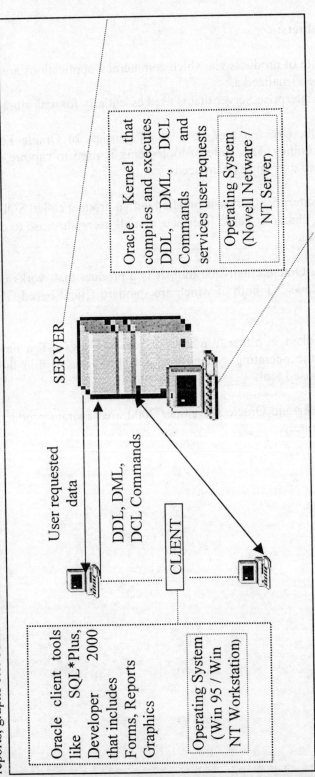

Diagram 1.4 : Various Oracle tools connected to the Oracle engine.

Once the Oracle engine is loaded in the computer's memory, all legitimate users of the network can connect to the Oracle engine and get work done.

Oracle's Suite of products:

Hence Oracle has a suite of products via which commercial applications are created. The suite of products can be visualized as:
Oracle Workgroup or Enterprise Server that is used essentially for data storage.

Oracle Developer 2000, *Oracle's tool box*, which consists of Oracle Forms, Oracle Reports and Oracle Graphics. This suite of tools being is used to capture, validate and display data according to user and system needs.

Oracle Workgroup or Enterprise Server is bundled with a product called SQL*Plus. This is the natural language, character based interface, that all users must use to communicate with Oracle Server products.

SQL*Plus is a separate Oracle client-side tool. It is a product that works on Microsoft Windows 95 and Windows NT both of which are standard Client based GUI operating systems.

Once SQL*Plus is invoked in either Windows 95 or Windows NT a new command window is opened by the operating system and SQL*Plus runs within this command window as a character based tool.

Oracle Workgroup Server and Oracle Developer 2000 are separate products, and they must be purchased separately.

Oracle Client Side Tools:

Oracle for Windows 95:
SQL*PLUS:
The SQL*Plus tool is made up of two distinct parts. These are

- Interactive SQL (iSQL)
- PL/SQL

Interactive SQL is designed to create, access and maintain all data structures like tables, indexes etc. It can also be used for interactive, data manipulation.

Programmers can use *PL/SQL* to create programs for validation and manipulation of table data. PL/SQL adds to the power of interactive SQL and provides the user with all the facilities of a standard, modern day (4GL) programming environment. Via PL/SQL the user can not only manipulate data but also can use procedural techniques such as writing loops or branching to another block of code.

To invoke SQL*Plus, click on the Program Icon *SQL*Plus in* the Oracle Group.

Tools included in Developer 2000:

Oracle Forms:
This Tool allows you to create a data entry screen along with suitable menu objects. Thus it is the Oracle Forms Tool, that handles data gathering and data validation in a commercial application.

To invoke the Oracle Forms Designer tool, click on the Program Icon *Forms Designer* in the *Developer 2000* Group.

Report Writer:
Report Writer allows programmers to prepare innovative reports using data from the Oracle Structures like tables, views etc. It is the Report Writer Tool that handles the reporting section of a commercial application.

To invoke the Oracle Report Designer tool, click on the Program Icon *Reports Designer* in the *Developer 2000* Group.

Oracle Graphics:

Some of the data can be better represented in the form of pictures. The Oracle Graphics Tool allows programmers to prepare graphs using data from Oracle Structures like tables, views etc. Oracle Graphics can also be considered as a part of the reporting section of a commercial application.

 To invoke Oracle Forms Designer tool, click on the Program Icon *Graphics Designer* in the *Developer 2000* Group.

SELF REVIEW QUESTIONS

FILL IN THE BLANKS

1. Human data is traditionally _____.

2. Multiple fields placed in the same horizontal plane are an object called a _____.

3. A group of '*Tables*' with related data in them is called a _____.

4. The various Oracle Tools are:

    *   _____

    *   _____

    *   _____

    *   _____

    *   _____

5. SQL* Plus is made up of _____and _____.

6. The Oracle Server Product is called _____ or _____.

7. All information stored in a database is represented only by data item values, which are stored in _____.

8. The person responsible for administrating all the Oracle's resources on the hard disk drive is called an _____.

TRUE OR FALSE

9. DBMS stands for Data Management System.

A) True   B) False

10. SQL*PLUS is the tool used for Database Administration.

A) True   B) False

➢ **An introduction to Understanding & Managing Data.**

➢ **The Basic Database Concepts.**

➢ **Introduction to the various Oracle Products like :**
- *SQL* Plus*
- *Forms Designer*
- *Reports Designer*
- *Graphics Designer*

➢ **The various components of Commercial Application using Oracle.**

Welcome to the world of Interactive SQL ......

CHAPTER TWO

Interactive SQL

IN THIS CHAPTER

> Client/Server Technology

> An Introduction to SQL*Plus

> The Oracle Data Types

> Creation of Tables and Data
  Manipulation commands for
  Insertion / Updation / Deletion
  of Data in Tables

> Viewing Records from Tables.

> Modifying / Renaming /
  Destroying table structures

2. INTERACTIVE SQL

ORACLE & CLIENT- SERVER TECHNOLOGY

Oracle Server is a multi-user tool that works in a Client/Server environment. Client / Server programming is a form of distributed application processing. It has three distinct components, each focusing on a specific job. The three components are:

1) Oracle Server.
2) Oracle Client Tools.
3) Network for connecting the first two components.

The *Oracle Server* 's (i.e. Oracle back-end) primary job is to manage data optimally, among multiple users that concurrently request for the same data. Access to data, in the data storage system is always via the Oracle Server. This gives a single entry point to access of data. Any one-point, data access system has the capacity of offering excellent data security.

The combination of user_id and password for both the Oracle Server and SQL*Plus tool offers a very high level of security to misuse of data held in any Oracle data storage system.

The *Oracle Client Tools* (i.e. Oracle front-end) is that part of the system that provides an interface to the user so that the data retrieved from the Server can be manipulated. It allows users to pass data manipulation requests to the Oracle Server. The Oracle Server then interacts with the user by displaying data and messages (if any) as requested by the user.

The Network and Communication software is the vehicle that transports data between Oracle Client Tools and the Oracle Server. Both the Oracle Client Tools and the Oracle Server run communication software that allows them to talk across a network. The name of this software is SQL*NET.

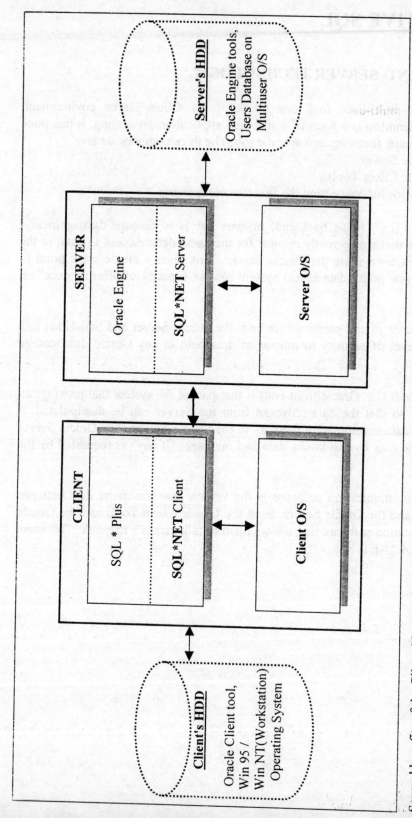

Several benefits of the Client / Server model stem from the fact that the client and server portions of the system run on separate computers. Hence each computer in the system can be carefully chosen to fit the needs of the system.

Operating System requirements for Oracle Server Software:

Before installing the Oracle Server Software, an operating system needs to be installed on the Server Computer.

Commonly used operating systems are:
Novell Netware
SCO-Unix
Windows NT

Note

An Operating System specific copy of the Oracle Server Software must be loaded on the computer.
For example: If the Operating system is Windows NT then Oracle Server for Win NT must be installed on the Server machine.

Operating System requirements for Oracle Client Tools:

Before installing Oracle Client tools, an appropriate operating system like Windows 95 or Windows NT Workstation needs to be installed on the client computer.

Oracle Client side tools, that come bundled in a tool kit called *Developer 2000*, comprises of:
a) Oracle SQL*Plus
b) Oracle Forms Designer
c) Oracle Reports Designer
d) Oracle Graphics

For example: If the Operating system on the client machine is Windows NT then the user needs to load Oracle Developer 2000 for Win NT on the Client machine.

Developer 2000 allows programmers to create forms based Commercial Application with Client/Server Architecture.

Oracle SQL Plus* is a separate tool that comes as a part of Oracle Enterprise Server as well as Oracle Workgroup Server via which users can communicate interactively with the Oracle Server. Please refer to diagram 2.1 which is a graphical representation if the above.

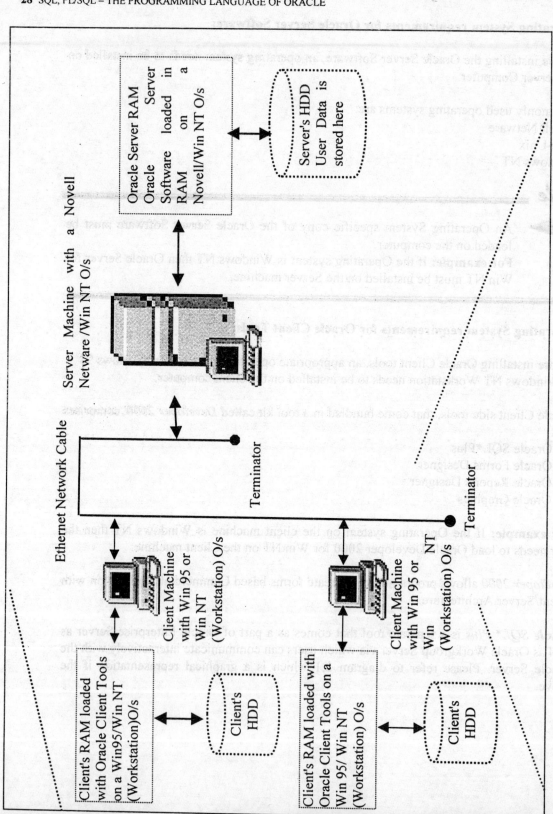

Diagram 2.1 : Oracle and the Client/Server Model

INVOKING SQL*PLUS

The product Oracle Server can be called Oracle DBA, Oracle Engine or Oracle Server interchangeably. This is when the product is loaded into a computer's memory. To avoid confusion between the *product Oracle Server* and the *'Server computer'* from now on (both the Oracle Workgroup Server and the Oracle Enterprise Server) will be referred to as the **Oracle Engine.**

To work with Oracle Engine the user needs to be able to communicate with it when loaded in a server's memory. The natural language of the Oracle Engine is ANSI SQL (Structured Query Language). Oracle provides an Interactive SQL tool called *SQL*Plus*, which allows users to enter ANSI SQL sentences and pass them to the Oracle Engine for execution.

These sentences allow the user to create, access and maintain data structures like tables, indexes etc. To use ANSI SQL the user must load the SQL*PLUS tool in a client's memory, link to the server and then communicate with the Oracle Engine loaded on the Server.

SQL*Plus is a character based interactive tool, that runs in a GUI environment. It is loaded on the client machine. This is the first tool to be used by most programmers when they begin their study of Oracle.

The Steps In Invoking SQL*Plus:

1. Start Windows 95 in the normal way.

2. Click on the **Start** button as shown in diagram 2.2 and click on **Programs**. It displays a list of programs. Click on **Oracle for Win 95** and then select **SQL*Plus**.

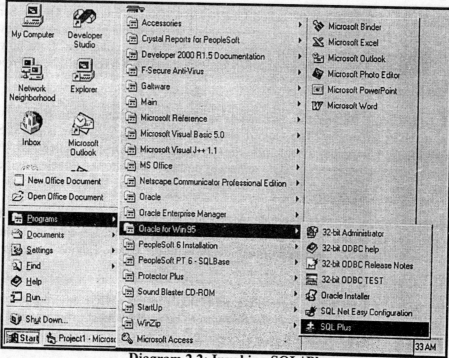

Diagram 2.2: Invoking SQL*Plus

3. You are prompted for your Oracle Login-id and password as shown in diagram 2.3. This is done in-order to connect to the Oracle Server.

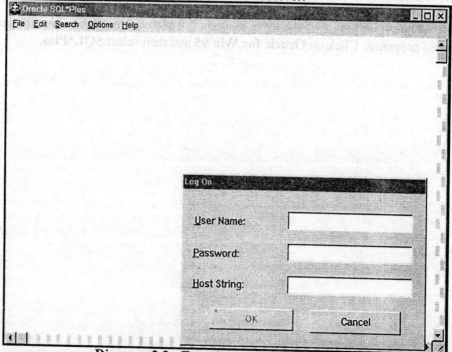

Diagram 2.3 : Entering user id and password

4. The SQL* Plus tool needs to know what protocol to use to communicate with the Server. The most commonly used protocols are:

IPX/SPX   Novell Netware
Net BEUI   Win NT
TCP/IP   SCO UNIX

Additionally, the SQL*Plus tool needs to know the name of the Server to connect to. This is because the tool SQL*Plus maybe invoked in a multi Server, multi protocol network.

If no values are passed to the 'Host String' variable then the SQL* Plus tool reads the Windows Registry for this information.

Tip

If connectivity protocol and the Server name is not known to the SQL*Plus tool, it will fail to connect to a Server and will not find an Oracle Engine to link to.

The Windows Registry has appropriate connectivity protocol information in addition to a Server name as part of its content.

The entries in the Windows registry are made when SQL*Plus and other Oracle client tools are installed and configured on the client computer.

Once Login-id and password are entered, an *SQL>* prompt appears, as shown in diagram 2.4.

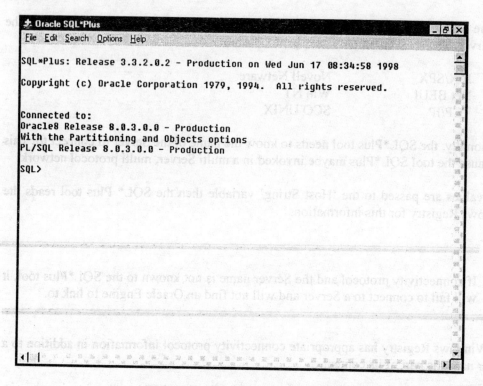

Diagram 2.4 : Working with SQL*Plus

At this point in time, you are connected to the Oracle engine that is on the Server. The SQL*Plus tool allows you to pass SQL statements to the engine. SQL*Plus also allows access to *PL/SQL* i.e. the *Procedural Language* of the Oracle engine. PL/SQL will be covered in-depth in later chapters.

STEPS FOR CREATING SHORTCUTS ON THE DESKTOP

Create an MS Window95 shortcut for invoking any Oracle Product like SQL*Plus, Forms Designer, etc. This is very useful, as each time there is no need click on **Start..Programs..Oracle for Win 95..SQL*Plus** etc. to start an application.

The steps involved in creating a shortcut are:

1. When Win 95 is invoked, it displays a startup screen. This startup screen is called Windows 95 Desktop. *Right click* on the Windows 95 Desktop. It displays a pop up menu with several menu items one of which is *New* as shown in Diagram 2.5.

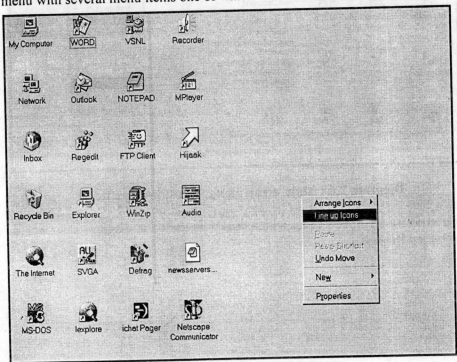

Diagram 2.5 : Windows 95 Desktop

2. Click on the Menu Item New. It displays submenu items *Folder* and *Shortcuts*. See diagram 2.6

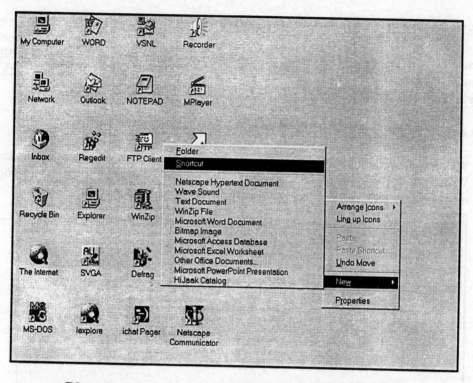

Diagram 2.6 : Main menu along with sub-menu items

3. Click on *Shortcuts*. It comes up with a screen as shown in diagram 2.7. Click on the push button **Browse**.

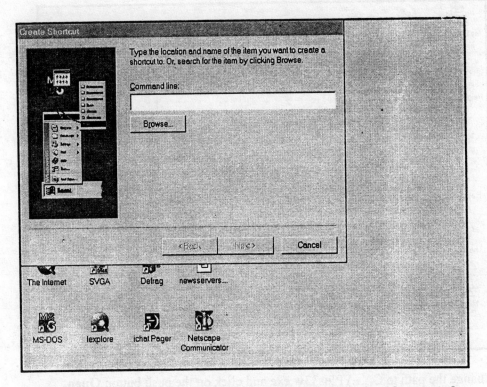

Diagram 2.7 : Location of the file for which shortcut is to be created.

4.   The screen appears as in Diagram 2.8.

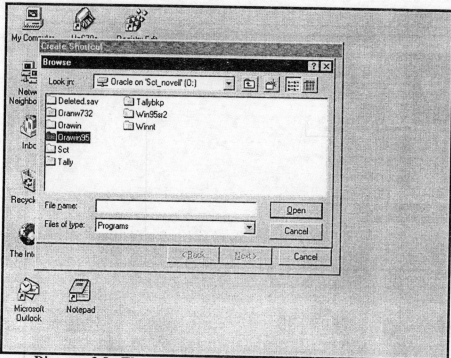

Diagram 2.8 : The screen after clicking the on the Browse button

5.   Change the path to C:\...\ Plus33w.exe and click on the push button **Open**.

Find out the correct path of your installation by asking the Installation Administrator

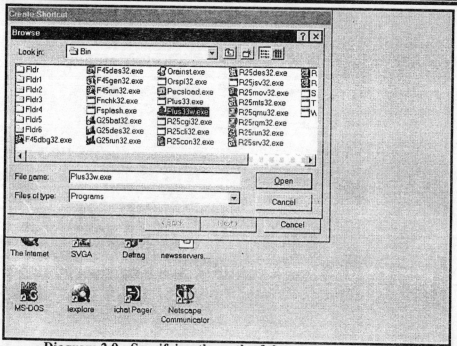

Diagram 2.9 : Specifying the path of the executable file.

6. The next screen as in Diagram 2.10 appears. Specify the name of the shortcut. By default the name of the .exe file appears in the text box. Then Click on **Finish.**

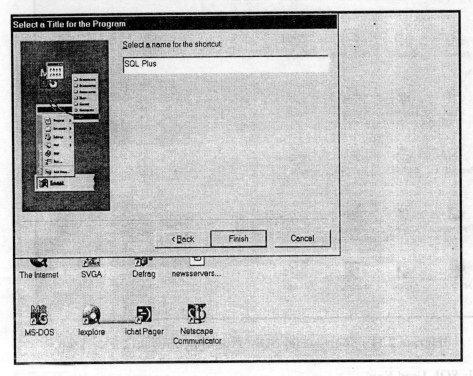

Diagram 2.10 : Giving the shortcut a name.

7. The shortcut for SQL Plus is now created and appears on the desktop as shown in diagram 2.11. By double clicking on the shortcut it opens up SQL*Plus. Similarly the user can create other shortcuts to other applications.

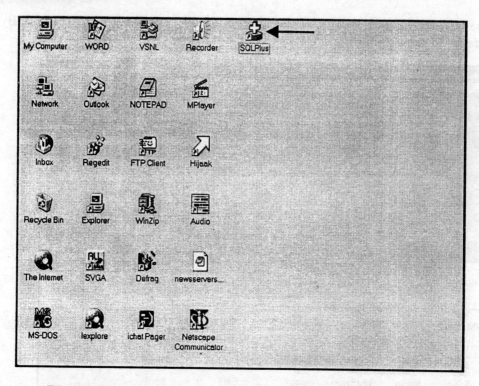

Diagram 2.11 : Shortcut for SQL*Plus appearing on the desktop.

What Is SQL Used For:

Using SQL one can create and maintain data manipulation objects such as tables, views, sequences etc. These data manipulation objects will be created and stored on the server's hard disk drive, in a tablespace, to which the user has been assigned.

Once these data manipulation objects are created, they are used extensively in commercial applications.

DML, DCL, DDL:

In addition to the creation of data manipulation objects, the actual manipulation of data within these objects is done using SQL.

The SQL sentences that are used to create these objects are called DDL's or **D**ata **D**efinition **L**anguage. The SQL sentences used to manipulate data within these objects are called DML's or **D**ata **M**anipulation **L**anguage. The SQL sentences, which are used to control the behavior of these objects, are called DCL's or **D**ata **C**ontrol **L**anguage.

Hence, once access to the SQL*Plus tool is available and SQL syntax is known, the creation of data storage and the manipulation of data within the storage system, required by commercial applications, is possible.

DATA MANIPULATION IN DATA BASE MANAGEMENT SYSTEMS

All organizations need to collect, process and store data for its human, financial, material needs. For example, an organization could store information for Payroll, Accounts Receivable and Payable, Sales Receivable and Forecast or Design and Manufacturing.

Table / Entity:

To represent this information one can use DBMS modeling. In a DBMS a group of similar information or data which is of interest to an organization is called an **Entity**. Entity information is stored in an object called **Table**. For example, a *client* is considered an entity. Information about the client entity can be stored in a client_master table. A *table* is really a two dimensional matrix that consists of rows and columns.

The table must have a unique name (i.e. ***client_master***) via which it can be referred to, after its creation. The Oracle engine can manipulate data stored in such an object, (i.e. a table) at very high speed.

The Component Parts Of A Two Dimensional Matrix:

Attributes / Columns / Fields:
Each entity can have a number of characteristics. A client can have characteristics like name, address, telephone number, fax number, balance due etc. The characteristics of an entity are called **Attributes**. The values for these characteristics are called **Attribute values**.

When entity information is stored in a table, the attributes associated with the entity are stored in the table columns / table fields. The client_master table can have columns like name, address, telephone_number, fax_number, bal_due in which the user can store attributes values like 'Datamatics', 'Vile Parle (E)', '6124571', '6111646', '4500.00'.

Thus information in the client_master table will be

Name	Address	Telephone Number	Fax Number	Balance Due
Datamatics	Vile Parle (E)	6124571	6111646	4500.00

Tuple / Record / Row:
An organization will deal with many clients and the same information must be recorded for each client. Multiple *fields* placed in a *horizontal plane*, is called a **Record** or **Row** or **Tuple**.

Thus information in the client_master table will be:

Name	Address	Telephone Number	Fax Number	Balance Due
Datamatics	Vile Parle (E)	6124571	6111646	4500.00
Sampoorna	Santacruz (W)	5755342	7456443	90.00
Videocon	Fort	7977353	5745342	7000.00
Citicorp	Seepz	34364754	6007734	300.00

To create a column / field, to store, maintain and manipulate data, the engine requires a minimum of three parameters to be passed by the creator. These parameters are *column name*, *column size* and *column data type*. These parameters are passed to the engine, via its natural language, SQL. The tool used is SQL*Plus.

The field *Name* is of type **char** (character) with size 20, the field *address* is of type **char** with size 100 and the field *balance_due* is of type **number** with size 8 and so on.

There are several other parameters that a creator can pass to the engine at column creation time. Some of these parameters will place *constraints* on the data that a user can load into the column.

The various data types, recognized by the Oracle engine and permitted to be used for creating an Oracle table column are defined below.

THE DATA TYPES THAT A CELL CAN HOLD

Data Type		Description
CHAR(size)	:	This data type is used to store character strings values of fixed length. The size in brackets determines the number of characters the cell can hold. The maximum number of characters (i.e. the size) this data type can hold is 255 characters. ORACLE compares CHAR values using blank-padded comparison semantics i.e. if a value that is inserted in a cell of CHAR datatype is shorter than the size it is defined for then it will be padded with spaces on the right until it reaches the size characters in length.
VARCHAR (size) / VARCHAR2 (size)	:	This data type is used to store variable length alphanumeric data. The maximum this data type can hold is 2000 characters. One difference between this data type and the CHAR data type is ORACLE compares VARCHAR values using non-padded comparison semantics i.e. the inserted values will not be padded with spaces.

Data Type		Description
NUMBER(P, S)	:	The NUMBER data type is used to store numbers (fixed or floating point). Numbers of virtually any magnitude maybe stored up to 38 digits of precision. Numbers as large as 9.99 * 10 to the power of 124, i.e. 1 followed by 125 zeros can be stored. The precision, (P), determines the maximum length of the data, whereas the scale, (S), determines the number of places to the right of the decimal. If scale is omitted then the default is zero. If precision is omitted, values are stored with their original precision upto the maximum of 38 digits.
DATE	:	This data type is used to represent date and time. The standard format is DD-MON-YY as in 21-JUN-98. To enter dates other than the standard format, use the appropriate functions. DateTime stores date in the 24-hour format. By default, the time in a date field is 12:00:00 am, if no time portion is specified. The default date for a date field is the first day of the current month.
LONG	:	This data type is used to store variable length character strings containing upto 2GB. LONG data can be used to store arrays of binary data in ASCII format. LONG values cannot be indexed, and the normal character functions such as SUBSTR cannot be applied to LONG values.
RAW / LONG RAW	:	The RAW /LONG RAW data types is used to store binary data, such as digitized picture or image. Data loaded into columns of these data types are stored without any further conversion. RAW data type can have a maximum length of 255 bytes. LONG RAW data type can contain up to 2GB. Values stored in columns having LONG RAW data type cannot be indexed.

TWO DIMENSION MATRIX CREATION

One needs to communicate with the Oracle engine to create a two dimensional matrix (i.e. a table) for the storage and manipulation of data. This must be done using the natural language of the Oracle Engine i.e. SQL.

By using an SQL sentence we can command the engine to create a table with cell parameters of our choice. Hence, it is necessary to understand how to construct standard SQL sentences. A look at a *generic* SQL sentence will help understand SQL syntax.

The Generic SQL Sentence Construct:

Verb:
[Clause **1**]<para1:1 para1:2 para1:**n**>,
[Clause **2**]<para2:1 para2:2 para2:**n**>, ... [Clause **n**];

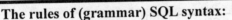

Note

The rules of (grammar) SQL syntax:
- An SQL statement starts with a *verb*. This verb may have additional *nouns* and *adjectives*.
- Each *verb* is followed by a number of *clauses*.
- Each *clause* has one or more *parameters*. Beyond this no further decomposition is allowed i.e. parameters cannot in turn have sub-parameters.
- A *space* separates *clauses* within an SQL statement.
- A *comma* separates *parameters* within a clause.
- A *semi colon* is used to *terminate* the SQL statement.

The Create Table Command:

<u>Syntax:</u>

> **CREATE TABLE** *tablename*
> *(columnname datatype(size), columnname datatype(size))*;

As seen in the CREATE TABLE syntax, the SQL statement starts with 'CREATE' i.e. a verb, followed by 'TABLE' i.e. a noun and '<tablename>' i.e. adjective.

The CREATE TABLE command includes a single clause for the column definition. Each column is a parameter for the clause and thus it is separated by comma.

Finally, the SQL statement is terminated with a semi colon.

<u>Example:</u>

1. Create a client_master table who structure is:

Column Name	Data Type	Size
client_no	varchar2	6
name	varchar2	20
address1	varchar2	30
address2	varchar2	30
city	varchar2	15
state	varchar2	15
pincode	number	6
remarks	varchar2	60
bal_due	number	10,2

> **CREATE TABLE** *client_master*
> *(client_no varchar2(6), name varchar2(20), address1 varchar2(30),*
> *address2 varchar2(30), city varchar2(15), state varchar2(15),*
> *pincode number(6), remarks varchar2(60), bal_due number(10,2));*

2. Create a product_master table whose structure is:

Column Name	Data Type	Size
product_no	varchar2	6
description	varchar2	25
profit_percent	number	4,2
unit_measure	varchar2	10
qty_on_hand	number	8
reorder_lvl	number	8
sell_price	number	8,2
cost_price	number	8,2

CREATE TABLE *product_master*
  (product_no varchar2(6), description varchar2(25),
  profit_percent number(4,2), unit_measure varchar2(10),
  qty_on_hand number(8), reorder_lvl number(8),
  sell_price number (8,2), cost_price number (8,2));

In addition to creating a table as above, a table can be created from another existing table. The syntax for doing so is as described under.

INSERTION OF DATA INTO TABLES

Once a table is created the most natural thing to do is load this table with data to be manipulated later. The appropriate SQL sentence syntax is:

When inserting a single row of data into the table, the *insert operation*:

- Creates a new row in the database table
- Loads the values passed into all the columns specified.

Syntax:
  INSERT INTO *tablename*
    (columnname, columnname)
  VALUES (*expression, expression*);

Example:

1. Insert the following values into the client_master table

Column Name	Values
client_no	C02000,
name	Prabhakar Rane,
address1	A-5, Jay Apartments,
address2	Service Road, Vile Parle,
city	Bombay,
state	Maharashtra,
pincode	400057;

INSERT INTO *client_master*
  (client_no, name, address1, address2, city, state, pincode)
  VALUES (*'C02000', 'Prabhakar Rane', 'A-5, Jay Apartments',*
  'Service Road, Vile Parle', 'Bombay', 'Maharashtra', 400057);

Tip

The character expressions must be enclosed in single quotes.(')

In the *insert into* SQL sentence the columns and values have a one to one relationship i.e. the first value described into the first column, the second value described being inserted into the second column and so on.

Hence, if there are exactly the same number of values as there are columns and the values are given in accordance with the way the columns were created. There is no need to indicate the column names in the SQL sentence.

However, if there are less values being described than columns in the table then it is mandatory to indicate both the table column name and its corresponding value in the *insert into* SQL sentence.

VIEWING DATA IN THE TABLES

Once data has been inserted into a table, the next most logical operation would be to view what has been entered. The *'SELECT'* SQL verb is used to achieve this.

All Rows and all Column:

In order to view global table data the syntax is:

<u>Global data extract:</u>
I)   <u>Syntax:</u>

   SELECT (*columnname1........columnname n*) **FROM** *tablename*;

Note

Here *columnname1........columnname n* represents table columns.

II)   <u>Syntax:</u>

   SELECT * FROM *tablename*;

<u>Example:</u>
1. Retrieve the names of the employees and their salaries from the table emp_master;

   SELECT *name, salary* **FROM** *emp_master*;

2. Retrieve all records from table client_master;

   SELECT * FROM *client_master*;

Tip

When data from all rows and columns from the table are to be viewed the syntax of the SELECT statement will be:

   SELECT * from *tablename;*

Oracle allows the user to use the *meta character asterisk (*)*, which is expanded by Oracle to mean *all columns* in the table.

The Oracle Server compiles the sentence, executes it, and retrieves data for all columns/rows from the table.

<u>Filtering Table Data:</u>

While viewing data from a table it is rare that all the data from the table will be required **each time**. Hence, SQL must give us a method of filtering out data that is not required.

The ways of filtering table data will be
- Selected columns and all rows
- Selected rows and all columns
- Selected columns and selected rows

Selected Columns and All Rows:

The retrieval of specific columns from a table:

<u>Syntax:</u>
> **SELECT** *columnname, columname*
> **FROM** *tablename*;

<u>Examples:</u>
1. Retrieve the contents of the columns *client_no* and *name* from the table client_master

> **SELECT** *client_no, name*
> **FROM** *client_master* ;

Selected Rows and All Columns:

If information of a particular client must be retrieved from the table, its retrieval must be based on a specific condition.

The SELECT statement used until now displayed all rows. This is because there was no condition set that informed Oracle about the need to view a specific data set from the table.

Oracle provides the option of using a *'where clause'* in an SQL sentence to apply a filter on the *rows* the select statement will retrieve.

When a *'Where Clause'* is added to the SQL sentence, the Oracle Server compares each record from the table with the condition specified in the *where clause*. Oracle displays only those records that satisfy the specified condition.

<u>Syntax:</u>
> **SELECT** *
> **FROM** *tablename*
> **WHERE** *search condition*;

Example:
1. Retrieve all client_information from the table client_master where the value in the bal_due field is greater than *0*;

> **SELECT** *
>   **FROM** *client_master*
>   **WHERE** bal_due > *0*;

Tip

In the *search condition* all standard operators such as logical, arithmetic, predicates etc. can be used. Their usage in SQL sentences is extensive in later chapters.

Selected Columns and Selected Rows:

To view a specific data set from the table and also a select number of columns the syntax will be:

Syntax:

> **SELECT** *columnname, columnname*
>   **FROM** *tablename*
>   **WHERE** *search condition*;

Example:
2. Retrieve the *client_no, name* from the table client_master where the value in the bal_due field is greater than *5000*;

> **SELECT** *client_no, name*
>   **FROM** *client_master*
>   **WHERE** bal_due > *5000*;

Elimination of duplicates from the Select statement:

A table could hold duplicate rows. In such a case, to see only unique rows the syntax is:

Syntax:

> **SELECT DISTINCT** *columnname,columnname*
>   **FROM** *tablename*;

The *SELECT DISTINCT* SQL syntax scans through the values of the column/s specified and displays unique values from amongst them.

Syntax:

> **SELECT DISTINCT** *
>   **FROM** *tablename*;

The SELECT DISTINCT SQL syntax scans through entire rows, and eliminates rows that have exactly the same contents in each column.

Example:
1. Eliminate the duplicate job descriptions when retrieving data from the job column of the table employee.

> **SELECT DISTINCT** *job*
> **FROM** *employee*;

2. Select only unique rows from the table client_master;

> **SELECT DISTINCT** *
> **FROM** *client_master*;

Sorting data in a table:

Oracle allows data from a table to be viewed in a sorted order. The rows retrieved from the table will be sorted in either ascending or descending order depending on the condition specified in the select sentence. The syntax for viewing data in a sorted order is:

Syntax:

> **SELECT** *
> **FROM** *tablename*
> **ORDER BY** *columnname, columnname[sort order]*;

Example:
1. Retrieve all rows from the table client_master and display this data sorted on the value contained in the field client_no in ascending order;

> **SELECT** *
> **FROM** *client_master*
> **ORDER BY** *client_no*;

Tip

For viewing the data in descending sorted order the word *'desc'* must be mentioned after the column name and before the semi colon in the *order by* clause. In case there is no mention of the sort order, the Oracle engine sorts in *ascending order* by default.

For example:

> **SELECT** *client_no, name, address1, address2, city, pincode*
> **FROM** *client_master*
> **ORDER BY** *client_no* **desc**;

CREATING A TABLE FROM A TABLE

Syntax:
      CREATE TABLE *tablename*
          [(*columnname, columnname*)]
              AS SELECT *columnname, columnname* **FROM** *tablename*;

Tip

The Source table is the table identified in the *'SELECT'* section of this SQL sentence. The Target table is one identified in the *'CREATE'* section of this SQL sentence. This SQL sentence populates the Target table with data from the Source table.

To create a Target table without the records from the source table (i.e. create the structure only), the *select* statement used will have a *'where clause'*. The condition specified in the *where clause* **must not** be satisfied. This means the select statement in the **CREATE TABLE** definition must not retrieve any rows.

Example:
1. Create a table supplier_master from client_master. Select all fields, rename *client_no* with supplier_no and *name* with supplier_name.

      CREATE TABLE *supplier_master*
             (*supplier_no, supplier_name, address1,*
                     address2, city, state, pincode, remarks)
             AS SELECT *client_no, name, address1, address2,*
                 city, state, pincode, remarks
                 FROM *client_master;*

Note

If the Source Table *client_master* was populated with records these will be uploaded in *supplier_master* table.

INSERTING DATA INTO A TABLE FROM ANOTHER TABLE

In addition to inserting data one row at a time into a table, it is quite possible to populate a table with data that already exists in another table. The syntax for doing so is described under:

Syntax:

        INSERT INTO *tablename*

            SELECT *columnname, columnname,*

            FROM *tablename;*

Example:

1.   Insert records into table supplier_master from the table client_master;

        INSERT INTO *supplier_master*

            SELECT *client_no, name, address1, address2,*

                    city, state, pincode, remarks

            FROM *client_master;*

Insertion of a data set into a table from another table:

Syntax:

        INSERT INTO *tablename*

            SELECT *columnname, columnname*

            FROM *tablename*

            WHERE *column = expression;*

Example:

1.   Insert records into the table supplier_master from the table client_master where the field client_no contains the value 'C01001';

        INSERT INTO *supplier_master*

            SELECT *client_no, name, address1, address2,*

                    city, pincode, state, remarks

            FROM *client_master*

            WHERE ***CLIENT_NO = 'C01001';***

DELETE OPERATIONS

The verb DELETE in SQL is used to remove rows from table. To **remove**
- All the rows from a table
                    Or
- A select set of rows from a table

Removal of All Rows:

<u>Syntax:</u>
        DELETE FROM *tablename*;

<u>Example:</u>
1. Delete all rows from the table client_master;

        DELETE FROM *client_master*;

Removal of a Specified Row/s:

<u>Syntax:</u>
        DELETE FROM *tablename* **WHERE** *search condition*;

<u>Example:</u>
2. Delete rows from the table client_master where the value in the bal_due field is less than 500;

        DELETE FROM *client_master* **WHERE** *bal_due < 500*;

UPDATING THE CONTENTS OF A TABLE

The UPDATE command is used to change or modify data values in a table. To **update**
- All the rows from a table
                    Or
- A select set of rows from a table

Updating of All Rows:

<u>Syntax:</u>
        UPDATE *tablename*
            SET *columnname = expression, columnname = expression*;

Example:

1. Give every employee a bonus of 15%. Calculate the 15% amount based on the value held in the column basic_sal of the table emp_master and update the values held in the column net_sal.

> **UPDATE** *emp_master*
> **SET** *netsal = net_sal+ basic_sal* 0.15;*

Updating records conditionally:

Syntax:

> **UPDATE** *tablename*
> **SET** *columnname = expression, columnname = expression...*
> **WHERE** *columnname = expression;*

Example:

2. Update the table client_master change the contents of the field *name* to 'Vijay Kadam' and the contents of the field *address* to 'SCT Jay Apartments' for the record identified by the field *client_no* containing the value 'C02000';

> **UPDATE** *client_master*
> **SET** *name = 'Vijay Kadam' , address1 = 'SCT Jay Apartments'*
> **WHERE** *client_no = 'C02000';*

MODIFYING THE STRUCTURE OF TABLES

Adding New Columns:

Syntax:

> **ALTER TABLE** *tablename*
> **ADD**(*newcolumnname datatype(size), newcolumnname datatype(size)...*);

Example:

1. Add the field's client_tel, which is a field that can hold a number upto 8 digits in length and client_fax, which is a field that can hold number upto 15 digits in length.

> **ALTER TABLE** *client_master*
> **ADD** (*client_tel number(8), client_fax number(15)*);

Modifying Existing Columns:

Syntax:

> **ALTER TABLE** *tablename*
> **MODIFY** (*columnname newdatatype(newsize)*);

Example:
1. Modify the field *client_fax* of the table client_master to now hold a maximum of 25 character values.

> **ALTER TABLE** *client_master*
> **MODIFY** (*client_fax varchar2(25)*);

Restrictions on the ALTER TABLE:

Using the **ALTER TABLE** clause the following tasks **cannot** be performed:

- Change the name of the table.
- Change the name of the column.
- Drop a column.
- Decrease the size of a column if table data exists.

RENAMING TABLES

To rename a table, the syntax is:

Syntax:
> **RENAME** *oldtablename* **TO** *newtablename;*

Example:
1. Rename the table client_master to client_master1;

> **RENAME** *client_master* **TO** *client_master1*;

DESTROYING TABLES

Syntax:
> **DROP TABLE** *tablename*;

Example:
1. Destroy the table client_master and all the data held in it;

> **DROP TABLE** *client_master*;

EXAMINING OBJECTS CREATED BY A USER

Finding out the table/s created by a user:

To determine which tables the user has access to the syntax is:

Syntax:

SELECT * FROM TAB;

The objects name and type are displayed. The Object types i.e. the TABTYPE column in the table TAB will be TABLE, since this is the only object created so far.

Example:

TNAME	TABTYPE	CLUSTERID
CLIENT_MASTER	TABLE	
PRODUCT_MASTER	TABLE	
SALES_ORDER	TABLE	
SALES_ORDER_DETAILS	TABLE	
EMPLOYEE	TABLE	

Finding out the column details of a table created:

To **find** information about the columns defined in the table use the following syntax:

Syntax:

DESCRIBE *tablename;*

This command displays the column names, the data types and the special attributes connected to the table.

Example:
1. Display the columns and their attributes of the table client_master

   DESCRIBE *client_master;*

Output:

Name	Type	Null?
CLIENT_NO	NOT NULL	VARCHAR2(6)
NAME	NOT NULL	VARCHAR2(20)
ADDRESS1		VARCHAR2(30)
ADDRESS2		VARCHAR2(30)
CITY		VARCHAR2(15)
STATE		VARCHAR2(15)
PINCODE		NUMBER(6)
BAL_DUE		NUMBER(10,2)

Note

The DESCRIBE verb displays the names of the columns, their data type and size along with the NOT NULL constraint. The syntax for viewing **additional constraints** that may be placed on the table columns has been explained in detail in Chapter 3.

WORKING WITH AN ASCII EDITOR

SQL is a single sentence language. The sentence once typed at the SQL> prompt cannot be retrieved and corrected if a spelling or syntax error was discovered after it was dispatched to the Oracle engine for processing.

The technique used to overcome this constant retyping of sentences is to create an ASCII file. Place the SQL sentence as the contents of the ASCII file. When the sentence has to be executed, appropriate commands in SQL*Plus opens the ASCII file and passes its contents (the SQL sentences) to the Oracle Server for execution.

Any ASCII editor can be used. One convenient editor to use will be *Windows Notepad Editor, which* is a part of the MS Windows Operating System. Hence, *Notepad* can be invoked while the SQL prompt is on the screen as the *editor of choice*.

- To invoke **Notepad,** Window's full page ASCII editor, from SQL*Plus Tool type **Ed** followed by the *file name* at the SQL Prompt like shown in diagram 2.12. If the file does not exist then the system comes up with a message asking the user to create a new file. Refer diagram 2.12. Click on the push button **Yes.**

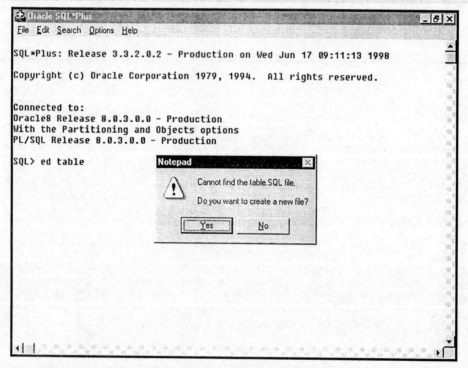

Diagram 2.12 : Creating an ASCII File.

- At this point an ASCII file of the filename specified is opened in memory. See Diagram 2.13. Start to type in SQL sentences in the ASCII File. *Each SQL sentence is to be terminated with a / (backslash) in the first column of the next line.* Refer Diagram 2.13.

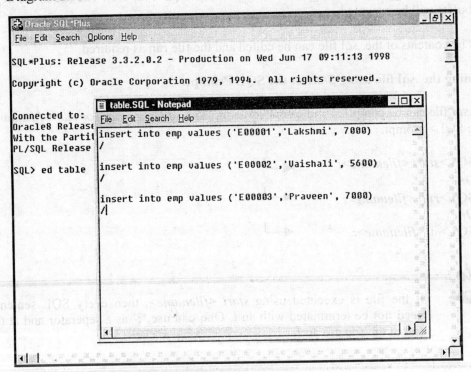

Diagram 2.13 : Using the ASCII Editor File

- Save the file using the Notepad Menu choices **File, Save**.

- This file can be invoked and used repeatedly at the SQL> prompt.

- To exit from the tool click on **File, Exit**

Running the .sql file using *Get* at the SQL Prompt:

- To run this *.sql* file, after saving the file and exiting from notepad, at the **SQL>** prompt, type the command *get <filename>*
        SQL> *get <filename>*;

Or

- Click on **Open** from the **File** menu item of the SQL*Plus tool. It displays the *Open* dialog box. Select the name of the file and click on OK.

- To execute the *.sql* file at the SQL> prompt type, **/**

  SQL> /

- **Or** Click on **Run** from the **File** menu item of the SQL*Plus tool. The file in the SQL buffer will be executed.

- The contents of the .sql file can be edited and the file run as required.

Running the .sql file using *Start* at the SQL Prompt:

The *.sql* file can be compiled and executed using *start <filename.sql>or run <filename>* at the SQL> prompt.

SQL>*start <filename>;*
Or
SQL>*run <filename>;*
Or
SQL>*@ <filename>;*

Note

If the file is executed using *start <filename>*, then every SQL sentence **need not** be terminated with an **/**. One can use '**;**' as a seperator and at the end of the file use an **/**.

SAVING INTO AN ASCII FILE FROM THE SQL PROMPT

The steps involved in saving an SQL statement into an ASCII file from the SQL prompt are:

- At the SQL> prompt, you can execute any valid SQL statement.
  E.g. *Select * from client_master;*

- If you want to save the SQL statement in a file, at the SQL> prompt type-in *save <filename>*. This command automatically creates a file by the *<filename>* in the current working directory.

  SQL> save *<filename>;*

SELF REVIEW QUESTIONS

READ THE QUESTIONS AND WRITE DOWN APPROPRIATE SQL STATEMENTS, AS ANSWERS.

1) **Create the tables described below:**

a) **Table Name**: Client_master
   Description: Used to store information about clients.

Column Name	Data Type	Size
client_no	varchar2	6
name	varchar2	20
address1	varchar2	30
address2	varchar2	30
city	varchar2	15
pincode	number	8
state	varchar2	15
bal_due	number	10,2

b) **Table Name**: product_master
   Description: Use to store information about products.

Column Name	Data Type	Size
product_no	varchar2	6
description	varchar2	15
profit_percent	number	4,2
unit_measure	varchar2	10
qty_on_hand	number	8
reorder_lvl	number	8
sell_price	number	8,2
cost_price	number	8,2

c) **Table Name** : salesman_master

Description : Use to store information about salesmen working in the company.

Column Name	Data Type	Size
salesman_no	varchar2	6
salesman_name	varchar2	20
address1	varchar2	30
address2	varchar2	30
city	varchar2	20
pincode	number	8
state	varchar2	20
sal_amt	number	8,2
tgt_to_get	number	6,2
ytd_sales	number	6,2
remarks	varchar2	60

2) **Insert the following data into their respective tables:**

a) Data for **client_master** table

client_no	name	city	pincode	state	bal_due
C00001	Ivan Bayross	Bombay	400054	Maharashtra	15000
C00002	Vandana Saitwal	Madras	780001	Tamil Nadu	0
C00003	Pramada Jaguste	Bombay	400057	Maharashtra	5000
C00004	Basu Navindgi	Bombay	400056	Maharashtra	0
C00005	Ravi Sreedharan	Delhi	100001		2000
C00006	Rukmini	Bombay	400050	Maharashtra	0

b) Data for **product_master** table

product_no	description	profit_percent	unit_measure	qty_on_hand	reorder_lvl	sell_price	cost_price
P00001	1.44 Floppies	5	Piece	100	20	525	500
P03453	Monitors	6	Piece	10	3	12000	11280
P06734	Mouse	5	Piece	20	5	1050	1000
P07865	1.22 Floppies	5	Piece	100	20	525	500
P07868	Keyboards	2	Piece	10	3	3150	3050
P07885	CD Drive	2.5	Piece	10	3	5250	5100
P07965	540 HDD	4	Piece	10	3	8400	8000
P07975	1.44 Drive	5	Piece	10	3	1050	1000
P08865	1.22 Drive	5	Piece	2	3	1050	1000

c) Data for **salesman_master** table

salesman_no	salesman_name	address1	address2	city	pincode	state	sal_amt	tgt_to_get	Ytd_sales	remarks
S00001	Kiran	A/14	Worli	Bombay	400002	Maharashtra	3000	100	50	Good
S00002	Manish	65	Nariman	Bombay	400001	Maharashtra	3000	200	100	Good
S00003	Ravi	P-7	Bandra	Bombay	400032	Maharashtra	3000	200	100	Good
S00004	Ashish	A/5	Juhu	Bombay	400044	Maharashtra	3500	200	150	Good

3) **Exercise on retrieving records from a table:**

a) Find out the names of all the clients.
b) Retrieve the entire contents of the client_master table.
c) Retrieve the list of names and the cities of all the clients.
d) List the various products available from the product_master table.
e) List all the clients who are located in Bombay.
f) Find the names of the salesman who have a salary equal to Rs.3000.

4) **Exercise on updating records in a table:**

a) Change the city of client_no 'C00005' to 'Bombay'.
b) Change the bal_due of client_no 'C00001' to Rs. 1000.
c) Change the cost price of '1.22 Floppies' to Rs. 950.00.
d) Change the city of the salesman to Mumbai.

5) **Exercise on deleting records in a table:**

a) Delete all salesmen from the salesman_master whose salaries are equal to Rs. 3500.
b) Delete all products from product_master where the quantity on hand is equal to 100.
c) Delete from client_master where the column state holds the value 'Tamil Nadu'.

6) **Exercise on Altering the table structure:**

a) Add a column called 'telephone' of data type 'number' and size ='10' to the client_master table.
b) Change the size of sell_price column in product_master to 10,2.

7) **Exercise on deleting the table structure along with the data:**

a) Destroy the table client_master along with its data.

8) **Exercise on renaming the table:**

a) Change the name of the salesman_master table to sman_mast.

A QUICK REVIEW

➢ **Client/Server Technology & Oracle**

➢ **SQL*Plus and its Uses**

➢ **Creating a short cut to invoke SQL*Plus**

➢ **Data Types used in Oracle**
  - *Char*
  - *Varchar/Varchar2*
  - *Number*
  - *Date*
  - *Long*
  - *Raw*
  - *Long Raw*

➢ **Creating Tables and Inserting data into tables.**

➢ **Retrieving data from tables**
  - *Global retrieval*
  - *Conditional retrieval*

➢ **Deleting Records from tables**
  - *Deletion of all the records.*
  - *Deletion of a specific set of records.*

➢ **Updating records in tables**
  ▪ *Updation of all the records.*
  ▪ *Updation of a specific set of records.*

➢ **Modifying table structures**

➢ **Renaming Tables**

➢ **Dropping Tables**

➢ **Viewing the attributes of table columns created by users.**

➢ **Working with ASCII Editor**
  ▪ *Invoking the ASCII Editor*
  ▪ *Creating a ASCII file (i.e. .sql file)*
  ▪ *Running the ASCII file at the SQL Prompt.*

More On SQL

IN THIS CHAPTER

➢ **Selecting data using computations**
  ▪ *Arithmetic & Logical Operators*
  ▪ *Range Searching & Pattern Matching*
  ▪ *Functions*

➢ **Data Constraints**

➢ **Retrieving data using the Grouping function.**

➢ **Date Manipulation using SQL**

➢ **Joins & Subqueries**

➢ **Union, Intersect and Minus Clause**

More On SQL

IN THIS CHAPTER

3. MORE ON SQL

COMPUTATIONS ON TABLE DATA

None of the techniques used till now allows display of data from a table after some arithmetic has been done with it.

To display an employee_name, and the employee's salary from the employee master table along with the annual salary of the employee (i.e. Salary* 12). The arithmetic (Salary * 12) is an example of table data arithmetic.

Arithmetic and logical operators give a new dimension to SQL sentences.

Arithmetic Operators:

Oracle allows arithmetic operators to be used while viewing records from a table or while performing Data Manipulation operations such as Insert, Update and Delete. These are

+	Addition	*	Multiplication
-	Subtraction	**	Exponentiation
/	Division	( )	Enclosed operation

For Example:
1. Retrieve the contents of the column product_no, description and compute 5% of the values contained in the column sell_price and 105% of the values contained in the field sell_price for each row from the table product_master.

> **SELECT** *product_no, description, sell_price * 0.05, sell_price * 1.05*
> **FROM** *product_master*;

Here, *sell_price * 0.05* and *sell_price * 1.05* are not columns in the table *product_master*. However, the calculations are done on the contents of the column *sell_price* of the table *product_master*.

By default, the Oracle engine will use column names of the table *product_master* as column headers when displaying column output on the VDU screen.

Since there are no columns with the names *sell_price * 0.05* and *sell_price * 1.05* in the table *product_master*, the engine will perform the required operations and use each formula as the *default column header* when displaying output as shown below:

Output:

Product No	Description	Sell Price * 0.05	Sell Price * 1.05
P00001	1.44 Floppies	25	525
P03453	Monitors	600	12600
P06734	Mouse	50	1050
P07865	1.22 Floppies	25	525
P07868	Keyboards	150	3150
P07885	CD Drive	250	5250
P07965	HDD	400	8400
P07975	1.44 Drive	50	1050
P08865	1.22 Drive	50	1050

Renaming Columns Used with Expression Lists:

Rename the *default output column names* with an **alias**, when required.

Syntax:

> **SELECT** *columnname* **result_columnname**, *columnname* **result_columnname**
>   **FROM** *tablename;*

Example:

1. Retrieve the contents of the column product_no, description and compute 5% and 105% of the field sell_price for each row retrieved. Rename sell_price * 0.05 as *Increase* and sell_price * 1.05 as *New_Price*.

> **SELECT** *product_no, description,*
>   *sell_price * 0.05 Increase, sell_price * 1.05 New_Price*
>   **FROM** *product_master;*

Output:

Product No	Description	Increase	New_Price
P00001	1.44 Floppies	25	525
P03453	Monitors	600	12600
P06734	Mouse	50	1050
P07865	1.22 Floppies	25	525
P07868	Keyboards	150	3150
P07885	CD Drive	250	5250
P07965	HDD	400	8400
P07975	1.44 Drive	50	1050
P08865	1.22 Drive	50	1050

Logical Operators:

Logical operators that can be used in SQL sentences are:

The *AND* Operator:
The Oracle engine will process all rows in a table and display the result only when *all of* the conditions specified using the *AND* operator are satisfied.

Example:
1. Retrieve the contents of the columns product_no, description, profit_percent, sell_price from the table product_master where the values contained in the field profit_percent is between 10 *and* 20 *both inclusive*.

> **SELECT** *product_no, description, profit_percent, sell_price*
> **FROM** *product_master*
> **WHERE** *profit_percent >= 10* **AND** *profit_percent <= 20*;

The *OR* Operator:
The Oracle engine will process all rows in a table and display the result only when *any of* the conditions specified using the *Or* operator are satisfied.

Example:
2. Retrieve client information like client_no, name, address1, address2, city and pincode for all the clients where the field pincode has the value 400054 *OR* 400057;

> **SELECT** *client_no, name, address1, address2, city, pincode*
> **FROM** *client_master*
> **WHERE** *(pincode = 400054* **OR** *pincode = 400057)*;

The contents of the fields client_no, name, address1, address2, city, pincode satisfying the·condition of *pincode* being 400054 *OR* 400057 in the client_master table will be displayed on the VDU screen.

The **NOT** Operator:

The Oracle engine will process all rows in a table and display the result only when *none of* the conditions specified using the *Not* operator are satisfied.

Example:

3. Retrieve specified client information for the clients who are **NOT** in 'Bombay' **OR** 'Delhi'.

    SELECT client_no, name, address1, address2, city, pincode
        FROM client_master **WHERE NOT** *(city = 'Bombay' or city ='Delhi')*;

The Oracle engine will not display the rows from the client_master table where the value of the field *city* is either *Bombay* or *Delhi*.

Range Searching:

In order to select data that is within a range of values, the **BETWEEN** operator is used. The BETWEEN operator allows the selection of rows that contain values within a specified lower and upper limit. The range coded after the word BETWEEN is *inclusive*.

The lower value must be coded first. The two values in between the range must be linked with the keyword **AND**. A BETWEEN operator can be used with both character and numeric data types. However, one cannot mix the data types i.e. the lower value of a range of values from a character column and the other from a numeric column.

Example for the BETWEEN Operator:

1. Retrieve product_no, description, profit_percent, sell_price from the table product_master where the values contained within the field profit_percent is *between* 10 and 20 *both inclusive.*

    SELECT *product_no, description, profit_percent, sell_price*
        FROM *product_master*
        WHERE *profit_percent* **BETWEEN** *10* **AND** *20*;

The above select will retrieve all the records from the product_master table where the profit_percent is in between 10 and 20 (both values inclusive).

2. Retrieve product_no, description, profit_percent, and sell_price from the product_master table where the values contained in the field profit_percent are *not between* 10 and 15 *both inclusive.*

    SELECT *product_no, description, profit_percent, sell_price*
        FROM *product_master*
        WHERE *profit_percent* **NOT BETWEEN** *10* **AND** *15*;

The above select will retrieve all the records from the product_master table **except** where the profit_percent is in between 10 and 15 (both values inclusive).

Pattern Matching:

The use of the LIKE predicate:
The comparison operators discussed so far have compared one value, exactly to one other value. Such a precision may not always be desired or necessary. For this purpose Oracle provides a predicate **LIKE**.

The **LIKE** predicate allows for a comparison of one string value with another string value, which is not identical. This is achieved by using wildcard characters. Two wildcard characters that are available are:

For character data types: The percent sign (**%**) matches any string
                             The Underscore (_) matches any single character

Example:
1. Retrieve all information about suppliers whose names begin with the letters **'ja'** from supplier_master .

    > **SELECT * FROM** *supplier_master*
    >   **WHERE** *supplier_name* **LIKE** 'ja%';

2. Retrieve all information about suppliers where the second character of names are either **'r'** or **'h'**.

    > **SELECT** *
    >   **FROM** *supplier_master*
    >   **WHERE** *supplier_name* **LIKE** '_r%' **OR** *supplier_name* **LIKE** '_h%';

3. Retrieve the supplier_name, address1, address2, city and pincode from the table supplier_master where the supplier_name is **3** characters long and the first two characters are **'ja'**.

    > **SELECT** *supplier_name, address1, address2, city, pincode*
    >   **FROM** *supplier_master* **WHERE** *supplier_name* **like** 'ja_';

The *IN* and *NOT IN* predicates:
The arithmetic operator (=) compares a single value to another single value. In case a value needs to be compared to a list of values then the **IN** predicate is used. One can check a single value against multiple values by using the **IN** predicate.

Example:
1. Retrieve the supplier_name, address1, address2, city and pincode from the table supplier_master where the supplier_name is either Ramos or Clark or Pramada or Aruna.

> **SELECT** *supplier_name, address1, address2, city, pincode*
> **FROM** *supplier_master*
> **WHERE** *supplier_name* **IN** *('Ramos', 'Clark', 'Pramada', 'Aruna')*;

The **NOT IN** predicate is the opposite of the IN predicate. This will select all the rows where values *do not match all of the values* in the list.

Example:
> **SELECT** *supplier_name, address1, address2, city, pincode*
> **FROM** *supplier_master*
> **WHERE** *supplier_name* **NOT IN** *('Ramos', 'Clark', 'Pramada', 'Aruna')*;

In the above example by just changing the predicate to NOT IN the Select statement will now retrieve all the rows from the supplier_master table where the supplier_name is not equal to the ones supplied. In other words, information about suppliers whose names are not *Ramos, Clark, Pramada, Aruna* will be displayed.

The Oracle Table 'DUAL':

Dual is a small Oracle worktable, which consists of only one row and one column, and contains the value x in that column. Besides arithmetic calculations, it also supports date retrieval and it's formatting.

Often a simple calculation needs to be done, for example, 2*2. The only SQL verb to cause an output to be written to a VDU screen is SELECT. However, a SELECT must have a table name in its FROM clause, otherwise the SELECT fails.

When an arithmetic exercise is to be performed such as 2*2 or 4/2 etc., there really is no table being referenced, only numeric literals are being used.

To facilitate such calculations via a SELECT, Oracle provides a dummy table called DUAL, against which SELECT statements that are required to manipulate numeric literals can be fired, and output obtained.

Example:
  SQL> **SELECT** 2*2 **FROM** *dual*;

Output:
```
        2*2
    ---------
        4
```

The current date can be obtained from the table DUAL in the required format as shown below.

SYSDATE:

Sysdate is a pseudo column that contains the current date and time. It requires no arguments when selected from the table DUAL and returns the current date.

Example:
  SQL> **SELECT** *sysdate* **FROM** *dual*;

Output:
```
    SYSDATE
    --------------
    06-FEB-98
```

ORACLE FUNCTIONS

Oracle Functions serve the purpose of manipulating data items and returning a result. Functions are also capable of accepting user-supplied variables or constants and operating on them. Such variables or constants are called as *arguments*. Any number of arguments (or no arguments at all) can be passed to a function in the following format:

Function_name(argument1, argument2,..).

Oracle Functions can be clubbed together depending upon whether they operate on a single row or a group of rows retrieved from a table. Accordingly, functions can be classified as follows:

Group Functions (Aggregate Functions):

Functions that act on a set of values are called as Group Functions. For example, *SUM*, is a function which calculates the total of a set of numbers. A group function returns a single result row for a group of queried rows.

Scalar Functions (Single Row Functions):

Functions that act on only one value at a time are called as Scalar Functions. For example, *LENGTH*, is a function, which calculates the length of one particular string value. A single row function returns one result for every row of a queried table or view.

Single row functions can be further grouped together by the data type of their arguments and return values. For example, *LENGTH* relates to the *String* Data type. Functions can be classified corresponding to different data types as:

String Functions   : Work for *String* Data type
Numeric Functions   : Work for *Number* Data type
Conversion Functions : Work for Conversion of one data type to another.
Date Functions   : Work for *Date* Data type

Aggregate Functions:

AVG   Syntax   AVG ([DISTINCT|ALL] n)

         Purpose   Returns average value of 'n', ignoring null values.

         Example   **SELECT AVG(sell_price) "Average"**

                             FROM product_master;

         Output   Average

                      2012.3654

Note

In the above SELECT statement, AVG function is used to calculate the average selling price of all products. The selected column is renamed as 'Average' in the output.

MIN   Syntax   MIN([DISTINCT|ALL] expr)

         Purpose   Returns minimum value of 'expr'.

         Example   **SELECT MIN(bal_due) "Minimum Balance"**

                             FROM client_master ;

         Output   Minimum Balance

                                0

COUNT(expr)   Syntax   COUNT([DISTINCT|ALL] expr)

         Purpose   Returns the number of rows where 'expr' is not null.

         Example   **SELECT COUNT(product_no) "No of Products"**

                             FROM product_master;

         Output   No of Products

                                9

COUNT(*)   Syntax   COUNT(*)

         Purpose   Returns the number of rows in the table, including duplicates and those with nulls.

         Example   **SELECT COUNT(*) "Total"**

                             FROM client_master;

         Output   Total

                      15

MAX	Syntax	MAX([DISTINCT|ALL] expr)
	Purpose	Returns maximum value of 'expr'.
	Example	**SELECT MAX(bal_due) "Maximum"** 　　　**FROM client_master ;**
	Output	Maximum ------------- 15000

SUM	Syntax	SUM([DISTINCT|ALL] n)
	Purpose	Returns sum of values of 'n'.
	Example	**SELECT SUM(bal_due) "Total Balance Due"** 　　　**FROM client_master ;**
	Output	Total Balance Due ----------------------- 22000

Numeric Functions:

ABS	Syntax	ABS(n)
	Purpose	Returns the absolute value of 'n'.
	Example	**SELECT ABS(-15) "Absolute"** 　　　**FROM dual;**
	Output	Absolute ----------- 15

POWER	Syntax	POWER(m,n)
	Purpose	Returns 'm' raised to 'nth' power. 'n' must be an integer, else an error is returned.
	Example	**SELECT POWER(3,2) "Raised"** 　　　**FROM dual;**
	Output	Raised -------- 9

ROUND	Syntax	ROUND(n[,m])
	Purpose	Returns 'n' , rounded to 'm' places right of the decimal Point. If 'm' is omitted, 'n' is rounded to 0 places. 'm' can be negative to round off digits left of the decimal point. 'm' must be an integer.
	Example	**SELECT ROUND(15.19,1) "Round"** **FROM dual;**
	Output	Round -------- 15.2

SQRT	Syntax	SQRT(n)
	Purpose	Returns square root of 'n'. If 'n'<0, NULL. SQRT returns a *real* result.
	Example	**SELECT SQRT(25) "Square Root"** **FROM dual;**
	Output	Square Root -------------- 5

String Functions:

LOWER	Syntax	LOWER(char)
	Purpose	Returns char, with all letters in lowercase.
	Example	**SELECT LOWER('IVAN BAYROSS') "Lower"** **FROM dual;**
	Output	Lower ---------------- ivan bayross

INITCAP	Syntax	INITCAP(char)
	Purpose	Returns string with the first letter in upper case.
	Example	**SELECT INITCAP('IVAN BAYROSS') "Title Case"** **FROM dual;**
	Output	Title Case ---------------- Ivan Bayross

UPPER	Syntax	UPPER (char)
	Purpose	Returns char, with all letters forced to uppercase.
	Example	**SELECT UPPER('Ms. Carol')**
		FROM dual;
	Output	UPPER('Ms. Carol')

		MS. CAROL

SUBSTR	Syntax	SUBSTR(char,m[,n])
	Purpose	Returns a portion of char, beginning at character 'm', exceeding upto 'n' characters. If 'n' is omitted, result is returned upto the end char. The first position of char is 1.
	Example	**SELECT SUBSTR('SECURE',3,4) "Substring"**
		FROM dual;
	Output	Subs

		CURE

LENGTH	Syntax	LENGTH(char)
	Purpose	Returns the length of char.
	Example	**SELECT LENGTH('ELEPHANT') "Length"**
		FROM dual;
	Output	Length

		8

LTRIM	Syntax	LTRIM(char[,set])
	Purpose	Removes characters from the left of char with initial characters removed upto the first character not in set.
	Example	**SELECT LTRIM ('NISHA','N')**
		"Left trim example" FROM dual;
	Output	Left

		ISHA

RTRIM	Syntax	RTRIM (char,[set])
	Purpose	Returns char, with final characters removed after the last character not in the set. 'set' is optional, it defaults to spaces.
	Example	**SELECT RTRIM('SUNILA','A') "RTRIM Example"**
		FROM dual;
	Output	RTRIM

		SUNIL

LPAD	Syntax	LPAD(char1,n [,char2])
	Purpose	Returns 'char1', left padded to length 'n' with the Sequence of characters in 'char2', 'char2' defaults to blanks.
	Example	**SELECT LPAD('Page 1',10,'*') "Lpad"**
		FROM dual;
	Output	Lpad

		****Page 1

RPAD	Syntax	RPAD(char1,n[,char2])
	Purpose	Returns 'char1', right-padded to length 'n' with the characters in 'char2', replicated as many times as necessary. If 'char2' is omitted, right-pad is with blanks.
	Example	**SELECT RPAD(name,10,'x') "RPAD Example"**
		FROM client_master
		WHERE name = 'TURNER';
	Output	RPAD Example

		TURNERxxxx

Conversion Functions:

TO_NUMBER Syntax   TO_NUMBER(char)

               Purpose   Converts 'char', a CHARACTER value containing a
                                 number, to a value of NUMBER datatype.

               Example   **UPDATE product_master**
                                 SET sell_price = sell_price +
                                                TO_NUMBER (SUBSTR('$100',2,3));

 Note

Here, the value 100 will be added to every products selling price in the product_master table.

TO_CHAR   Syntax   TO_CHAR (n[,fmt])
(number
conversion) Purpose   Converts a value of NUMBER datatype to a value of
                                 CHAR datatype , using the optional format string . It
                                 accepts a number (n) and a numeric format (fmt) in
                                 which the number has to appear. If 'fmt' is omitted, 'n' is
                                 converted to a char value exactly long enough to hold
                                 significant digits.

               Example   **SELECT TO_CHAR(17145,'$099,999') "Char"**
                                      FROM dual;

               Output   Char

                                 $017,145

TO_CHAR   Syntax   TO_CHAR(date[,fmt])
(date
conversion) Purpose   Converts a value of DATE datatype to CHAR value. It
                                 accepts a date (date), as well as the format (fmt) in
                                 which the date has to appear. 'fmt' must be a date format.
                                 If 'fmt' is omitted, 'date' is converted to a character value
                                 in the default date format, i.e. "DD-MON-YY".

               Example   **SELECT TO_CHAR(order_date,'Month DD, YYYY')**
                                      "New Date Format" FROM sales_order
                                      WHERE order_no = 'O42453';

               Output   New Date Format

                                 January 26, 1996

Date Conversion Functions:

The DATE data type is used to store date and time information. The DATE data type has special properties associated with it. It stores information about century, year, month, day, hour, minute and second for each date value.

The value in the column of a DATE data type, is always stored in a specific *default* format: This default format is 'DD-MON-YY HH:MI:SS'. Hence, when a date has to be inserted in a date field, its value has to be specified in the same format. Also, values of DATE columns are displayed in the *default* format when *retrieved* from the table.

In case a user wishes to view the date column information in any other format other than the default format, Oracle provides the TO_DATE function that can be used to specify the required format.

The same function can be used for inserting a date into a DATE field in a particular format (other than default). This can be achieved by specifying the date value, along with the format in which it is to be inserted. This function also allows part insertion of a DATE, for example, only the day and month portion of the value.

To enter the time portion of a date, the TO_DATE function must be used with a *format mask* indicating the time portion.

TO_DATE	Syntax	TO_DATE(char [, fmt])
	Purpose	Converts a character field to a date field.
	Example	**INSERT INTO sales_order (order_no, order_date)**
		VALUES ('O87650', TO_DATE('30-SEP-8510:55 A.M.',
		'DD-MON-YY HH:MI A.M.');

Date Functions:

Also to manipulate and extract values from the date column of a table some date functions have been provided by Oracle. These are discussed below:

ADD_MONTHS	Syntax	ADD_MONTHS(d,n)
	Purpose	Returns date after adding the number of months specified with the function
	Example	**SELECT ADD_MONTHS(SYSDATE,4)**
		FROM dual;
	Output	ADD_MONTH

		04-JUN-98

LAST_DAY	Syntax	LAST_DAY(d)
	Purpose	Returns the last date of the month specified with the function
	Example	**SELECT SYSDATE, LAST_DAY(SYSDATE) "LAST" FROM DUAL;**
	Output	SYSDATE LAST
		-------------- ---------
		04-FEB-98 28-FEB-98

MONTHS_BETWEEN	Syntax	MONTHS_BETWEEN(d1, d2)
	Purpose	Returns number of months between 'd1' and 'd2'
	Example	**SELECT MONTHS_BETWEEN('02-FEB-92', '02-JAN-92') "MONTHS" FROM DUAL;**
	Output	MONTHS

		1

NEXT_DAY	Syntax	NEXT_DAY(date,char)
	Purpose	Returns the date of the first weekday named by 'char' that is after the date named by 'date'. 'char' must be a day of the week.
	Example	**SELECT NEXT_DAY('04-FEB-98', 'FRIDAY') "NEXT DAY" FROM DUAL;**
	Output	NEXT DAY

		06-FEB-98

Note

In the above case, the **FRIDAY** that followed **4ᵗʰ FEB'98 was the 6th FEB'98.**

The above Oracle functions are just a few selected from the many functions that are built into Oracle. These Oracle functions are commonly used in commercial application development. They will serve to indicate how Oracle functions are used. Before you develop your own functions using SQL or PL/SQL refer to the Oracle manuals and check to see if an in built Oracle function already exists that would allow you to process data as required.

DATA CONSTRAINTS

All businesses of the world run on business data being gathered, stored and analyzed. Business managers determine a set of rules that must be applied to the data being stored to ensure its integrity. For instance, no employee in the sales department can have a salary of less than Rs.1000/-.

Such limitations have to be enforced on the data, and only that data which satisfies the conditions set will actually be stored for analysis. If the data gathered fails to satisfy the conditions set, it is rejected. This technique ensures that the data that is stored in the database will be valid, and has integrity.

Rules that have to be applied to data are completely _System dependent_. The rules applied to data gathered and processed by a _Saving bank system_ will be very different, to the business rules applied to data gathered and processed by an _Inventory system_, which in turn will be very different, to the business rules applied to data gathered and processed by a _Personnel management system._

Rules which are enforced on data being entered, and prevents the user from entering invalid data into tables are called _Constraints_. Thus, constraints super control data being entered in tables for permanent storage.

Tables created in Oracle are used to store data belonging to commercial applications. The commercial application could be one of many systems (e.g. a Saving bank system, Inventory System or a Personnel management system).

Oracle permits data constraints to be attached to table columns via SQL syntax that will check data for integrity. Once data constraints are part of a table column construction, the Oracle engine checks the data being entered into a table column against the data constraints. If the data passes this check, it is stored in the table, else the data is rejected. Even if a single column of the record being entered into the table fails a constraint, the _entire record is rejected and not stored in the table_. Any business decisions made by business managers based on this data should be appropriate for the growth of the company.

Both the '_Create Table_' and '_Alter Table_' SQL verbs can be used to write SQL sentences that attach constraints to a table column.

Until now tables created have **not** had any data constraints attached to their table columns. Hence the tables have **not** been given any instructions to filter what is being stored in the table. _This situation can and does, result in erroneous data being stored in the table._

Once a constraint is attached to a table column, any SQL *Insert* or *Update* statement causes these constraints to be applied to the data prior to it being inserted into the tables for storage.

Types of Data Constraints:

There are two types of data constraints that can be applied to data being inserted into an Oracle table. One type of constraint is called an **i/o** constraint (input / output). This data constraint determines the speed at which data can be inserted or extracted from an Oracle table. The other type of constraint is called a **business rule** constraint.

I/O Constraints:

The input / output data constraint, is further divided into two distinctly different constraints.

The Primary Key constraint:
Here the data constraint attached to a table column (or columns) ensures:

- That the data entered in the table column (or columns) is **Unique** across the entire column (or columns)
- That none of the cells belonging to the table column (or columns) are left **empty**.

The Foreign Key Constraint:
This constraint establishes a relationship between records (*i.e. data*) across a Master and a Detail table. This relationship ensures:

- Records cannot be inserted into a *detail table* if corresponding records in the *master table* do not exist.
- Records of the *master table* cannot be deleted if corresponding records in the *detail table* exist.

In addition to Primary and Foreign Key, Oracle has *NOT NULL* and *UNIQUE* as column constraints. The NOT NULL column constraint ensures that a table column cannot be left empty. The *UNIQUE* constraint ensures that the data across the entire table column is unique (*i.e. no repeating values can be inserted into the column*).

Note

The *Unique* column constraint permits multiple entries of the NULL value into the column. These NULL values are clubbed at the top of the column in the order in which they were entered into the table. This is the essential difference between the Primary Key and the Unique constraints when applied to a table column(s).

Business Rule Constraints:

Oracle allows the application of **business rules** to table columns. Business managers determine business rules. These rules are applied to data prior the data being inserted into table columns. This ensures that the data (*records*) in the table have integrity. Thus, business processes initiated after business managers analyze this data will result in business growth.

For example, the rule that no employee in the company shall get salary less than Rs.1000/- is a business rule. Business rules differ from business to business and organization to organization.

Business rules can be implemented in Oracle by using CHECK constraints. Business rule validation checks are performed when the user performs a write operation on the table i.e. insert, update or delete data. Any insert, update or delete statement causes the relevant constraint to be evaluated. The constraint must be satisfied for the statement to succeed. Thus these constraints ensure integrity of the data in the tables.

Constraints can be connected to a *column* or a *table* by the CREATE TABLE or ALTER TABLE command. Constraints are recorded in Oracle's data dictionary.

Conceptually, data constraints are connected to a column, by the Oracle engine, as *flags*. Whenever user attempts to load the column with data, the Oracle engine will observe the flags and recognize the presence of constraints. Then, the Oracle engine will apply the defined constraint, to the data being entered.

If the data being entered into a column fails any of the data constraint checks, the entire record is rejected. The Oracle engine will then flash an appropriate **error message** to the user.

Oracle allows programmers to define constraints at:
* Column Level
* Table Level

Column Level Constraints:

If data constraints are defined along with the column definition when creating or altering a table structure, they are *column level constraints*.

Caution

 Column level constraints are applied to the **current column**. The current column is the column that immediately *precedes* the constraint i.e. they are local to a specific column.

A column level constraint **cannot** be applied if the data constraint spans across multiple columns in a table.

Table Level Constraints:

If data constraints are defined *after defining all the table columns* when creating or altering a table structure, it is a *table level constraint*.

Note

 Table level constraint **must** be applied if the data constraint spans across multiple columns in a table.

Constraints are stored as a part of the global table definition by the Oracle engine in its *system tables*.

The SQL syntax used to attach the constraint will change depending upon whether it is a column level or table level constraint.

NULL value concepts:

Often there may be records in a table that do not have values for every field, either because the information is not available at the time of data entry or because the field is not applicable in every case. If the column was created as NULLABLE (i.e. the default column construction of Oracle), Oracle will place a NULL value in the column in the absence of a user defined value.

A NULL value is different from a blank or a zero. NULL values are treated specially by Oracle. *A NULL value can be inserted into the columns of any data type.*

Principles of NULL values:
- Setting a NULL value is appropriate when the actual value is unknown, or when a value would not be meaningful.
- A NULL value is *not equivalent* to a value of *zero* if the data type is *number* and *spaces* if the data type is *character*.
- A NULL value will evaluate to NULL in any expression e.g. NULL multiplied by 10 is NULL.
- NULL value can be inserted into columns of *any data type*
- If the column has a NULL value, Oracle ignores the UNIQUE, FOREIGN KEY, CHECK constraints that may be attached to the column. Please refer to page 89, 92, 95 for UNIQUE, FOREIGN KEY, CHECK constraints.

NOT NULL constraint defined at the column level:

When a column is defined as *not null*, then that column becomes a *mandatory* column. It implies that a value must be entered into the column if the record is to be accepted for storage in the table.

Syntax:
> *columnname datatype(size)* **NOT NULL**

Example:
Create a table client_master with the following mandatory fields:
client_no, name, address1, and address2 columns.

CREATE TABLE *client_master*
> *(client_no varchar2(6)* **NOT NULL,**
> *name varchar2(20)* **NOT NULL,**
> *address1 varchar2(30)* **NOT NULL,**
> *address2 varchar2(30)* **NOT NULL,**
> *city varchar2(15), state varchar2(15), pincode number(6),*
> *remarks varchar2(60), bal_due number(10,2));*

Caution

The **NOT NULL** constraint can only be applied at column level. Although **NOT NULL** can be applied as a **CHECK** constraint, *however Oracle recommends that this be not done.*

The UNIQUE Constraint:

Unique Key concepts:
The purpose of a unique key is to ensure that information in the column(s) is unique, i.e. a value entered in column(s) defined in the unique constraint must not be repeated across the column(s). A table may have many unique keys.

UNIQUE constraint defined at the column level:

Syntax:
>   columnname datatype(size) **UNIQUE**

Example:
Create a table client_master such that the contents of the column *client_no* are unique across the entire column.

>   **CREATE TABLE** *client_master*
>   *(client_no varchar2(6)* **UNIQUE***,*
>   *name varchar2(20), address1 varchar2(30), address2 varchar2(30),*
>   *city varchar2(15), state varchar2(15), pincode number(6),*
>   *remarks varchar2(60), bal_due number(10,2));*

UNIQUE constraint defined at the table level:

Syntax:
>   **UNIQUE** *(columnname [, columnname, ...])*

Example:
Create a table client_master such that the unique constraint on the column *client_no* is described as a table level constraint.

>   **CREATE TABLE** *client_master*
>   *(client_no varchar2(6), name varchar2(20),*
>   *address1 varchar2(30), address2 varchar2(30),*
>   *city varchar2(15), state varchar2(15), pincode number(6),*
>   *remarks varchar2(60), bal_due number(10,2),*
>   **UNIQUE***(client_no));*

The PRIMARY KEY Constraint:

Primary Key concepts:
A primary key is one or more column(s) in a table used to uniquely identify each row in the table. *A primary key column* in a table has special attributes:

- It defines the column as a mandatory column i.e. the column cannot be left blank. The NOT NULL attribute is active.
- The data held across the column MUST be UNIQUE.

A single column primary key is called a *Simple* key. A multicolumn primary key is called a *Composite* primary key. The only function of a primary key in a table is to uniquely identify a row. Only when a record cannot be uniquely identified using the value in a single column, will a composite primary key be defined.

For example, a sales_order_details table will hold multiple records that are sales orders. Each such sales order will have multiple products that have been ordered. Standard business rules do not allow multiple entries for the same product, However, multiple orders will definitely have multiple entries of the same product.

Under these circumstances, the only way to uniquely identify a row in the sales_order_details table is via a composite primary key, consisting of order_no and product_no. Thus the combination of order number and product number will uniquely identify a row.

PRIMARY KEY constraint defined at the column level:

Syntax:
> columnname datatype(size) **PRIMARY KEY**

Example:
Create a table sales_order where the column order_no is its primary key. Since this is a simple key, define the constraint at column level.

> **CREATE TABLE** sales_order
> (order_no varchar2(6) **PRIMARY KEY**,
>   order_date date,client_no varchar2(6), dely_addr varchar2(25),
>   salesman_no varchar2(6), dely_type char(1), billed_yn char(1),
>   dely_date date, order_status varchar2(10));

PRIMARY KEY constraint defined at the table level:

Syntax:
> **PRIMARY KEY** (columnname [, columnname, ...])

Example:
Create a table sales_order_details where there is a composite primary key on the column detlorder_no and product_no. Since the constraint spans across columns, describe it at table level.

Column Name	Data Type	Size
detlorder_no	varchar2	6
product_no	varchar2	6
qty_ordered	number	8
qty_disp	number	8
product_rate	number	8,2

> CREATE TABLE sales_order_details
>   (detlorder_no varchar2(6), product_no varchar2(6),
>   qty_ordered number(8), qty_disp number(8),
>   product_rate number(8,2),
>   PRIMARY KEY (detlorder_no, product_no));

The FOREIGN KEY Constraint:

Foreign Key concepts:
Foreign keys represent relationships between tables. A foreign key is a column (or a group of columns) whose values are derived from the *primary key* or *unique key* of some other table.

The table in which the foreign key is defined is called a **Foreign table** or **Detail table**. The table that defines the *primary* or *unique* key and is referenced by the *foreign key* is called the **Primary table** or **Master table**.

The master table can be referenced in the foreign key definition by using the REFERENCES adverb. If the name of the column is not specified, by default, Oracle references the primary key in the master table.

Insert or update operation in the foreign table:
The existence of a foreign key implies that the table with the foreign key is **related** to the master table from which the foreign key is derived. A foreign key must have a corresponding primary key or unique key value in the master table.

For example a personnel information system includes two tables i.e. *department* and *employee*. An employee cannot belong to a department that does not exist. Thus the department number specified in the employee table must be present in the department table.

Delete operation on the primary table:
Oracle displays an error message if the user tries to delete a record in the master table
WHEN corresponding records exists in the detail table.

Note

The default behavior of the foreign key can be changed by using the ON
DELETE CASCADE option. When the ON DELETE CASCADE option is
specified in the foreign key definition, if the user deletes a record in the
master table, all corresponding records in the detail table along with the
record in the master table will be deleted.

Principles of Foreign Key/References constraint:
- Rejects an INSERT or UPDATE of a value, if a corresponding value does not
  currently exist in the master key table.
- If the ON DELETE CASCADE option is set, a DELETE operation in the master
  table will trigger the DELETE operation for corresponding records in the detail table.
- Rejects a DELETE for the Master table if corresponding records in the DETAIL table
  exist.
- Must reference a PRIMARY KEY or UNIQUE column(s) in primary table.
- Will automatically reference the PRIMARY KEY of the MASTER table if no
  column or group of columns is specified when creating the FOREIGN KEY.
- Requires that the FOREIGN KEY column(s) and the CONSTRAINT column(s) have
  matching data types.
- May reference the same table named in the CREATE TABLE statement.

FOREIGN KEY constraint defined at the column level:

Syntax:
> *columnname datatype(size)* **REFERENCES** *tablename [(columnname)]*
> *[ON DELETE CASCADE]*

Example:
Create a table **sales_order_details** table with its **primary key** as *detlorder_no* and
product_no. The **foreign key** is *detlorder_no,* referencing column *order_no* in the
sales_order table.

> **CREATE TABLE** *sales_order_details*
> *(detlorder_no varchar2(6)* **REFERENCES** *sales_order,*
> *product_no varchar2(6),*
> *qty_ordered number(8), qty_disp number(8),*
> *product_rate number(8,2),*
> **PRIMARY KEY** *(detlorder_no, product_no));*

The REFERENCES key word points to the table sales_order. The table sales_order has the column order_no as its primary key column. Since no column is specified in the foreign key definition, Oracle applies an automatic (default) link to the primary key column i.e. order_no of the table sales_order. The foreign key definition will be specified as

(detlorder_no varchar2(6) **REFERENCES** *sales_order(order_no)*

FOREIGN KEY constraint defined at the table level:

Syntax:
FOREIGN KEY (*columnname [,columnname]*)
REFERENCES *tablename [(columnname [,columnname])*

Example:
Create table sales_order_details with the **primary key** as *detlorder_no* and *product_no* and **foreign key** at table level as detlorder_no *referencing column order_no in the sales_order table.*

CREATE TABLE *sales_order_details*
(detlorder_no varchar2(6),
product_no varchar2(6),
qty_ordered number(8), qty_disp number(8),
product_rate number(8,2),
PRIMARY KEY *(detlorder_no, product_no),*
FOREIGN KEY *(detlorder_no)* **REFERENCES** *sales_order);*

Assigning User Defined Names to Constraints:

When constraints are defined as explained above, Oracle assigns a unique name to each constraint. The convention used by Oracle is

SYS_Cn where **n** is a numeric value that makes the constraint name unique.

For example, Oracle can create a constraint with the constraint name as SYS_C004871.

Constraints can be given a unique user-defined name along with the constraint definition. A constraint can be dropped by referring to the constraint by its name. Under these circumstances a user defined constraint name becomes very convenient.

If Oracle generated names are to be used, it becomes difficult to search for and identify the required constraint to be dropped. Hence, user named constraints simplifies the task of dropping constraints. A constraint can be given a user-defined name by preceding the constraint definition with the reserve word CONSTRAINT and a user-defined name.

Thus the syntax is:

CONSTRAINT *<constraintname><constraint definition>*

Example:
1. Create a table client_master with a **primary key** constraint on the column client_no. The *constraint name* must be p_clientkey.

    CREATE TABLE *client_master*
    (client_no varchar2(6) **CONSTRAINT** *p_clientkey* **PRIMARY KEY,**
    name varchar2(25),
    address1 varchar2(15), address2 varchar2(15),
    city varchar2(10), pincode number(8),
    bal_due number(10,2));

2. Create a table sales_order_details with a table-level **foreign key** as detlorder_no referencing column order_no in the sales_order table. The *constraint name* must be f_orderkey.

    CREATE TABLE *sales_order_details*
    (detlorder_no varchar2(6),
    product_no varchar2(6),
    qty_ordered number(8), qty_disp number(8),
    product_rate number(8,2),
    CONSTRAINT *f_orderkey* **FOREIGN KEY**
    (detlorder_no) **REFERENCES** *sales_order);*

The CHECK Constraint:

Business Rule validations can be applied to a table column by using CHECK constraint. CHECK constraints must be specified as a logical expression that evaluates either to TRUE or FALSE.

Note

A CHECK constraint takes longer to execute as compared to NOT NULL, PRIMARY KEY, FOREIGN KEY or UNIQUE. Thus CHECK constraints must be avoided if the constraint can be defined using the Not Null, Primary key or Foreign key constraint.

CHECK constraint defined at the column level:

<u>Syntax:</u>
>   *Columnname datatype (size)* **CHECK** *(logical expression)*

<u>Example:</u>
Create a table client_master with the following check constraints:
- Data values being inserted into the column *client_no* must start with the capital letter *'C'*.
- Data values being inserted into the column *name* should be in *upper case* only.
- Only allow *"Bombay", "Delhi", "Madras" and "Calcutta"* as legitimate values for the column *city*.

>   **CREATE TABLE** client_master
>   >   (*client_no varchar2(6)* **CHECK** *(client_no like 'C%'),*
>   >   *name varchar2(20)* **CHECK** *(name = upper(name)),*
>   >   *address1 varchar2(30), address2 varchar2(30),*
>   >   *city varchar2(15)* **CHECK** *(city IN ('Delhi', 'Bombay',*
>   >   >   >   >   *'Calcutta', 'Madras')),*
>   >   *state varchar2(15), pincode number(6),*
>   >   *remarks varchar2(60), bal_due number(10,2));*

CHECK constraint defined at the table level:

<u>Syntax:</u>
>   **CHECK** *(logical expression)*

<u>Example:</u>
>   **CREATE TABLE** *client_master*
>   >   *(client_no varchar2(6), name varchar2(20),*
>   >   *address1 varchar2(30), address2 varchar2(30),*
>   >   *city varchar2(15), state varchar2(15), pincode number(6),*
>   >   *remarks varchar2(60), bal_due number(10,2),*
>   >   **CHECK** *(client_no like 'C%'),*
>   >   **CHECK** *(name = upper(name)),*
>   >   **CHECK** *(city IN ('Delhi', 'Bombay', 'Calcutta', 'Madras')));*

When using CHECK constraints, consider the ANSI / ISO standard which states that a CHECK constraint is violated only if the condition evaluates to *False*. A check constraint is not violated if the condition evaluates to *True*.

*If the expression in a check constraint does not return a true / false, the value is **Indeterminate** or **Unknown**. <u>Unknown values do not violate a check constraint condition.</u>* For example, consider the following CHECK constraint for *sell_price* column in the *product_master* table:

$$\text{CHECK (sell\_price > 0)}$$

At first glance, this rule may be interpreted as "do not allow a row in the *product_master* table unless the *sell_price is greater than 0*.

*However, note that if a row is inserted with a **null** sell_price, the row does not violate the CHECK constraint because the entire check condition is evaluated as unknown.*

In this particular case, you can prevent such violations by placing the *not null* integrity constraint along with the check constraint on *sell_price* column of the table *product_master*.

Restrictions on *CHECK* Constraints:

A CHECK integrity constraint requires that a condition be **true** or **unknown** for the row to be processed. If an SQL statement causes the condition to evaluate to **false**, an appropriate error message is displayed and processing stops. A CHECK constraint has the following limitations:

- The condition must be a Boolean expression that can be evaluated using the values in the row being inserted or updated.
- The condition cannot contain subqueries or sequences.
- The condition cannot include the SYSDATE, UID, USER or USERENV SQL functions.

DEFINING DIFFERENT CONSTRAINTS ON A TABLE:

Create a sales_order_details table where:

Column Name	Data Type	Size	Attributes
detlorder_no	varchar2	6	Primary Key, Foreign Key references of order_no of sales_order table.
product_no	varchar2	6	Primary Key, Foreign Key references product_no of product_master table
qty_ordered	number	8	
qty_disp	number	8	Cannot be greater than qty_ordered
product_rate	number	8,2	not null

CREATE TABLE *sales_order_details*
    (detlorder_no varchar2(6),
    product_no varchar2(6),
    qty_ordered number(8),
    qty_disp number(8),
    product_rate number(8,2) **NOT NULL,**
    CONSTRAINT *pk_or_pr_no* **PRIMARY KEY** *(detlorder_no, product_no),*
    CONSTRAINT *fk_orderno* **FOREIGN KEY** *(detlorder_no)*
                REFERENCES *sales_order(order_no),*
    CONSTRAINT fk_prno **FOREIGN KEY** *(product_no)*
                REFERENCES *product_master,*
    CONSTRAINT *ck_qty* **CHECK** *(qty_disp <= qty_ordered));*

THE USER_CONSTRAINTS TABLE

A table can be created with multiple constraints attached to its columns. If the user wishes to see the table structures, Oracle provides the DESCRIBE <tablename> command. But this command displays only the column names, data type, size and the NOT NULL constraint.

The information about the other constraints that may be attached to the table columns such as the PRIMARY KEY, FOREIGN KEY, etc. is not available using the DESCRIBE verb. Oracle stores such information in a structure called USER_CONSTRAINTS.

Querying USER_CONSTRAINTS provides information pertaining to the names of all the constraints on the table. USER_CONSTRAINTS comprises of multiple columns, some of which are described below:

USER_CONSTRAINTS Table:

Column Name	Description
Owner	The owner of the constraint.
Constraint_Name	The name of the constraint
Constraint_Type	The type of constraint P : Primary Key Constraint R : Foreign Key Constraint U : Unique Constraint C : Check Constraint
Table_Name	The name of the table associated with the constraint
Search_Condition	The search condition used (for CHECK Constraints)
R_Owner	The owner of the table referenced by the FOREIGN KEY constraints
R_Constraint_Name	The name of the constraint referenced by a FOREIGN KEY constraint.

To view the constraints of the table sales_order_details the syntax is:

> **SELECT** Owner, Constraint_Name, Constraint_type
> **FROM** USER_CONSTRAINTS
> **WHERE** Table_Name = 'SALES_ORDER_DETAILS' ;

Output:

Owner	Constraint_Name	Constraint_Type
VAISHALI	pk_or_pr_no	P
VAISHALI	fk_orderno	R
VAISHALI	fk_prno	R
VAISHALI	ck_qty	C

DEFINING INTEGRITY CONSTRAINTS IN THE ALTER TABLE COMMAND

You can also define integrity constraints, using the constraint clause, in the **ALTER TABLE** command.

> Oracle will not allow constraints defined using the **ALTER TABLE**, to be applied to the table if data in the table violates such constraints.
>
> If a Primary key constraint was being applied to a table in retrospect and the column has duplicate values in it, the Primary key constraint will not be set to that column.

The following examples show the definitions of several integrity constraints:

Example:
1. Add a PRIMARY KEY data constraint on the column supplier_no belonging to the table supplier_master.

       ALTER TABLE *supplier_master*
             ADD *PRIMARY KEY (suppplier_no)*;

2. Add FOREIGN KEY constraint on the column order_no belonging to the table sales_order_details, which references the table sales_order. Modify column qty_ordered to include the NOT NULL constant;

       ALTER TABLE sales_order_details
             ADD CONSTRAINT *order_fkey*
                   FOREIGN KEY (detlorder_no) REFERENCES sales_order
             MODIFY *(qty_ordered number(8) NOT NULL)*;

DROPPING INTEGRITY CONSTRAINTS IN THE ALTER TABLE COMMAND

You can drop an integrity constraint if the rule that it enforces is no longer true or if the constraint is no longer needed. Drop the constraint using the ALTER TABLE command with the DROP clause. The following examples illustrate the dropping of integrity constraints:

Examples:
1. Drop the PRIMARY KEY constraint from supplier_master.

> **ALTER TABLE** *supplier_master*
> **DROP** *PRIMARY KEY*;

2. Drop FOREIGN KEY constraint on column product_no in table sales_order_details.

> **ALTER TABLE** *sales_order_details*
> **DROP CONSTRAINT** fk_prno;

Note

⟹ Dropping UNIQUE and PRIMARY KEY constraints drops the associated indexes.

DEFAULT VALUE CONCEPTS

At the time of table creation a '*default value*' can be assigned to a column. When the user is loading a 'record' with values and leaves this column empty, the Oracle engine will automatically load this column with the default value specified. The data type of the default value should match the data type of the column. You can use the DEFAULT clause to specify a default value for a column.

Syntax:
> *columnname data type (size)* **DEFAULT** *(value);*

Example:
Create a sales_order table where the default value for the column dely_type is the character, upper case 'F'. The attributes of each column of the sales_order table are described below:

Column Name	Data Type	Size	Attributes
order_no	varchar2	6	Primary Key
order_date	date		
client_no	varchar2	6	
dely_Addr	varchar2	25	
salesman_no	varchar2	6	
dely_type	char	1	delivery : part(P) / full (F) **Default 'F'**
billed_yn	char	1	
dely_date	date		
order_status	varchar2	10	

CREATE TABLE *sales_order*
(order_no varchar2(6) PRIMARY KEY,
order_date date, client_no varchar2(6),
dely_Addr varchar2(25), salesman_no varchar2(6),
dely_type char(1) **DEFAULT 'F',**
billed_yn char(1), dely_date date,
order_status varchar2(10)) ;

Note

- The data type of the default value should match the data type of the column.
- Character and date values will be specified in single quotes.
- If a column level constraint is defined on the column with a default value, *the default value clause must precede the constraint definition.* Thus the syntax will be:

Columnname datatype(size) **DEFAULT** *value constraint definition*

GROUPING DATA FROM TABLES IN SQL

The concept of grouping:

Till now, we have seen SQL **select** statements which:
- retrieve all the rows from database tables
- retrieve selected rows from tables with the use of a **where** clause, which returns only those rows that meet the conditions specified
- retrieve unique rows from the table, with the use of **distinct** clause
- retrieve rows in the sorted order i.e. ascending or descending order, as specified, with the use of **order by** clause.

Other than the above clauses, there are two other clauses, which facilitate selective retrieval of rows. These are the **GROUP BY** and **HAVING** clauses. These are parallel to the **order by** and **where** clause, except that they act on record sets, and not on individual records.

GROUP BY Clause:
The **GROUP BY** clause is another section of the **select** statement. This optional clause tells Oracle to *group rows based on distinct values* that exist for *specified columns* **i.e.** it creates a data set, containing several sets of records *grouped* together based on a condition.

Example:
Retrieve the product numbers and the total quantity ordered for each product from the sales_order_details table.

Table name: sales_order_details

Detorder No	Product No	Qty Ordered	Qty Disp
O19001	P00001	10	10
O19001	P00004	3	3
O19001	P00006	7	7
O19002	P00002	4	4
O19002	P00005	10	10
O19003	P00003	2	2
O19004	P00001	6	6
O19005	P00006	4	4
O19005	P00004	1	1
O19006	P00006	8	8

SELECT *product_no, sum (qty_ordered) "Total Qty Ordered"*
    FROM *sales_order_details*
    GROUP BY *product_no;*

Output:

Product No	Total Qty Ordered
P00001	16
P00002	4
P00003	2
P00004	4
P00005	10
P00006	19

In the above example, the common rows in the column product_no are grouped together and the total quantity ordered for each product is displayed on screen.

HAVING Clause:

The **HAVING** clause can be used in conjunction with the **GROUP BY** clause. **HAVING** imposes a condition on the *group by* clause, which further filters the groups created by the *group by* clause.

Example:

Retrieve the product no and the total quantity ordered for products 'P00001', 'P00004' from the sales_order_details table.

Table name: sales_order_details

Detorder No	Product No	Qty Ordered	Qty Disp
O19001	P00001	10	10
O19001	P00004	3	3
O19001	P00006	7	7
O19002	P00002	4	4
O19002	P00005	10	10
O19003	P00003	2	2
O19004	P00001	6	6
O19005	P00006	4	4
O19005	P00004	1	1
O19006	P00006	8	8

SELECT product_no, sum(qty_ordered) "Total Qty Ordered"
    FROM sales_order_details
    GROUP BY product_no
    HAVING product_no = 'P00001' **OR** product_no = 'P00004';

Output:

Product No	Total Qty Ordered
P00001	16
P00004	4

In the above example, the common rows in the column product_no are grouped together and the total quantity ordered for only the product numbers specified in the *having clause* are displayed on screen.

MANIPULATING DATES IN SQL

A column of data type 'Date' is always displayed in a default format, which is 'DD-MON-YY'. If this default format is not used when entering data into a column of the 'date' data type, *Oracle rejects the data and returns an error message.*

If a 'date' has to be retrieved or inserted into a table in a format other than the default one, Oracle provides the TO_CHAR and TO_DATE functions to do this.

TO_CHAR:

The TO_CHAR function facilitates the retrieval of data in a format different from the default format. It can also extract a part of the date, i.e. the date, month, or the year from the date value and use it for sorting or grouping of data according to the date, month, or year.

Syntax:
    TO_CHAR (date value [, fmt])

where 'date value' stands for the date and 'fmt' is the specified format in which date is to be displayed.

Example:
        TO_CHAR ('23-DEC-97', 'DD/MM/YY')

TO_DATE:

TO_DATE converts a char value into a date value. It allows a user to insert date into a date column in any required format, by specifying the **character** value of the date to be inserted and its format.

Syntax:
    TO_DATE(char value [, fmt])

where 'char value' stands for the value to be inserted in the date column, and 'fmt' is a date format in which the 'char value' is specified.

Example:

TO_DATE ('23/12/98, 'DD/MM/YY')

Examples on Date Manipulation:

Table name: **sales_order**

Order No	Client No	Order Date
O19001	C00006	12-apr-97
O19002	C00002	25-dec-97
O19003	C00007	03-oct97
O19004	C00005	18-jun-97
O19005	C00002	20-aug-97
O19006	C00007	02-jan-97

1. Retrieve order information like order_no, client_no, order_date for all the orders placed by the client in the *ascending* order of date. The order_date should be displayed in 'DD/MM/YY' format.

> **SELECT** *order_no, client_no* , **to_char**(*order_date*, **'DD/MM/YY'**)
>   **FROM** *sales_order*
>   **ORDER BY to_char** (*order_date*, **'MM'**);

Output:

Order_No	Client_No	Order_Date
O19006	C00007	02/01/97
O19001	C00006	12/04/97
O19004	C00005	18/06/97
O19005	C00002	20/08/97
O19003	C00007	03/10/97
O19002	C00002	25/12/97

  Note

Here the ordering of the output data set is based on the "MONTH" segment of the data in the column order_date. This is due to the to_char( ) in the order by clause extracting only the "MONTH" segment of the order_date to sort on.

2. Insert the following data in the table sales_order, wherein the time component has to be stored along with the date in the column order_date.

Order No	Client No	Order Date
O19100	C00100	31/DEC/97 11:32:45

INSERT INTO *sales_order*
    (order_no, client_no, order_date)
    VALUES('O19100', 'C00100', **to_date**('31/DEC/97 11:32:45',
                                    'DD/MON/YY hh:mi:ss'));

Special Date Formats using the To_Char function

Sometimes, the date value is required to be displayed in special formats, for example, instead of 12-JAN-97, display the date as 12th of January, 1997. For this, Oracle provides with *special alphabets*, which can be used in the format specified with the TO_CHAR and TO_DATE functions. The significance and use of these characters are explained in the examples below.

All three examples below are with respect to the sales_order table:

Table name: sales_order

Order No	Client No	Order Date
O19001	C00006	12-Apr-97
O19002	C00002	25-Dec-97
O19003	C00007	03-Oct-97
O19004	C00005	18-Jun-97
O19005	C00002	20-Aug-97
O19006	C00007	12-Jan-97

The query
               SELECT *order_no, order_date*
                  FROM *sales_order;*

Would give the following output:

Order_No	Order_Date
O19001	12-Apr-97
O19002	25-Dec-97
O19003	03-Oct-97
O19004	18-Jun-97
O19006	02-Jan-97
O19005	20-Aug-97

Variations in this output can be achieved as follows:

1. Use of **TH** in the to_char function:
    'TH' places TH, RD, ND for the date (DD), for example, 2ND, 3RD, 08TH etc

    SELECT *order_no*, **to_char***(order_date,*'DDTH-MON-YY')
        FROM *sales_order;*

    Output:

Order_No	To_Char (Order_Date,'DDTH-MON-YY')
O19001	12TH-APR-97
O19002	25TH-DEC-97
O19003	03RD-OCT-97
O19004	18TH-JUN-97
O19006	02ND-JAN-97
O19005	20TH-AUG-97

2. Use of **'SP'** in to_char function
    'DDSP' indicates that the date (DD) must be displayed by spelling the date such as ONE, TWELVE etc.

    SELECT *order_no*, **to_char**(*order_date,*'DDSP')
        FROM *sales_order;*

Output:

Order No	To_Char(Order_Date,'DDSP')
O19001	TWELVE
O19002	TWENTY-FIVE
O19003	THREE
O19004	EIGHTEEN
O19006	TWO
O19005	TWENTY

3. Use of **'SPTH'** in the to_char function
'SPTH' displays the date (DD) with **th** added to the spelling fourteen**th**, twelf**th**.

> **SELECT** *order_no,* **to_char***(order_date,*'DDSPTH')
> **FROM** sales_order;

Output:

Order No	To_Char(Order_Date,'DDSPTH')
O19001	TWELF**TH**
O19002	TWENTY-FIF**TH**
O19003	THI**RD**
O19004	EIGHTEEN**TH**
O19006	SECO**ND**
O19005	TWENTIE**TH**

SUBQUERIES

A subquery is a form of an SQL statement that appears inside another SQL statement. It is also termed as *nested query*. The statement containing a subquery is called a *parent* statement. The parent statement uses the rows returned by the subquery.

It can be used by the following commands:
- To insert records in a target table.
- To create tables and insert records in the table created.
- To update records in a target table.
- To create views.
- To provide values for *conditions* in WHERE, HAVING, IN etc. used with SELECT, UPDATE, and DELETE statements.

Examples:
1. Retrieve all orders placed by a client named 'Rahul Desai' from the sales_order table.

Table name: sales_order

Order No	Client No	Order Date
O19001	C00006	12-Apr-97
O19002	C00002	25-Dec-97
O19003	C00007	03-Oct97
O19004	C00005	18-Jun-97
O19005	C00002	20-Aug-97
O19006	C00007	12-Jan-97

Table name: client_master

Client No	Name	Bal Due
C00001	Ashok Mehra	500
C00002	Vishal Parikh	1000
C00003	Ajay Mehta	0
C00004	Rohit Roy	0
C00005	Nalini Deewan	0
C00006	Prem Iyer	0
C00007	Rahul Desai	0

SELECT * FROM *sales_order*
WHERE *client_no* =
(SELECT *client_no* FROM *client_master*
WHERE *name* = 'Rahul Desai');

The table sales_order contains client_no and all associated sales order information about this client. However the sales_order does not contain a client's name. In the client_master table, each client is identified by a unique client_no. This table also holds the client's name.

If we wish to see all the orders placed by a client 'Rahul Desai', we have to retrieve Rahul Desai's client_no from the client_master table. Having done this, we can retrieve the orders placed by 'Rahul Desai' from the sales_order table.

This type of processing works very well using a subquery.

Output:

Order_No	Client_No	Order_Date
O19003	C00007	03-Oct-97
O19006	C00007	12-Jan-97

2. Find out all the products that are not being sold from the product_master table, based on the *products actually sold* as shown in the sales_order_details table.

Table name: sales_order_details

Detorder No	Product No	Qty Ordered	Qty Disp
O19001	P00001	10	10
O19001	P00007	3	3
O19001	P00006	7	7
O19002	P00002	4	4
O19002	P00005	10	10
O19003	P00003	2	2
O19004	P00001	6	6
O19005	P00006	4	4
O19005	P00001	1	1
O19006	P00008	8	8

Table name: product_master

Product No	Description
P00001	1.44 Floppies
P00002	Monitors
P00003	Mouse
P00004	1.22 Floppies
P00005	Keyboards
P00006	CD Drive
P00007	HDD
P00008	1.44 Drive
P00009	1.22 Drive

> **SELECT** *product_no, description*
> **FROM** *product_master*
> **WHERE** *product_no NOT IN*
> *(***SELECT** *product_no* **FROM** *sales_order_details);*

Output:

```
Product No        Description
--------------    --------------------
P00004            1.22 Floppies
P00009            1.22 Drive
```

3. Retrieve the names of all personnel who work in Mr. Pradeep's department and have worked on an inventory control system as well, from the tables **emp** and **inv_sys**.

Table name: emp

Emp No	Ename	Dept No
1	Rahul	D01
2	Joshi	D02
3	Lenna	D01
4	Ashwariya	D01
5	Pradeep	D01
6	Arjun	D01
7	Pritam	D01
8	Sangeeta	D02
9	Prashant	D02
10	Melba	D02

Table name: inv_sys

Ename	Performance
Rahul	Good
Joshi	Average
Lenna	Excellent
Pradeep	Excellent
Pritam	Ok
Sangeeta	Excellent
Melba	Good

> **SELECT** *ename, dept_no*
>   **FROM** *emp*
>   **WHERE** *dept_no* **IN** (**SELECT** *dept_no* **FROM** *emp*
>   **WHERE** *ename = 'Pradeep'*)
>   **AND** *ename* **IN** (**SELECT** *ename*
>   **FROM** *inv_sys*);

If a select statement is defined as a subquery, the innermost select statement gets executed first. Thus in the above example, Oracle executes

> **SELECT** *ename*
>   **FROM** *inv_sys*

The data retrieved by the above select statement will be passed to the where clause of the query as in

> *ename* **IN** ('*Rahul'*, '*Joshi'*, '*Lenna'*, '*Pradeep'*, '*Pritam'*, '*Sangeeta'*, '*Melba'*)

Similarly when Oracle executes

> **SELECT** *dept_no* **FROM** *emp*
>   **WHERE** *ename = 'Pradeep'*

the output will be passed to the where clause as in

> *dept_no* **IN** ('*D01'*)

Thus the final query after replacing the inner queries with retrieved values will be
> **SELECT** *ename, dept_no* **FROM** *emp*
>   **WHERE** *dept_no* **IN** ('*D01'*) **AND**
>   *ename* **IN** ('*Rahul'*, '*Joshi'*, '*Lenna'*, '*Pradeep'*, '*Pritam'*,
>   '*Sangeeta'*, '*Melba'*);

Thus the final output will be:

<u>Output:</u>

Ename	Dept No
Lenna	D01
Pradeep	D01
Pritam	D01
Rahul	D01

JOINS

Joining Multiple Tables (Equi Joins):

Sometimes we require to treat multiple tables as though they were a single entity. Then a single SQL sentence can manipulate data from all the tables. To achieve this, we have to join tables. Tables are joined on columns that have the same **data type** and **data width** in the tables.

Example1:
Retrieve the order numbers, client names and their order dates from the client_master and sales_order tables. The order date should be displayed in 'DD/MM/YY' format and sorted in ascending order.

Here the data required is in two tables *sales_order* and *client_master*. These tables have to be accessed as though they were one entity.

Table name: sales_order

Order No	Client No	Order Date
O19001	C00006	12-apr-97
O19002	C00002	25-dec-97
O19003	C00001	03-oct97
O19004	C00005	18-jun-97
O19005	C00004	20-aug-97
O19006	C00001	12-jan-97

Table name: client_master

Client No	Name	Bal Due
C00001	Ashok Mehra	500
C00002	Vishal Parikh	1000
C00003	Ajay Mehta	0
C00004	Rohit Roy	0
C00005	Nalini Deewan	0
C00006	Prem Iyer	0
C00007	Rahul Desai	0

SELECT *order_no, name, to_char (order_date,'DD/MM/YY')* ***"Order Date"***
    FROM *sales_order, client_master*
    WHERE *client_master.client_no = sales_order.client_no*
    ORDER BY *to_char (order_date, 'DD/MM/YY');*

Note

If the columnnames on which the 'join' is to be specified are the same in each table refer to the column as ***tablename.columnname*** in the WHERE condition.

Output:

Order_No	Name	Order Date
O19003	Rahul Desai	03/10/97
O19006	Rahul Desai	12/01/97
O19001	Prem Iyer	12/04/97
O19004	Nalini Deewan	18/06/97
O19005	Vishal Parikh	20/08/97
O19002	Vishal Parikh	25/12/97

Example2:

Retrieve the product numbers, their description and the total quantity ordered for each product.

Table name: sales_order_details

Detorder No	Product No	Qty Ordered	Qty Disp
O19001	P00001	10	10
O19001	P00004	3	3
O19001	P00006	7	7
O19002	P00002	4	4
O19002	P00005	10	10
O19003	P00003	2	2
O19004	P00001	6	6
O19005	P00006	4	4
O19005	P00004	1	1
O19006	P00006	8	8

Table name: product_master

Product No	Description
P00001	1.44 Floppies
P00002	Monitors
P00003	Mouse
P00004	1.22 Floppies
P00005	Keyboards
P00006	CD Drive
P00007	HDD
P00008	1.44 Drive
P00009	1.22 Drive

SELECT *sales_order_details.product_no, description,*
       sum(qty_ordered) "Total Qty Ordered"
    FROM *sales_order_details, product_master*
    WHERE *product_master.product_no = sales_order_details.product_no*
    GROUP BY *sales_order_details.product_no, description;*

Output:

Product No	Description	Total Qty Ordered
P00001	1.44 Floppies	16
P00002	Monitors	4
P00003	Mouse	2
P00004	1.22 Floppies	4
P00005	Keyboards	10
P00006	CD Drive	19

Joining A Table to Itself (Self Joins):

In some situations, you may find it necessary to join a table to itself, as though you were joining two separate tables. This is referred to as a self-join. In a self-join, two rows from the same table combine to form a result row.

To join a table to itself, two copies of the very same table have to be opened in memory. Hence in the FROM clause, the table name needs to be mentioned twice. Since the table names are the same, the second table will overwrite the first table and in effect, result in only one table being in memory. This is because a table name is translated into a specific memory location. To avoid this, each table is opened under an alias. Now these table aliases will cause two identical tables to be opened in different memory locations. This will result in two identical tables to be physically present in the computer's memory.

Using the table alias names these two identical tables can be joined .

FROM tablename [alias1], tablename [alias2] ....

Example1:
Retrieve the names of the employees and the names of their respective managers from the employee table.

Table name: employee

Employee_No	Name	Manager_No
E00001	Basu Navindgi	E00002
E00002	Rukmini	E00005
E00003	Carol D'Souza	E00004
E00004	Cynthia Bayross	-
E00005	Ivan Bayross	-

> **SELECT** *emp.name, mngr.name manager*
> **FROM** *employee* **emp**, *employee* **mngr**
> **WHERE** *emp.manager_no = mngr.employee_no;*

Note

In this query, the employee table is treated as two separate tables named **emp** and **mngr**, using the table *alias* feature of SQL

Table name: **emp**

Employee No	Name	Manager No
E00001	Basu Navindgi	E00002
E00002	Rukmini	E00005
E00003	Carol D'Souza	E00004
E00004	Cynthia Bayross	-
E00005	Ivan Bayross	-

Table name: **mngr**

Employee No	Name	Manager No
E00001	Basu Navindgi	E00002
E00002	Rukmini	E00005
E00003	Carol D'Souza	E00004
E00004	Cynthia Bayross	-
E00005	Ivan Bayross	-

The join operation is evaluated as follows:

Using the compound condition
emp.client_no = **mngr**.client_no

where, each manager_no record (E00002, E00005, E00004) from the *emp* table is joined with the employee_no record (E00001, E00002, E00003, E00004, E00005) from the *mngr* table to form the following result :

Table name: **emp**

Employee No	Name	Manager No
E00001	Basu Navindgi	E00002
E00002	Rukmini	E00005
E00003	Carol D'Souza	E00004

Table name: **mngr**

Employee No	Name	Manager No
E00001	Rukmini	E00002
E00002	Ivan Bayross	E00005
E00003	Cynthia Bayross	E00004

Output:

Name	Manager
Basu Navindgi	Rukmini
Rukmini	Ivan Bayross
Carol D'Souza	Cynthia Bayross

Example2:
Retrieve the order number, Client number and Salesman No where a client has been serviced by more than one salesman from the *Sales_order* table.

Table name: sales_order

Order No	Client No	Salesman_No
O19001	C00006	S00002
O19002	C00002	S00001
O19003	C00007	S00004
O19004	C00005	S00003
O19005	C00002	S00003
O19006	C00007	S00002

> **SELECT** *first.order_no, first.client_no, first.salesman_no*
> **FROM** *sales_order first, sales_order second*
> **WHERE** *first.client_no = second.client_no* **AND**
> *first.salesman_no <> second.salesman_no;*

Note

In this query, the sales_order table is treated as two separate tables named **first** and **second**, using the table *alias* feature of SQL

Table name: **first**

Order No	Client No	Salesman_No
O19001	C00006	S00002
O19002	C00002	S00001
O19003	C00007	S00004
O19004	C00005	S00003
O19005	C00002	S00003
O19006	C00007	S00002

Table name: **second**

Order No	Client No	Salesman_No
O19001	C00006	S00002
O19002	C00002	S00001
O19003	C00007	S00004
O19004	C00005	S00003
O19005	C00002	S00003
O19006	C00007	S00002

The join operation is evaluated as follows:

First the following *Where clause* is applied:

Where **first**.client_no = **second**.client_no

Now the query holds the following intermediate output:

Order_no	First. Client_no	Second. Client_no	First. Salesman_no	First. Salesman_no
O19002	C00002	C00002	S00001	S00001
O19005	C00002	C00002	S00003	S00001
O19002	C00002	C00002	S00001	S00003
O19005	C00002	C00002	S00003	S00003
O19004	C00005	C00005	S00003	S00003
O19001	C00006	C00006	S00002	S00002
O19003	C00007	C00007	S00004	S00004
O19006	C00007	C00007	S00002	S00004
O19003	C00007	C00007	S00004	S00002
O19006	C00007	C00007	S00002	S00002

Then to this data set Oracle applies the second part of the where clause as

where **first**.salesman_no <> **second**.salesman_no

The resultant output to the query is as follows:

Order_no	First. Client_no	Second. Client_no	First. Salesman_no	First. Salesman_no
O19005	C00002	C00002	S00003	S00001
O19002	C00002	C00002	S00001	S00003
O19006	C00007	C00007	S00002	S00004
O19003	C00007	C00007	S00004	S00002

Since we need to display columns from table **first** only, the output will be

<u>Output:</u>

Order No	Client No	Salesman No
O19005	C00002	S00003
O19002	C00002	S00001
O19006	C00007	S00002
O19003	C00007	S00004

CONSTRUCTING AN ENGLISH SENTENCE WITH DATA FROM TABLE COLUMNS

Example:
Create an english sentence, by joining predetermined string values with column data retrieved from the sales_order table.

The string literals are: Order No.
                        was placed by Client No.
                        on
The columns are: order_no
                        client_no
                        order_date

Table name: sales_order

Order No	Client No	Order Date
O19001	C00006	12-apr-97
O19002	C00002	25-dec-97
O19003	C00007	03-oct97
O19004	C00005	18-jun-97
O19005	C00002	20-aug-97
O19006	C00007	12-jan-97

SELECT 'Order No. ' || order_no || ' was placed by Client No. ' ||
     •   Client_no || ' on ' || order_date
        FROM sales_order ;

Since the above SELECT cannot find an appropriate column header to print on the VDU screen, the SELECT uses the 'formula' i.e. the entire SELECT content as the column header as described below.

Output:
    'Orderno.'||Order_No||'Wasplacedbyclientno.'||Client_No||'On'||Order_Date
----
Order No. O19002 was placed by Client No. C00002 on 25-DEC-97
Order No. O19003 was placed by Client No. C00007 on 03-OCT-97
Order No. O19004 was placed by Client No. C00005 on 18-JUN-97
Order No. O19006 was placed by Client No. C00007 on 12-JAN-97
Order No. O19005 was placed by Client No. C00002 on 20-AUG-97
Order No. O19001 was placed by Client No. C00006 on 12-APR-97
Order No. O19100 was placed by Client No. C00001 on 31-DEC-97

To avoid a data header that appears meaningless, use an **alias** as shown below:

SELECT 'Order No. ' || order_no || ' was placed by Client No. ' ||
Client_no || ' on ' || order_date **"Orders Placed"**
FROM sales_order ;

Output:

Orders Placed

Order No. O19002 was placed by Client No. C00002 on 25-DEC-97
Order No. O19003 was placed by Client No. C00007 on 03-OCT-97
Order No. O19004 was placed by Client No. C00005 on 18-JUN-97
Order No. O19006 was placed by Client No. C00007 on 12-JAN-97
Order No. O19005 was placed by Client No. C00002 on 20-AUG-97
Order No. O19001 was placed by Client No. C00006 on 12-APR-97
Order No. O19100 was place by Client No. C00001 on 31-DEC-97

USING THE UNION, INTERSECT AND MINUS CLAUSE

Union Clause:

Multiple queries can be put together and their output combined using the union clause. The Union clause merges the output of two or more queries into a single set of rows and columns.

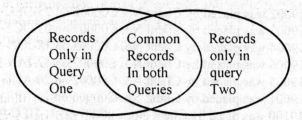

Output of the Union Clause

The output of both the queries will be as displayed above. The final output of the union clause will be:

Output = Records only in query one + records only in query two +
A single set of records which is common in both queries.

Example:
Retrieve the names of all the clients and salesmen in the city of 'Mumbai' from the tables client_master and salesman_master.

Table name: client_master

Client No	Name	City
C00001	Ashok Mehra	Mumbai
C00002	Vishal Parikh	Delhi
C00003	Ajay Mehta	Mumbai
C00004	Rohit Roy	Calcutta
C00005	Nalini Deewan	Mumbai
C00006	Prem Iyer	Delhi
C00007	Rahul Desai	Baroda

Table name: salesman_master

Salesman No	Name	City
S00001	Manish Patel	Mumbai
S00002	Kiran Dixit	Delhi
S00003	Nitesh Khanna	Mumbai
S00004	Mahesh Patil	Calcutta

      SELECT *salesman_no "ID", name*
          FROM *salesman_master*
          WHERE *city* = 'Mumbai'
UNION
      SELECT *client_no "ID", name*
          FROM *client_master*
          WHERE *city* = 'Mumbai' ;

Oracle executes the queries as follows:

      SELECT *client_no "ID", name*
          FROM *client_master*
          WHERE *city* = 'Mumbai' ;

The target table will be as follows:

ID	Name
C00001	Ashok Mehra
C00003	Ajay Mehta
C00005	Nalini Deewan

Then,

      SELECT *salesman_no "ID", name*
          FROM *salesman_master*
          WHERE *city* = 'Mumbai'

The target table will be as follows:

ID	Name
S00001	Manish Patel
S00003	Nitesh Khanna

The UNION clause picks up the common records as well as the individual records in both queries. Thus, the output after applying the UNION clause will be:

Output:

```
ID              NAME
------          --------------------
C00001          Ashok Mehra
C00003          Ajay Mehta
C00005          Nalini Deewan
S00001          Manish Patel
S00003          Nitesh Khanna
```

The Restrictions on using a union are as follows:
- Number of columns in all the queries should be the same.
- The datatype of the columns in each query must be same.
- Unions cannot be used in subqueries.
- Aggregate functions cannot be used with union clause.

Intersect Clause:

Multiple queries can be put together and their output combined using the intersect clause. The *Intersect* clause outputs only rows produced by both the queries intersected i.e. the output in an Intersect clause will include only those rows that are retrieved by both the queries.

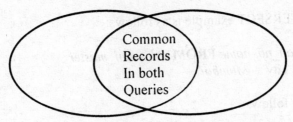

Common
Records
In both
Queries

Output of the Intersect Clause

The output of both the queries will be as displayed above. The final output of the Intersect clause will be:

Output = A single set of records which are common in both queries.

Example:
Retrieve the salesman name in 'Mumbai' whose efforts have resulted into atleast one sales transaction.

Table name: salesman_master

Salesman No	Name	City
S00001	Manish Patel	Mumbai
S00002	Kiran Dixit	Delhi
S00003	Nitesh Khanna	Mumbai
S00004	Mahesh Patil	Calcutta

Table name: sales_order

Order No	Order Date	Salesman No
O19001	12-Apr-97	S00001
O19002	25-Dec-97	S00003
O19003	03-Oct97	S00001
O19004	18-Jun-97	S00004
O19005	20-Aug-97	S00003
O19006	12-Jan-97	S00002

SELECT *salesman_no, name* **FROM** *salesman_master*
    WHERE city = '*Mumbai*'
INTERSECT
SELECT *salesman_master.salesman_no, name*
    FROM *salesman_master, sales_order*
    WHERE *salesman_master.salesman_no = sales_order. salesman_no;*

The first query in the INTERSECT example is as follows:

SELECT *salesman_no, name* **FROM** *salesman_master*
    WHERE city = '*Mumbai*'

The target table will be as follows:

Salesman No	Name
S00001	Manish Patel
S00003	Nitesh Khanna

The second query in the INTERSECT example is as follows:

SELECT salesman_master.salesman_no, name
    FROM salesman_master, sales_order
    WHERE salesman_master.salesman_no = sales_order. salesman_no;

The target table will be as follows:

Salesman No	Name
S00001	Manish Patel
S00003	Nitesh Khanna
S00001	Manish Patel
S00004	Mahesh Patil
S00003	Nitesh Khanna
S00002	Kiran Dixit

The INTERSECT clause picks up records that are comon in both queries. Thus, the output after applying the INTERSECT clause will be:

Output:

Salesman No	Name
S00001	Manish Patel
S00003	Nitesh Khanna

Minus Clause:

Multiple queries can be put together and their output combined using the minus clause. The *Minus* clause outputs the rows produced by the first query, after filtering the rows retrieved by the second query.

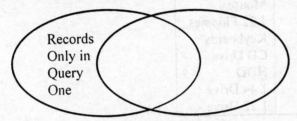

Output of the Minus Clause

Note

> The output of both the queries will be as displayed above. The final output of the minus clause will be:

Output = Records only in query one

Example:
Retrieve all the product numbers of non-moving items from the product_master table.

Table name: sales_order_details

Order No	Product No
O19001	P00001
O19001	P00004
O19001	P00006
O19002	P00002
O19002	P00005
O19003	P00003
O19004	P00001
O19005	P00006
O19005	P00004
O19006	P00006

Table name: product_master

Product No	Description
P00001	1.44 Floppies
P00002	Monitors
P00003	Mouse
P00004	1.22 Floppies
P00005	Keyboards
P00006	CD Drive
P00007	HDD
P00008	1.44 Drive
P00009	1.22 Drive

SELECT product_no **FROM** product_master
MINUS
SELECT product_no **FROM** sales_order_details;

The first query in the MINUS example is as follows:

SELECT product_no **FROM** product_master

The target table will be as follows:

Product No
P00001
P00002
P00003
P00004
P00005
P00006
P00007
P00008
P00009

The second query in the MINUS example is as follows:

SELECT product_no **FROM** sales_order_details

The target table will be as follows:

Product No
P00001
P00004
P00006
P00002
P00005
P00003
P00001
P00006
P00004
P00006

The MINUS clause picks up records in the first query after filtering the records retrieved by the second query. Thus, the output after applying the MINUS clause will be:

Output:

```
     Product No
    --------------
      P00007
      P00008
      P00009
```

SELF REVIEW QUESTIONS

READ THE QUESTIONS AND WRITE DOWN APPROPRIATE SQL STATEMENTS, AS ANSWERS.

1) Create the tables described below:

a) **Table Name**: Client_master
   Description: Used to store client information.

Column Name	Data Type	Size	Attributes
client_no	varchar2	6	Primary Key / first letter must start with 'C'
name	varchar2	20	Not Null
address1	varchar2	30	
address2	varchar2	30	
city	varchar2	15	
pincode	number	8	
state	varchar2	15	
bal_due	number	10,2	

b) **Table Name**: product_master
   Description: Used to store product information.

Column Name	Data Type	Size	Attributes
product_no	varchar2	6	Primary Key / first letter must start with 'P'
description	varchar2	15	Not Null
profit_percent	number	4,2	Not Null
unit_measure	varchar2	10	Not Null
qty_on_hand	number	8	Not Null
reorder_lvl	number	8	Not Null
sell_price	number	8,2	Not Null, cannot be 0.
cost_price	number	8,2	Not Null, cannot be 0.

c) **Table Name**: salesman_master
Description: Used to store salesman working for the company.

Column Name	Data Type	Size	Attributes
salesman_no	varchar2	6	Primary Key / first letter must start with 'S'
salesman_name	varchar2	20	Not Null
address1	varchar2	30	Not Null
address2	varchar2	30	
city	varchar2	20	
pincode	varchar2	8	
state	varchar2	20	
sal_amt	number	8,2	Not Null, cannot be 0
tgt_to_get	number	6,2	Not Null, cannot be 0
ytd_sales	number	6,2	Not Null
remarks	varchar2	60	

d) **Table Name**: sales_order
Description: Used to store client's orders

Column Name	Data Type	Size	Attributes
order_no	varchar2	6	Primary Key / first letter must start with 'O'
order_date	date		
client_no	varchar2	6	Foreign Key references client_no of client_master table
dely_Addr	varchar2	25	
salesman_no	varchar2	6	Foreign Key references salesman_no of salesman_master table
dely_type	char	1	Delivery : part(P) / full (F) Default 'F'
billed_yn	char	1	
dely_date	date		cannot be less than order_date
order_status	varchar2	10	Values ('In Process', 'Fulfilled', 'BackOrder', 'Cancelled')

e) **Table Name**: sales_order_details

Description: Used to store client's orders with details of each product ordered.

Column Name	Data Type	Size	Attributes
order_no	varchar2	6	Primary Key / Foreign Key references order_no of the sales_order table
product_no	varchar2	6	Primary Key / Foreign Key references product_no of the product_master table.
qty_ordered	number	8	
qty_disp	number	8	
product_rate	number	10,2	

2) Insert the following data into their respective tables:

a) Data for **client_master** table:

client no	name	City	pincode	state	bal. due
C00001	Ivan Bayross	Bombay	400054	Maharashtra	15000
C00002	Vandana Saitwal	Madras	780001	Tamil Nadu	0
C00003	Pramada Jaguste	Bombay	400057	Maharashtra	5000
C00004	Basu Navindgi	Bombay	400056	Maharashtra	0
C00005	Ravi Sreedharan	Delhi	100001	Delhi	2000
C00006	Rukmini	Bombay	400050	Maharashtra	0

b) Data for **product_master** table:

product no	description	profit percent	uom	qty on hand	reorder level	sell price	cost price
P00001	1.44 Floppies	5	Piece	100	20	525	500
P03453	Monitors	6	Piece	10	3	12000	11280
P06734	Mouse	5	Piece	20	5	1050	1000
P07865	1.22 Floppies	5	Piece	100	20	525	500
P07868	Keyboards	2	Piece	10	3	3150	3050
P07885	CD Drive	2.5	Piece	10	3	5250	5100
P07965	540 HDD	4	Piece	10	3	8400	8000
P07975	1.44 Drive	5	Piece	10	3	1050	1000
P08865	1.22 Drive	5	Piece	2	3	1050	1000

c) Data for **salesman_master** table:

salesman no	salesman name	address 1	address 2	city	pincode	state	salamt	tgt_to get	ytd sales	remarks
S00001	Kiran	A/14	Worli	Bombay	400002	Maharastra	3000	100	50	Good
S00002	Manish	65	Nariman	Bombay	400001	Maharastra	3000	200	100	Good
S00003	Ravi	P-7	Bandra	Bombay	400032	Maharastra	3000	200	100	Good
S00004	Ashish	A/5	Juhu	Bombay	400044	Maharastra	3500	200	150	Good

d) Data for **sales_order** table:

order no	order date	client no	dely type	bill yn	salesman no	dely date	order status
O19001	12-Jan-96	C00001	F	N	S00001	20-Jan-96	In Process
O19002	25-Jan-96	C00002	P	N	S00002	27-Jan-96	Cancelled
O46865	18-Feb-96	C00003	F	Y	S00003	20-Feb-96	Fulfilled
O19003	03-Apr-96	C00001	F	Y	S00001	07-Apr-96	Fulfilled
O46866	20-May-96	C00004	P	N	S00002	22-May-96	Cancelled
O19008	24-May-96	C00005	F	N	S00004	26-May-96	In Process

e) Data for **sales_order_details** table:

order no	product no	qty ordered	qty disp	product rate
O19001	P00001	4	4	525
O19001	P07965	2	1	8400
O19001	P07885	2	1	5250
O19002	P00001	10	0	525
O46865	P07868	3	3	3150
O46865	P07885	3	1	5250
O46865	P00001	10	10	525
O46865	P03453	4	4	1050
O19003	P03453	2	2	1050
O19003	P06734	1	1	12000
O46866	P07965	1	0	8400
O46866	P07975	1	0	1050
O19008	P00001	10	5	525
O19008	P07975	5	3	1050

3) Exercises on computations on table data:

a) Find the names of all clients having 'a' as the second letter in their names.

b) Find out the clients who stay in a city whose second letter is 'a'.

c) Find the list of all clients who stay in 'Bombay' or 'Delhi'

d) Print the list of clients whose bal_due is greater than value 10000.

e) Print the information from sales_order table for orders placed in the month of January.

f) Display the order information for client_no 'C00001' and 'C00002'.

g) Find products whose selling price is greater than 2000 and less than or equal to 5000.

h) Find products whose selling price is more than 1500. Calculate a new selling price as, original selling price * .15. Rename the new column in the above query as new_price.

i) List the names, city and state of clients who are not in the state of 'Maharashtra'.

j) Count the total number of orders.

k) Calculate the average price of all the products.

l) Determine the maximum and minimum product prices. Rename the output as max_price and min_price respectively.

m) Count the number of products having price greater than or equal to 1500.

n) Find all the products whose qty_on_hand is less than reorder level.

4) Exercise on Date Manipulation:

a) Display the order number and day on which clients placed their order.
b) Display the month (in alphabets) and date when the order must be delivered.
c) Display the order_date in the format 'DD-Month-YY'. e.g. 12-February-96.
d) Find the date, 15 days after today's date.
e) Find the number of days elapsed between today's date and the delivery date of the orders placed by the clients.

5) Exercises on using Having and Group By Clauses:

a) Print the description and total qty sold for each product.
b) Find the value of each product sold.
c) Calculate the average qty sold for each client that has a maximum order value of 15000.00.
d) Find out the sum total of all the billed orders for the month of January.

6) Exercises on Joins and Correlation:

a) Find out the products, which have been sold to 'Ivan Bayross'.
b) Find out the products and their quantities that will have to be delivered in the current month.
c) Find the product_no and description of constantly sold i.e. rapidly moving products.
d) Find the names of clients who have purchased 'CD Drive'.
e) List the product_no and order_no of customers having qty_ordered less than 5 from the sales_order_details table for the product '1.44 Floppies'.
f) Find the products and their quantities for the orders placed by 'Ivan Bayross' and 'Vandana Saitwal'.
g) Find the products and their quantities for the orders placed by client_no 'C00001' and 'C00002'.

7) Exercise on Sub-queries:

a) Find the product_no and description of non-moving products i.e. products not being sold.
b) Find the customer name, address1, address2, city and pincode for the client who has placed order no 'O19001'.
c) Find the client names who have placed orders before the month of May'96.
d) Find out if the product '1.44 Drive' has been ordered by any client and print the client_no, name to whom it was sold.
e) Find the names of clients who have placed orders worth Rs. 10000 or more.

8) Exercise on Constructing Sentences with data:

a) Print information from product_master, sales_order_detail tables in the following format for all the records :-
{description} worth Rs. {total sales for the product} was sold.

b) Print information from product_master, sales_order_detail tables in the following format for all the records :-
{description} worth Rs. {total sales for the product} was ordered in the month of {order_date in month format}.

c) Print information from client_master, product_master, sales_order tables in the following format for all the records :-
{cust_name} has placed order {order_no} on {order_date}.

➢ **Performing Computations On Data using**
   ▪ *Arithmetic operators like +, -, *, /*
   ▪ *Logical operators like AND, OR & NOT*
   ▪ *Range searching using the BETWEEN operator*
   ▪ *Pattern matching using the LIKE and IN predicates*

➢ **Dual Table & Sysdate**

➢ **Oracle Functions**
   ▪ *Group Functions*
   ▪ *Scalar functions*
      - String
      - Numeric
      - Date
      - Conversion functions

➢ **Data Constraints**
  ▪ *Types*
          - I/O constraints like Primary Key, Foreign Key
            Null & Unique constraints
          - Business constraints like Check constraints
  ▪ *Levels*
        - Table level constraints
        - Column level constraints
  ▪ *Significance of assigning user names to Constraints*

➢ **Setting default values for columns**

➢ **Creation and Deletion of constraints using the
    Alter Table clause**

➢ **The User_Constraints table.**

> **Retrieval of Data Grouped on conditions using**
>   - *Group By Clause*
>   - *Having Clause*

> **Date Manipulation with the use of**
>   - *to_char functions.*
>   - *to_date functions.*

> **Sub-queries**

> **Joins**
>   - *Joining Multiple Tables (Equi Joins)*
>   - *Joining a Table to itself (Self Joins)*

REVIEW CONTINUED ...

➢ **Constructing an English sentence using table data**

➢ **Union Clause**

➢ **Intersect Clause**

➢ **Minus Clause**

SQL Performance Tuning

IN THIS CHAPTER

> *Indexes*

> *Views*

> *Sequences*

4. SQL PERFORMANCE TUNING

INDEXES

When the user fires a SELECT statement to search for a particular record, the Oracle engine must first locate the table on the hard disk. The Oracle engine reads system information and locates the starting location of a table's records on the current storage media. The Oracle engine then performs a sequential search to locate records that match user-defined criteria.

For example, to locate all the orders placed by client 'C00001' held in the sales_order table the Oracle engine must first locate the sales_order table and then perform a sequential search on the client_no column seeking a value equal too 'C00001'.

The records in the sales_order table are stored in the order in which they are keyed in and thus to get all orders where client_no is equal to 'C00001' the Oracle engine must search the entire table column.

Indexing a table is an 'access strategy', that is, a way to sort and search records in the table. Indexes are essential to improve the speed with which the record/s can be located and retrieved from a table.

An index is an ordered list of the contents of a column, (or a group of columns) of a table.

Indexing involves forming a two dimensional matrix completely independent of the table on which the index is being created.

- A column, which will hold sorted data, extracted from the table on which the index is being created.
- An address field that identifies the location of the record in the Oracle database. This address field is called **Rowid**.

When data is inserted in the table, the Oracle engine inserts the data value in the index. For every data value held in the index the Oracle engine inserts a unique rowid value. This is done for every data value inserted into the index, without exception. This rowid indicates exactly where the record is stored in the table.

Hence once the appropriate index data values have been located, the Oracle engine locates an associated record in the table using the rowid found in the table.

The records in the index are sorted in the ascending order of the index column/s.

If the SELECT statement has a where clause for the table column that is indexed, the Oracle engine will scan the index sequentially looking for a match of the search criteria rather than the table column itself. The sequential search is done using an ASCII compare routine to scan the columns of an index.

Since the data is sorted on the indexed column/s, the sequential search ends as soon as the Oracle engine reads an index data value that does not meet the search criteria.

Address field in the Index:

The address field of an index is called ROWID. ROWID is an internal generated and maintained, binary value, which identifies a record. The information in the ROWID columns provides Oracle engine the location of the table and a specific record in the Oracle database.

The ROWID format used by Oracle is as follows:

BBBBBBB.RRRR.FFFF

Where,

- **FFFF** is a unique number given by the Oracle engine to each **Data File**. Data files are the files used by the Oracle engine to store user data.

For example, a database can be a collection of data files as follows:

Data File Name	Data File Number	Size of the Data Files
Sysorcl.ora	1	10 MB
Temporcl.ora	2	5 MB
Sctstaff.ora	3	30 MB
Sctstudent.ora	4	30 MB

Each data file is given a unique number at the time of data file creation. The Oracle engine uses this number to identify the data file in which sets of table records are stored.

- Each data file is further divided into **Data Blocks** and each block is given a unique number. The unique number assigned to the first data block in a data file 0. Thus block number can be used to identify the data block in which a record is stored. **BBBBBBB** is the block number in which the record is stored.

- Each data block can store one or more **Records**. Thus each record in the data block is given a unique record number. The unique record number assigned to the first record in each data block is 0. Thus record number can be used to identify a record stored in a block. **RRRR** is a unique record number.

Each time a record is inserted into the table, Oracle locates free space in the **Data Blocks** in the data files. Oracle then inserts a record in the table and makes an entry in the index. The entry made in the index consists of table data combined with the Oracle engine created **rowid** for the table record.

Thus, data in an index will be represented as follows:

Data Field	Address Field
S00001	00000440.0000.0003
S00002	00000440.0001.0003
S00003	00000440.0002.0003
S00004	00000441.0000.0003
S00005	00000441.0001.0003

To retrieve data from an Oracle table at the fastest speed possible, the Oracle engine requires 'Search Criteria' i.e. the value to look for in the index.

Since the data in the index is sorted, the sequential search ends as soon as the Oracle engine reads an index data value that does not meet the search criteria. Thus, Oracle engine need not search the entire index. This reduces data retrieval time.

Once the data value in an index is located, the address field in an index specifies a rowid which points to a data file, block and the record number directly. Thus the time taken by the Oracle engine to locate table data is reduced and data retrieval time is improved.

Example 1:
Retrieve order_no, order_date, client_no from sales_order table where client_no is equal to 'C00001'. ***There is no index on client_no created for the sales_order table***.

Table Name: sales_order

Order_no	Order_date	Client_no
S00001	12-Nov-97	C00001
S00002	30-Nov-97	C00003
S00003	1-Dec-97	C00001
S00004	28-Dec-97	C00002
S00005	17-Jan-98	C00003
S00006	19-Jan-98	C00001

Syntax:
      SELECT *order_no, order_date, client_no*
         FROM *sales_order*
         WHERE *client_no = 'C00001'*;

When the above select statement is executed, since an index is not created on client_no column, the Oracle engine will scan the Oracle system information to locate the table in the data file. The Oracle engine will then perform a sequential search to retrieve records that match the search criteria i.e. client_no = 'C00001' by comparing the value in the search criteria with the value in the client_no column from the first record to the last record in the table.

Example 2:
Retrieve order_no, order_date, client_no from sales_order table where client_no is equal to 'C00001'.

_Table sales_order is indexed on client_no._

The table data will be stored as follows:

Table Name: sales_order

Order_no	Order_date	Client_no
S00001	12-Nov-97	C00001
S00002	30-Nov-97	C00003
S00003	01-Dec-97	C00001
S00004	28-Dec-97	C00002
S00005	17-Jan-98	C00003
S00006	19-Jan-98	C00001

Since an index exists on the client_no column of the sales_order table, the index data will be represented as follows:

Index Name: idx_client_no

Client_no	ROWID
C00001	00000240.0000.0004
C00001	00000240.0002.0004
C00001	00000241.0002.0004
C00002	00000241.0000.0004
C00003	00000240.0001.0004
C00003	00000241.0001.0004

Note

The index is in the ascending order of client_no. The addresses have been assigned a data file number, block number and record number in the *order of creation*.

Syntax:

> **SELECT** *order_no, Order_date, client_no*
> **FROM** *sales_order*
> **WHERE** *client_no = 'C00001'* ;

When the above select statement is executed, since an index is created on client_no column, the Oracle engine will scan the index to search for a specific data value i.e. client_no equal to 'C00001'. The Oracle engine will then perform a sequential search to retrieve records that match the search criteria i.e. client_no = 'C00001'. When 'C00002' is read, the Oracle engine stops further retrieval from the index.

For the three records retrieved, the Oracle engine locates the address of the table records from the ROWID field and retrieves records stored at the specified address.

Client_no	ROWID
C00001	00000240.0000.0004
C00001	00000240.0002.0004
C00001	00000241.0002.0004

The Rowid in the current example indicates that the record with client_no 'C00001' is located in data file 0004. Two records are stored in block 00000240 with record number 0000 and 0002. The third record is stored in block 00000241 with record number 0002.

Thus data retrieval from a table by using an index is faster than data retrieval from the table where indexes are not defined.

Duplicate / Unique Index:

Oracle allows the creation of two types of indexes. These are:
- Indexes that **allow** duplicate values for the indexed columns i.e. **Duplicate Index**
- Indexes that **deny** duplicate values for the indexed columns i.e. **Unique Index**

Creation of Index:

An index can be created on one or more columns. Based on the number of columns included in the index, an index can be:
- Simple Index
- Composite Index

Creating Simple Index:

An index created on a single column of a table it is called **Simple Index**. The syntax for creating simple index that *allows duplicate values* is:

<u>Syntax:</u>
> **CREATE INDEX** *indexname*
> > **ON** *tablename (columnname)* ;

<u>Example:</u>
Create a simple index on client_no column of the client_master table.

<u>Syntax:</u>
> **CREATE INDEX** *idx_client_no*
> > **ON** *client_master (client_no)* ;

Creating Composite Index:

An index created on more than one column it is called **Composite Index**. The syntax for creating a composite index that *allows duplicate values* is:

<u>Syntax:</u>
> **CREATE INDEX** *indexname*
> > **ON** *tablename (columnname, columnname)* ;

<u>Example:</u>
Create a composite index on the sales_order_details tables on column order_no and product_no.

<u>Syntax:</u>
> **CREATE INDEX** *idx_sales_order_details*
> > **ON** *sales_order_details (order_no, product_no)* ;

Note

> The indexes in the above examples do not enforce uniqueness i.e. the columns included in the index can have duplicate values. To create unique index, the keyword UNIQUE should be included in the *Create Index* command.

Creation of Unique Index:

An unique index can also be created on one or more columns. If an index is created on a single column it is called **Simple Unique Index**. The syntax for creating a simple unique index is:

<u>Syntax:</u>
> **CREATE UNIQUE INDEX** *indexname*
> > **ON** *tablename (columnname)* ;

If an index is created on more than one column it is called **Composite Unique Index**. The syntax for creating a composite unique index is:

Syntax:
>   CREATE UNIQUE INDEX *indexname*
>   ON *tablename (columnname, columnname)* ;

Example:
Create a unique index on client_no column of the client_master table.

Syntax:
>   CREATE UNIQUE INDEX *idx_client_no*
>   ON *client_master (client_no)* ;

> When the user defines a primary key or a unique key constraint, the Oracle engine automatically creates a unique index on the primary key or unique key column/s.

Dropping Indexes:

Indexes associated with the tables can be removed by using the DROP INDEX command.

Syntax:
>   DROP INDEX *indexname* ;

Example:
>   Remove index idx_client_no created for the table client_master;
>
>   DROP INDEX idx_client_no;

> When a table, which has associated indexes (unique or non-unique) is dropped, the Oracle engine automatically drops all the associated indexes as well.

Multiple Indexes on a Table:

The Oracle engine allows creation of multiple indexes on each table. The Oracle engine prepares a query plan to decide on the index that must be used for specific data retrieval based on the where clause or the order by clause specified in the SELECT statement.

Whenever a SELECT statement is executed, the Oracle engine prepares a Query plan that identifies the data retrieval method. The query plan among other information indicates the name of the data retrieval table and the name of the index that must be used for data retrieval.

For example if a SELECT statement is fired without a where clause and without an order by clause the Oracle engine does not use indexes created on the table for data extraction.

Similarly if an Order By clause is not specified the Oracle engine does not use indexes created on the table for data extraction.

If a where clause or an Order By clause is specified, the Oracle engine uses the index created on a column on which the where clause or the order by clause is specified.

If there is no index for the column specified in the where clause or the order by clause is not created, data is retrieved without using indexes.

Instances when the Oracle engine uses an index for data extraction:

- A SELECT statement with WHERE clause specified on the column on which an index exists.
- A SELECT statement with ORDER BY clause specified on the column on which an index exists.

Instances when the Oracle engine does not use an index for data extraction:

- A SELECT statement without search criteria and order by clause.
- A SELECT statement with WHERE clause specified on the column on which an index is not defined.
- A SELECT statement with ORDER BY clause specified on the column on which an index is not defined.

Too many indexes - A Problem:

Each time a record is inserted into the table, Oracle locates free space in the blocks in the data files. The Oracle engine then inserts a record in all the indexes associated with the table. The index entries are sorted in the ascending order as well. If too many indexes were created the Oracle engine would take longer to insert a record in the table since index processing must be done after every record.

Thus though indexes speeds up data retrieval, the inserts would be slow. A balance must be maintained such that only the columns that are frequently used for retrieval are indexed.

USING ROWID TO DELETE DUPLICATE ROWS FROM A TABLE

If the user enters duplicate records in a table, a DELETE statement with a where clause will delete all the records that satisfy the where condition specified in the DELETE statement.

For example if the data in the client_master table is:

Client_no	Name	Bal_due
C00001	Ivan Bayross	300.00
C00001	Ivan Bayross	300.00
C00001	Ivan Bayross	300.00
C00003	Praveen Bangera	6000.00
C00002	Vaishali Bhayani	700.00
C00003	Praveen Bangera	6000.00
C00001	Ivan Bayross	300.00
C00004	Ashish Mehta	1000.000
C00003	Praveen Bangera	6000.00
C00005	Lakshmi Iyer	0.00
C00002	Vaishali Bhayani	700.00

And a delete statement is executed as

> **DELETE FROM** *client_master*
> **WHERE** *client_no in ('C00001' , 'C00002', 'C00003');*

All the records with client_no 'C00001', 'C00002' or 'C00003' will be deleted.

What is required is that the Oracle engine must retain one record and delete all other duplicate records. To retain one record, the where clause must be defined on the column that uniquely identifies a record.

As seen earlier, even if user enters duplicate records, Oracle will assign a unique rowid value that points to a record within a block in the data file for each record entered by the user.

A specific record in a table will be stored within a block in the data file. Each record in a block is given a unique record number. Thus at any time the value in the rowid column will always be unique.

A DELETE statement must be written such that the WHERE clause is defined using the rowid column. The values for the WHERE clause in the DELETE statement must be selected by using a SELECT statement that retrieves the rowid of the first row in each set of duplicate records in the table.

Thus when a WHERE clause is specified in the DELETE statement with the NOT IN operator it deletes all the duplicate rows but isolates one row in each set.

A subquery is an SQL statement that extracts values from table columns using a SELECT statement and passes these values as input to another SQL statement. The SELECT statement is called *Inner SQL statement* and the SQL statement to which the values of the select statement are passed is called *Parent SQL statement*. The parent SQL statement can be an INSERT, UPDATE, DELETE, SELECT or CREATE TABLE statement.

The Oracle engine executes the inner SELECT statement and then processes the parent SQL statement based on the values retrieved by the inner SELECT statement.

Inner Select Statement:

To create a record set of identical records from a table, the records must be grouped on all the columns in the table by using a GROUP BY clause in the SELECT statement.

A SELECT statement will then retrieve the rowid of the first row in each set of duplicate records. The first row in each set can be extracted by using the MIN function that returns the minimum value from a set of values. Thus the select statement will be

SELECT *min(rowid)* **FROM** *client_master*
GROUP BY *client_no, name, bal_due*

Parent SQL statement:

In the current example the Parent SQL statement will be a DELETE statement that will delete the records based on the rowid fetched by the Inner SQL statement.

Thus subquery used to delete duplicate rows will be

Syntax:

DELETE FROM *client_master*
WHERE *rowid* **NOT IN**
(**SELECT** *min (rowid)* **FROM** *client_master*
GROUP BY *client_no, name, bal_due*);

When the inner SELECT statement is executed, data is grouped on all the columns of the table and the MIN function returns the minimum rowid in the group as. Thus the output in memory will be as

ROWID	Client_no	Name	Bal_due
00000240.0000.0004	C00001	Ivan Bayross	300.00
00000240.0002.0004	C00003	Praveen Bangera	6000.00
00000241.0001.0004	C00002	Vaishali Bhayani	700.00
00000241.0002.0004	C00004	Ashish Mehta	1000.00
00000241.0003.0004	C00005	Lakshmi Iyer	0.00

The Oracle engine after the execution of the inner SELECT statement replaces the SELECT statement with the Minimum rowid for each group as retrieved by the SELECT statement. Thus the delete statement will be changed to:

> DELETE FROM *client_master*
> WHERE *rowid* NOT IN
> (*'00000240.0000.0004'*, *'00000240.0002.0004'*,
> *'00000241.0001.0004'*, *'00000241.0002.0004'*,
> *'00000241.0003.0004'*);

Thus all records with rowid other that those in the list specified above are deleted.

If a select statement is executed on the client_master table after such a delete operation, the Oracle engine displays the following output.

Syntax:

> SELECT *client_no, name, bal_due*
> FROM *client_master;*

Output:

Client_no	Name	Bal_due
C00001	Ivan Bayross	300. 00
C00003	Praveen Bangera	6000. 00
C00002	Vaishali Bhayani	700. 00
C00004	Ashish Mehta	1000.00
C00005	Lakshmi Iyer	0.00

Using this technique, duplicate records can be deleted from the table while maintaining one record in the table for reference.

USING ROWNUM IN SQL STATEMENTS

For each row returned by a query, the ROWNUM pseudo column returns a number indicating the order in which Oracle engine selects the row from a table or set of joined rows. The first row selected has a ROWNUM of 1; the second has 2, and so on.

Using ROWNUM to limit number of rows in a Query:

ROWNUM can be used to limit the number of rows retrieved.

Example:
Retrieve first seven rows by using ROWNUM

Table Name: Client_master

Client_No	Name
C00001	Ivan Bayross
C00002	Vandana Saitwal
C00003	Pramada Jaguste
C00004	Praveen
C00005	Ravi Sreedharan
C00006	Rukmini
C00007	Amar
C00008	Vijay Thakkar
C00009	Ashok Shroff
C00010	Anil Pathak
C00011	Sunil Verma
C00012	Rishabh Shah
C00013	Ramesh Gupta
C00014	Manjit Singh
C00015	Nikhilesh Choudhary
C00016	Ajit Mittal

Syntax:
> **SELECT** *ROWNUM, client_no, name*
> **FROM** *client_master*
> **WHERE** *ROWNUM < 8;*

Output:

ROWNUM	CLIENT_NO	NAME
1	C00001	Ivan Bayross
2	C00002	Vandana Saitwal
3	C00003	Pramada Jaguste
4	C00004	Praveen
5	C00005	Ravi Sreedharan
6	C00006	Rukmini
7	C00007	Amar

Caution

The Oracle engine assigns a ROWNUM value to each row as it is retrieved, before rows are sorted on the column/s in the ORDER BY clause. The order in which data is retrieved is dependent upon the indexes created on the table.

If an _index is created_ on the column/s used in the order by clause, the Oracle engine uses the index to retrieve data in a sorted order. Thus the ROWNUM will be _in the order of the rows retrieved from the index._

If an _index is not created_ on the column/s used in the order by clause, the Oracle engine will retrieve data from the table in the order of data insertion and thus an _ORDER BY_ clause _does not affect_ the ROWNUM of each row.

ORDER BY Clause, Index used and ROWNUM:

If the ORDER BY clause is specified and the Oracle engine does not use an index, the rows will be retrieved in the order in which the data was inserted and thus the ROWNUM assigned will also be in the same order.

Example:
Retrieve first seven rows by using ROWNUM. Sort the data in the ascending order of name.

No Index is defined on column 'Name'.

Syntax:

```
SELECT ROWNUM, client_no, name
    FROM client_master
    WHERE ROWNUM < 8
    ORDER BY name;
```

Output:

ROWNUM	CLIENT	NAME
7	C00007	Amar
1	C00001	Ivan Bayross
3	C00003	Pramada Jaguste
4	C00004	Praveen
5	C00005	Ravi Sreedharan
6	C00006	Rukmini
2	C00002	Vandana Saitwal

If an ORDER BY clause causes the Oracle engine to use an index to access the data, the Oracle engine will retrieve the rows in the order of the index used.

Example:

Create an index named idx_client_name is created on the Client_master table for the 'Name' column as follows:

Syntax:

> **CREATE INDEX** idx_client_name
> **ON** client_master (name);

Retrieve first seven rows by using ROWNUM. Sort the data in the ascending order of name.

Syntax:

> **SELECT** ROWNUM, client_no, name
> **FROM** client_master
> **WHERE** ROWNUM < 8
> **ORDER BY** name;

Output:

ROWNUM	CLIENT_NO	NAME
1	C00016	Ajit Mittal
2	C00007	Amar
3	C00010	Anil Pathak
4	C00009	Ashok Shroff
5	C00001	Ivan Bayross
6	C00014	Manjit Singh
7	C00015	Nikhilesh Choudhary

VIEWS

After a table is created and populated with data, it may become necessary to *prevent all users from accessing all columns* of a table, for data security reasons. This would mean creating several tables having the appropriate number of columns and assigning specific users to each table, as required. This will answer data security requirements very well but will give rise to a great deal of redundant data being resident in tables, in the database.

To reduce redundant data to the minimum possible, Oracle allows the creation of an object called a View. A View is mapped, to a SELECT sentence. The table on which the view is based is described in the FROM clause of the SELECT statement. The SELECT clause consists of a sub-set of the columns of the table. Thus a View, which is mapped to a table, will in effect have a sub-set of the actual columns of the table from which it is built. This technique offers a simple, effective way of hiding columns of a table.

An interesting fact about a View is that it is stored only as a definition in Oracle's system catalogue. When a reference is made to a View, its definition is scanned, the base table is opened and the View created on top of the base table. *Hence, a view holds no data at all, until a specific call to the view is made. This reduces redundant data on the HDD to a very large extent.* When a View is used to manipulate table data, the underlying base table will be completely invisible. *This will give the level of data security required.*

The Oracle engine treats a View just as though it was a base table. Hence a View can be queried exactly as though it was a base table. However, a query fired on a view will run slower that a query fired on a base table. This is because the View definition has to be retrieved from Oracle's system catalogue, the base table has to be identified and opened in memory and then the View has to be constructed on top of the base table, suitably masking table columns. Only then will the query actually execute and return the active data set.

Some View's are used only for looking at table data. Other View's can be used to Insert, Update and Delete table data as well as View data. If a View is used to only look at table data and nothing else the View is called a *Read-Only* View. A View that is used to Look at table data as well as Insert, Update and Delete table data is called an *Updateable* View.

The reasons why views are created are:
➢ When Data security is required
➢ When Data redundancy is to be kept to the minimum while maintaining data security

Lets spend some time in learning how a View is
➢ Created
➢ Used for only viewing *and / or* manipulating table data
  ➢ *i.e. a read-only or updateable view*
➢ Destroyed

Creation of views:

<u>Syntax</u>:

> **CREATE VIEW** *viewname* **AS**
> > *SELECT columnname, columnname*
> > *FROM tablename*
> > *WHERE columnname = expression list;*
> > *GROUP BY grouping criteria*
> > *HAVING predicate*

Note

The ORDER BY clause cannot be used while creating a view.

<u>Example</u>:

Create a view on the salesman_master table for the Sales Department.

> **CREATE VIEW** *vw_sales* **AS**
> > *SELECT * FROM salesman_master;*

Note

The columns of the table are related to the view on a one-to-one relationship.

<u>Example</u>:

Create a view on the client_master table for the Administration Department.

> **CREATE VIEW** *vw_clientadmin* **AS**
> > *SELECT name, address1, address2, city, pincode, state*
> > *FROM client_master;*

This creates a view by the name of *vw_clientadmin* based on the table *client_master*.

Renaming the columns of a view:

The columns of the view can take on different names from the table columns, if required.

<u>Example</u>:

> **CREATE VIEW** *vw_clientadmin* **AS**
> > *SELECT name, address1 add1, address2 add2, city, pincode, state*
> > *FROM client_master;*

Selecting a data set from a view:

Once a view has been created, it can be queried exactly like a base table.

<u>Syntax:</u>
> **SELECT** *columnname,columnname*
> **FROM** *viewname;*

Note

Instead of the table name in the FROM clause, a <u>*view name*</u> is used. The SELECT statement can have all the clauses like WHERE, ORDER BY etc.

<u>Example:</u>
> **SELECT** *name, address1, address2, city, pincode, state*
> **FROM** *vw_clientadmin*
> **WHERE** *city IN ('BOMBAY', 'DELHI');*

Updateable Views:

Views can also be used for data manipulation (i.e. the user can perform the Insert, Update and Delete operations). Views on which data manipulation can be done are called *Updateable Views*. When you give an updateable view name in the Update, Insert or Delete SQL statement, modifications to data will be passed to the underlying table.

For a view to be updateable, it should meet the following criteria:

<u>Views defined from Single table:</u>
- If the user wants to **INSERT** records with the help of a view, then the PRIMARY KEY column/s and all the NOT NULL columns must be included in the view.
- The user can **UPDATE, DELETE** records with the help of a view even if the PRIMARY KEY column and NOT NULL column/s **are excluded** from the view definition.

Example:

Table Name: Client_master

Column Name	Data type	Size	Attributes
Client_no	Varchar2	6	Primary key
Name	Varchar2	15	Not Null
Address1	Varchar2	15	Not Null
Address2	Varchar2	15	
City	Varchar2	10	
Pincode	Number	8	
Bal_due	Number	8,2	

Syntax for creating an Updateable View:

>   **CREATE VIEW** *vw_client* **AS**
>   **SELECT** *client_no, name, address1, bal_due*
>   **FROM** *client_master;*

- When an **INSERT** operation is performed using the view
  SQL> insert into vw_client values ('C0011', 'Robert', '1/101, Kurla', 1000);
  Oracle returns the following message:

  1 row created.

- When an **MODIFY** operation is performed using the view
  SQL> update vw_client set bal_due=10000 where client_no='C0011';
  Oracle returns the following message:

  1 row updated.

- When an **DELETE** operation is performed using the view
  SQL> delete from vw_client where client_no='C0011';
  Oracle returns the following message:

  1 rows deleted.

A view can be created from more than one table. For the purpose of creating the View these tables will be linked by a join condition specified in the where clause of the View's definition.

The behavior of the View will vary for Insert, Update, Delete and Select table operations depending upon the following:

- Whether the tables were created using a Referencing clause
- Whether the tables were created without any Referencing clause and are actually standalone tables not related in any way.

Views defined from Multiple tables (Which have no Referencing clause):

If a view is created from multiple tables, which were **not created** using a 'Referencing clause' (i.e. No logical linkage exists between the tables), then though the PRIMARY Key Column/ s as well as the NOT NULL columns *are included* in the View definition the view's behavior will be as follows:

- The INSERT, UPDATE or DELETE operation is **not allowed**. If attempted Oracle displays the following error message:

For insert/modify:
ORA –01779: cannot modify a column, which maps to a non key-preserved table.
For delete:
ORA –01752: cannot delete from view without exactly one key-preserved table.

Views defined from Multiple tables (Which have been created with a Referencing clause):

If a view is created from multiple tables, which **were created** using a 'Referencing clause' (i.e. a logical linkage exists between the tables), then though the PRIMARY Key Column/ s as well as the NOT NULL columns *are included* in the View definition the view's behavior will be as follows:

- An **INSERT** operation is not allowed.
- The **DELETE** or **MODIFY** operations *do not* affect the Master table.
- The view can be used to **MODIFY** the columns of the *detail table* included in the view.
- If a **DELETE** operation is executed on the view, the corresponding records from the *detail table* will be deleted.

Example:
a) **Table Name**: sales_order

Column Name	Data Type	Size	Attributes
order_no	varchar2	6	Primary Key / first letter must start with 'O'
order_date	date		
client_no	varchar2	6	Foreign Key references client_no of client_master table
dely_Addr	varchar2	25	
salesman_no	Varchar2	6	Foreign Key references salesman_no of salesman_master table
dely_type	char	1	Delivery : part(P) / full (F), Default 'F'
billed_yn	char	1	
dely_date	date		cannot be less than order_date
order_status	varchar2	10	Values ('In Process', 'Fulfilled', 'BackOrder', 'Cancelled')

b) **Table Name**: sales_order_details

Column Name	Data Type	Size	Attributes
detorder_no	varchar2	6	Primary Key / Foreign Key references order_no of the sales_order table
product_no	Varchar2	6	Primary Key / Foreign Key references product_no of the product_master table.
qty_ordered	Number	8	
qty_disp	Number	8	
product_rate	Number	10,2	

Syntax for creating a Master/Detail View:

> **CREATE VIEW** *vw_sales* **AS**
> **SELECT** *order_no,order_date, dely_addr, product_no, qty_ordered ,qty_disp*
> **FROM** *sales_order, sales_order_details*
> **WHERE** *sales_order.order_no =sales_order_details.detorder_no;*

- When an **INSERT** operation is performed using the view
  SQL> insert into vw_sales values ('O000011','12-Jan-98','Malad','P00001',100, 50);
  Oracle returns the following error message:

  ORA-01776: cannot modify more than one base table through a join view

- When an **MODIFY** operation is performed using the view
  SQL> update vw_sales set qty_disp =100 where detorder_no='O0007';
  Oracle returns the following message:

  1 row updated.

- When an **DELETE** operation is performed using the view
  SQL> delete from vw_sales where product_no ='P0001' and
                          detorder_no='O0001';
  Oracle returns the following message:

  1 rows deleted.

Common restrictions on updateable views:
The following condition holds true irrespective of the view being created from a single table or multiple tables.
  - For the view to be updateable the view definition must not include:
    - Aggregate functions.
    - DISTINCT, GROUP BY or HAVING clause.
    - Sub-queries.
    - Constants, Strings or Value Expressions like sell_price * 1.05.
    - UNION, INTERSECT or MINUS clause.
  - If a view is defined from another view, the second view should be updateable.

If the user tries to perform any of INSERT, UPDATE, DELETE operation, on a view which is created from a *non-updateable view* Oracle returns the following error message:

For insert/modify/delete:
ORA-01732: data manipulation operation not legal on this view

Destroying a view:

The **DROP VIEW** command is used to remove a view from the database.
Syntax:
       DROP VIEW *viewname;*
Example:
Remove the view vw_clientadmin from the database.
       DROP VIEW *vw_clientadmin;*

SEQUENCES

The quickest way to retrieve data from a table is to have a column in the table whose data uniquely identifies a row. By using this column and a specific value, in the Where condition of a Select sentence the Oracle engine will be able to identify and retrieve the row fastest.

To achieve this, a constraint is attached to a specific column in the table that ensures that the column is never left empty and that the data values in the column are unique. Since data entry is done by human beings it is quite likely that duplicate value will be entered, which violates the constraint and the entire row is rejected.

If the value to be entered into this column is machine generated it will always fulfil the constraint and the row will always be accepted for storage.

ORACLE provides an object called a _Sequence_ that can generate numeric values. The value generated can have a maximum of 38 digits. A sequence can be defined to
- generate numbers in ascending or descending
- provide intervals between numbers
- caching of sequence numbers in memory etc.

A sequence is an independent object and can be used with any table that requires its output.

Creating Sequences:

The minimum information required for generating numbers using a sequence is:
- The starting number
- The maximum number that can be generated by a sequence
- The increment value for generating the next number.

This information is provided to Oracle at the time of sequence creation. The SQL statement used for creating a sequence is:

Syntax:

```
CREATE SEQUENCE sequence_name
     [INCREMENT BY integervalue
      START WITH integervalue
      MAXVALUE integervalue / NOMAXVALUE
      MINVALUE integervalue / NOMINVALUE
      CYCLE / NOCYCLE
      CACHE integervalue / NOCACHE
      ORDER  / NOORDER]
```

Note

Sequence is always given a name so that it can be referenced later when required.

Keywords and Parameters:

INCREMENT BY:
Specifies the interval between sequence numbers. It can be any positive or negative value but not zero. If this clause is omitted, the default value is 1.

MINVALUE:
Specifies the sequence minimum value.

NOMINVALUE:
Specifies a minimum value of 1 for an ascending sequence and $-(10)^{26}$ for a descending sequence.

MAXVALUE:
Specifies the maximum value that a sequence can generate.

NOMAXVALUE:
Specifies a maximum of 10^{27} for an ascending sequence or -1 for a descending sequence. This is the default clause.

START WITH:
Specifies the first sequence number to be generated. The default for an ascending sequence is the sequence minimum value (1) and for a descending sequence, it is the maximum value (-1).

CYCLE:
Specifies that the sequence continues to generate repeat values after reaching either its maximum value.

NOCYCLE:
Specifies that a sequence cannot generate more values after reaching the maximum value.

CACHE:
Specifies how many values of a sequence ORACLE pre-allocates and keeps in memory for faster access. The minimum value for this parameter is **two.**

NOCACHE:
Specifies that values of a sequence are not pre-allocated.

Note

If the CACHE / NOCACHE clause is omitted ORACLE caches 20 sequence numbers by default.

ORDER:

This guarantees that sequence numbers are generated in the order of request. This is only necessary if you are using Parallel Server in Parallel mode option. In exclusive mode option, a sequence always generates numbers in order.

NOORDER:

This does not guarantee sequence numbers are generated in order of request. This is only necessary if you are using Parallel Server in Parallel mode option. If the ORDER / NOORDER clause is omitted, a sequence takes the NOORDER clause by default.

Note

The Order, NoOrder Clause has no significance, if Oracle is configured with Single Server option.

Example:

Create a sequence by the name order_seq, which will generate numbers from 1 upto 9999 in ascending order with an interval of 1. The sequence must restart from the number 1 after generating number 9999.

```
CREATE SEQUENCE order_seq
    INCREMENT BY 1
    START WITH 1
    MINVALUE 1
    MAXVALUE 9999
    CYCLE;
```

Referencing a Sequence:

Once a sequence is created SQL can be used to view the values held in its cache. To simply view sequence value use a Select sentence as described below:

SELECT sequence_name.**nextval** FROM dual;

This will display the next value held in the cache on the VDU screen. Every time **nextval** references a sequence its output is automatically incremented from the old value to the new value ready for use.

The example below explains how to access a sequence and use its generated value in the insert statement:

Example:
Insert values for order_no, order_date, client_no in the sales_order table. The **order_seq** sequence must be used to generate order_no and order_date must be set to system date.

Table Name: Sales_order

Column Name	Data Type	Size	Attributes
order_no	varchar2	6	Primary Key
order_date	date		
client_no	varchar2	6	
dely_Addr	varchar2	25	
salesman_no	varchar2	6	
dely_type	char	1	delivery : part(P) / full (F) **Default 'F'**
billed_yn	char	1	
dely_date	date		
order_status	varchar2	10	

Syntax:
       INSERT INTO *sales_order*
                (order_no, order_date, client_no)
                VALUES *(***order_seq.nextval**, *sysdate, 'C00001');*

To reference the current value of a sequence:

       SELECT *sequence_name*.**currval** FROM *dual*;

This is how, a numeric value generated by the system, using a sequence can be used to insert values into a primary key column.

The most commonly used technique in commercial application development is to concatenate a sequence-generated value with a user-entered value.

The order_no stored in the sales_order table, can be a concatenation of the month and year from the system date and the number generated by the sequence *order_seq*. For example order_no 01981 is generated with 01 (month in number format), 98 (year in number format) and 1(a sequence generated value).

To help keep the sequence generated number from becoming too large, each time either the month (or year) changes the sequence can be reset.

The sequence can be reset at the end of each month. If the company generated 50 sales orders for the month of January 98, the order_no will start with 01981 upto 019850. Again when the month changes to February and as the sequence is reset, the numbering will start with 02981, 02982....

Using this simple technique of resetting the sequence at the end of each month and concatenating the sequence with the system date, we can generate unique values for the order_no column and reduce the size of the number generated by the sequence.

Example:
<pre>
        INSERT INTO sales_order
            (order_no, order_date, client_no)
        VALUES (to_char(sysdate,'MMYY'||to_char(order_seq.nextval), sysdate,
            'C00001');
</pre>

Altering A Sequence:

A sequence once created can be altered. This is achieved by using the ALTER SEQUENCE statement.

Syntax:
<pre>
        ALTER SEQUENCE sequence_name
            [INCREMENT BY integervalue
            MAXVALUE integervalue / NOMAXVALUE
            MINVALUE integervalue / NOMINVALUE
            CYCLE / NOCYCLE
            CACHE integervalue / NOCACHE
            ORDER /NOORDER]
</pre>

Note

The START value of the sequence cannot be altered.

Example:
Change the Cache value of the sequence order_seq to 30 and interval between two numbers as 2.

<pre>
        ALTER SEQUENCE order_seq
            INCREMENT BY 2
            CACHE 30;
</pre>

Dropping A Sequence:

The DROP SEQUENCE command is used to remove the sequence from the database.

<u>Syntax</u>:
    DROP SEQUENCE *sequence_name*;

<u>Example</u>:
Remove the sequence *order_seq*.

    DROP SEQUENCE *order_seq*;

SELF REVIEW QUESTIONS

READ THE QUESTIONS AND WRITE DOWN APPROPRIATE SQL STATEMENTS, AS ANSWERS.

1. Create a sequence *inv_seq*, which will generate the numbers from 1 to 9999 in ascending order.

2. Use the sequence *inv_seq* to generate values for inv_no column in the invoice_hdr table. Note that the invoice number must start with 'I'.

   Table name: Invoice_hdr
   Description: Used to store invoice information.

Column Name	Data type	Size	Remarks
inv_no	Number	4	Primary key
inv_dt	Date		
clientname	Varchar	20	

3. Give the syntax to create a view *vw_prod* on the product_master table. Give example for **Inserting**, **Updating** and **Deleting** record/s using the view *vw_prod*.

   Table Name: product_master
   Description: Used to store product information.

Column Name	Data Type	Size	Attributes
Product_no	varchar2	6	Primary Key / first letter must start with 'P'
Description	varchar2	5	Not Null
Profit_percent	number	4,2	
Unit_measure	varchar2	10	
Qty_on_hand	number	8	Not Null
Reorder_lvl	number	8	
Cost_price	number	8,2	Not Null
Sell_price	number	8,2	

4. **FILL IN THE BLANKS**

1. _____ are masks placed upon tables.

   A) Views
   B) Sequences
   C) Tables
   D) Indexes.

2. The index created by the Primary key column is called _____ .

3. Views can be classified as _____ and _____.

4. The _____ parameter cannot be changed while altering a sequence.

5. Oracle caches _____ sequence numbers by default.

6. The _____ operation cannot be performed using views when the view definition includes more than one table.

7. When a view is defined from multiple tables, which have been created with a referencing clause, the *modify* and the *delete* operations affect only the _____ table.

8. List any three common restrictions on updatable views

   • _____.

   • _____.

   • _____.

9. When multiple table columns are included in the index, it is called a _____.

10. The _____ clause cannot be used while creating a view.

A QUICK REVIEW

➢ **Indexes**

- *Understanding indexes*
- *Creating indexes*
    - Simple indexes
    - Unique indexes
- *Altering indexes*
- *Dropping indexes*

➢ **Views**

- *Advantages to using views*
- *Creating and Using views*
    - ReadOnly Views
    - Updateable Views
- *Altering views*
- *Dropping views*

➢ **Sequences**

- *Creation and use of sequences*
- *Referencing a sequence*
- *Altering sequences*
- *Dropping sequences*

CHAPTER FIVE

Security Management Using SQL

> Granting Rights on User Obejcts

> Revoking Rights on User Obejcts

5. SECURITY MANAGEMENT USING SQL

GRANTING AND REVOKING PERMISSIONS

Oracle provides extensive security features in order to safeguard information stored in its tables from unauthorized viewing and damage. Depending on a user's status and responsibility, appropriate rights on Oracle's resources can be assigned to the user. The rights that allow the use of some or all of Oracle's resources on the Server are called *Privileges*.

Objects that are created by a user are owned and controlled by that user. If a user wishes to access any of the objects belonging to another user, the owner of the object will have to give permissions for such access. This is called *Granting of Privileges*.

Privileges once given can be taken back by the owner of the object. This is called *Revoking of Privileges*.

SQL Syntax for *Granting* and *Revoking* privileges is described below.

Granting Privileges using the GRANT statement.

The Grant statement provides various types of access to database objects such as tables, views and sequences.

<u>Syntax:</u>
> **GRANT** *{object privileges}*
> **ON** *objectname*
> **TO** *username*
> [**WITH** *GRANT OPTION*];

<u>OBJECT PRIVILEGES:</u>
Each object privilege that is granted authorizes the grantee to perform some operation on the object. The user can grant all the privileges or grant only specific object privileges.

The list of object privileges are as follows:

- ALTER : allows the grantee to change the table definition with the ALTER TABLE command.

- DELETE : allows the grantee to remove the records from the table with the DELETE command

- INDEX : allows the grantee to create an index on the table with the CREATE INDEX command.

- INSERT : allows the grantee to add records to the table with the INSERT command.

- SELECT : allows the grantee to query the table with the SELECT command.

- UPDATE : allows the grantee to modify the records in the tables with the UPDATE command.

WITH GRANT OPTION:

The WITH GRANT OPTION allows the grantee to **in turn** grant object privileges to other users.

Example1:
Give the user Pradeep all data manipulation permissions on the table product_master.

Syntax:

GRANT ALL
ON *product_master*
TO *pradeep;*

Example2:
Give the user Mita only the permission to view and modify records in the table client_master.

Syntax:

GRANT *SELECT, UPDATE*
ON *client_master*
TO *mita;*

Example3:
Give the user Ivan all data manipulation privileges on the table client_master along with an option to further grant permission on the client_master table to other users.

Syntax:

> **GRANT ALL**
> **ON** *client_master*
> **TO** *ivan*
> **WITH GRANT OPTION**;

Referencing a table belonging to another user:

Once a user has privileges to access another user's object/s, the user can access the table by prefixing the table with the name of the owner.

Example:
View the contents of the *product_master* table that belongs to *Sunita*.

Syntax:

> **SELECT * FROM**
> *sunita.product_master*;

Granting privileges when a grantee has been given the GRANT privilege:

If the user wants to grant privileges to other users, the user must be the owner of the object or must be given the GRANT option by the owner of the object.

Example:
Give the user Mili permission to view records from the product_master table. The table originally belongs to the user **Sunita**, who has granted you the privilege to GRANT privilege on product_master.

Syntax:

> **GRANT** *SELECT*
> **ON** *sunita.product_master*
> **TO** *mili;*

REVOKING PRIVILEGES GIVEN

Privileges once given can be denied to a user using the REVOKE command. The object owner can revoke privileges granted to another user. A user of an object who is not the owner, but has been granted the GRANT privilege, has the power to REVOKE the privileges from a grantee.

Revoking permissions using the REVOKE statement:

The **REVOKE** statement is used to deny the grant given on an object.

Syntax:

> **REVOKE** *{ object privileges }*
> **ON** *objectname*
> **FROM** *username*;

Note

The revoke command is used to revoke object privileges that the user previously granted directly to the Revokee.

The REVOKE command cannot be used to revoke the privileges granted through the operating system.

Example1:

All privileges on the table supplier_master have been granted to Florian. Take back the *Delete* privilege on the table.

Syntax:

> **REVOKE** *DELETE*
> **ON** *supplier_master*
> **FROM** *florian;*

Example2:

Take back *all* privileges on the table bonus from Florian.

Syntax:

> **REVOKE** *ALL*
> **ON** *bonus*
> **FROM** *florian* ;

Example3:

Norma has the permission to view records from *product_master*. Take back this permission. *Note that Sunita is the original owner of product_master table.*

Syntax:

> **REVOKE** *SELECT*
> **ON** *sunita.product_master*
> **FROM** *norma;*

SELF REVIEW QUESTIONS

READ THE QUESTIONS AND WRITE DOWN APPROPRIATE SQL STATEMENTS, AS ANSWERS.

1. Give the user Sanjay the permission only to view records in the tables sales_order and sales_order_details, along with an option to further grant permission on these tables to other users.

2. Give the user Ashish all data manipulation privileges on the table client_master without an option to further grant permission on the client_master table to other users.

3. View the *product_no, description* of the *product_master* table that belongs to *Ajay*.

4. Give the user Cedric permission to view records from the salesman_master table. The table originally belongs to the user Mita, who has granted privilege to GRANT further privilege on the table salesman_master to you.

5. Take back *all* privileges on the table client_master from Ashish.

6. Sanjay has the permission to view and delete records from the employee table. Take back the delete permission. *Melba is the original owner of employee table.*

A QUICK REVIEW

> **Granting Privileges on various type of database objects such as:**
> - Tables
> - Views
> - Sequences

> **The various types of object privileges**
> - Alter
> - Delete
> - Index
> - Insert
> - Select
> - Update

> **Revoking the privileges given to users on various database objects**

REFERENCE BOOKS

TITLE	AUTHOR	PUBLISHER
1. SQL Unleashed (W/CD)	Ladanyi	Techmedia
2. Understanding SQL	Gruber	BPB
3. SQL Spoken Here	Sayles	BPB
4. SQL and Relational Databases	Soren Vang	Galgotia

CHAPTER SIX

Introduction To PL/SQL

IN THIS CHAPTER

- ➢ SQL and PL/SQL - Differences

- ➢ PL/SQL Environment

- ➢ PL/SQL Syntax

- ➢ Conditional & Iterative Control
  - If...Then...End If
  - For Loop
  - While Loop
  - Goto Statement

6. INTRODUCTION TO PL/SQL

INTRODUCTION

Though SQL is the natural language of the DBA, it suffers from various inherent disadvantages, when used as a conventional programming language.

1. SQL does not have any procedural capabilities i.e. SQL does not provide the programming techniques of conditional checking, looping and branching that is vital for data testing before storage.

2. SQL statements are passed to the Oracle Engine one at a time. Each time an SQL statement is executed, a call is made to the engine's resources. This adds to the traffic on the network, thereby decreasing the speed of data processing, especially in a multi-user environment.

3. While processing an SQL sentence if an error occurs, the Oracle engine displays its own error messages. SQL has no facility for programmed handling of errors that arise during manipulation of data.

Although SQL is a very powerful tool, it's set of disadvantages prevent it from being a fully structured programming language. For a fully structured programming language, Oracle provides **PL/SQL**.

As the name suggests, PL/SQL is a superset of SQL. PL/SQL is a block- structured language that enables developers to combine the power of SQL with procedural statements. PL/SQL bridges the gap between database technology and procedural programming languages.

Advantages of PL/SQL:

1. PL/SQL is development tool that not only supports SQL data manipulation but also provides facilities of conditional checking, branching and looping.

2. PL/SQL sends an entire block of statements to the Oracle engine at one time. The communication between the program block and the Oracle engine reduces considerably. This in turn reduces network traffic. The Oracle engine gets the SQL statements as a single block, and hence it processes this code much faster than if it got the code one sentence at a time. There is a definite improvement in the performance time of the Oracle engine. As an entire block of code is passed to the DBA at one time for execution, all changes made to the data in the table are done or undone, in one go.

3.   PL/SQL also permits dealing with errors as required, and facilitates displaying user-friendly messages, when errors are encountered.

4.   PL/SQL allows declaration and use of variables in blocks of code. These variables can be used to store intermediate results of a query for later processing, or calculate values and insert them into an Oracle table later. PL/SQL variables can be used anywhere, either in SQL statements or in PL/SQL blocks.

5.   Via PL/SQL, all sorts of calculations can be done quickly and efficiently without the use of the Oracle engine. This considerably improves transaction performance.

6.   Applications written in PL/SQL are portable to any computer hardware and operating system, where Oracle is operational. Hence, PL/SQL code blocks written for a DOS version of Oracle will run on it's UNIX version, without any modifications at all.

THE GENERIC PL/SQL BLOCK

Every programming environment allows the creation of structured, logical blocks of code that describes processes, which have to be applied to data. Once these blocks are passed to the environment, the processes described are applied to the data, suitable data manipulation takes place, and useful output is obtained.

PL/SQL permits the creation of structured logical blocks of code that describes processes, which have to applied to data. A single PL/SQL code block consists of a set of SQL statements, clubbed together, and passed to the Oracle engine entirely. This block has to be logically grouped together for the engine to recognize it as a singular code block. A PL/SQL block has a definite structure. The minimum sections of a PL/SQL block are:

- The **Declare** section,
- The *Master* **Begin** and **End** section that contains the **Exception** section.

Each of these are explained below:

The Declare section:

Code blocks start with a declaration section, in which memory variables and other Oracle objects can be declared, and if required initialized. Once declared, they can be used in the SQL statements for data manipulation.

The Begin section:

It consists of a set of SQL and PL/SQL statements, which describe processes that have to be applied to the data. Actual data manipulation, retrieval, looping and branching constructs are specified in this section.

The Exception section:

This section deals with handling of errors that arise during execution of the data manipulation statements, which make up the PL/SQL code block. Errors can arise due to syntax, logic and/or validation rule violation.

The End section:

This marks the end of a PL/SQL block.

A PL/SQL code block can be diagrammatically represented as follows:

SQL executable statements for manipulating table data.

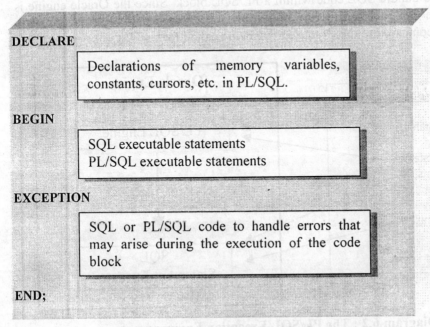

DECLARE

> Declarations of memory variables, constants, cursors, etc. in PL/SQL.

BEGIN

> SQL executable statements
> PL/SQL executable statements

EXCEPTION

> SQL or PL/SQL code to handle errors that may arise during the execution of the code block

END;

Diagram 6.1 : The PL/SQL block structure.

THE PL/SQL EXECUTION ENVIRONMENT

Wherever PL/SQL technology is required (i.e. in the RDBMS core or in its tools), the PL/SQL engine accepts any valid PL/SQL block as input.

PL/SQL in the Oracle Engine:

The PL/SQL engine resides in the Oracle engine, the Oracle engine can process not only single SQL statements but also entire PL/SQL blocks.

These blocks are sent to the PL/SQL engine, where procedural statements are executed; and SQL statements are sent to the SQL executor in the Oracle engine. Since the PL/SQL engine resides in the Oracle engine, this is an efficient and swift operation.

The call to the Oracle engine needs to be made only once to execute any number of SQL statements, if these SQL sentences are bundle inside a PL/SQL block.

Diagram 6.2 will give you an idea of how these statements are executed and how convenient it is to bundle SQL code within a PL/SQL block. Since the Oracle engine is called only once for each block, the speed of SQL statement execution is vastly enhanced, when compared to the Oracle engine being called for each SQL sentence.

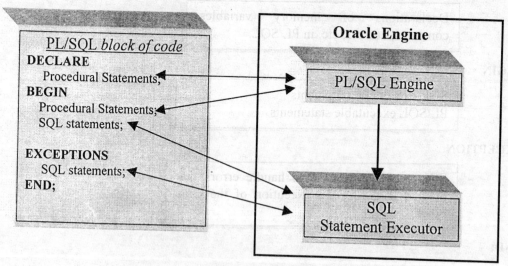

Diagram 6.2 : The PL/SQL Execution Environment.

PL/SQL

The character set:

The basic character set includes the following:
- uppercase alphabets { A - Z }
- lowercase alphabets { a - z }
- numerals { 0 - 9 }
- symbols : ( ) + - * / < > = ! ; : . ' @ % , " # $ ^ & _ \ { } ? [ ]

Words used in a PL/SQL block are called *Lexical Units*. Blank spaces can be freely insert between lexical units in a PL/SQL block. The spaces have no effect on the PL/SQL block.

The ordinary symbols used in PL/SQL blocks are:
$$( ) + - * / < > = ; \% ' " [ ] :$$
Compound symbols used in PL/SQL blocks are:
$$< > \quad != \quad \sim= \quad ^= \quad <= \quad >= \quad := \quad ** \quad .. \quad \| \quad << \quad >>$$

Literals:

A literal is a numeric value or a character string used to represent itself.

Numeric Literal:
These can be either integers or floats. If a float is being represented, then the integer part must be separated from the float part by a period.
Example: 25, 6.34, 7g2, 25e-03, .1, 1., 1.e4, +17, -5

String Literal:
These are represented by one or more legal characters and must be enclosed within single quotes. You can represent the single quote character itself, in a string literal by writing it twice. This will not be the same as a double quote.
Example: 'Hello World', 'Don''t go without saving your work'

Character Literal:
These are string literals consisting of single characters.
Example: '*', 'A', 'Y'

Logical (Boolean) Literal:
These are predetermined constants. The values it can take are: TRUE, FALSE, NULL

PL/SQL Data Types:

Both PL/SQL and Oracle have their foundations in SQL. Most PL/SQL datatypes are native to Oracle's data dictionary. Hence, there is a very easy integration of PL/SQL code with the Oracle Engine.

The default data types that can be declared in PL/SQL are *number* (for storing numeric data), *char* (for storing character data), *date* (for storing date and time data), *boolean* (for storing TRUE, FALSE or NULL). *number*, *char* and *date* data types can have NULL values.

The %TYPE attribute provides for further integration. PL/SQL can use the %TYPE attribute to declare variables based on definitions of columns in a table. Hence, if a column's attributes change, the variable's attributes will change as well. This provides for data independence, reduces maintenance costs, and allows programs to adapt to changes made to the table.

%TYPE declares a variable or constant to have the same datatype as that of a previously defined variable or of a column in a table or in a view. When referencing a table, you may name the table and column, or the owner of the table and column.

NOT NULL causes creation of a variable or a constant that cannot have a null value. If you attempt to assign the value NULL to a variable or a constant that has been assigned a NOT NULL constraint, it is an exception that Oracle senses automatically and an internal error condition is returned.

Note

As soon as a variable or constant has been declared as NOT NULL, it must be assigned a value. Hence every NOT NULL declaration of a variable or constant needs to be followed by a PL/SQL expression that loads a value into the variable or constant declared.

Variables:

Variables in PL/SQL blocks are *named* variables. A variable name must begin with a character and can be followed by a maximum of 29 other characters.

Reserved words cannot be used as variable names unless enclosed within double quotes. Variables must be separated from each other by at least one space or by a punctuation mark.

The case is insignificant when declaring variable names. A space cannot be used in variable name. A variable of any data type either native to the Oracle Engine such as number, char, date, etc. or native to PL/SQL such as boolean (i.e. logical variable content) can be declared.

<u>Assigning Values to Variables:</u>
The assigning of a value to a variable can be done in two ways:
- Using the assignment operator **: =** (i.e. a colon followed by an equal to sign).
- Selecting or fetching table data values into variables.

Note

An interesting point to note here is that if you use PL/SQL code blocks for loading and calculating variables, the power of the Oracle Engine is not used. This frees up the Oracle engine for other work and considerably improves response time.

Constants:

Declaring a constant is similar to declaring a variable except that you have to add the keyword 'constant' and immediately assign a value to it. Thereafter, no further assignments to the constant are possible, while the constant is within the scope of the PL/SQL block.

Logical comparisons:

PL/SQL supports the comparison between variables and constants in SQL and PL/SQL statements. These comparisons, often called Boolean expressions, generally consist of simple expressions separated by relational operators (<, >, =, < >, >=, <= that can be connected by logical operators (AND, OR, NOT). A Boolean expression will always evaluate to TRUE, FALSE or NULL.

Displaying user Messages on the Screen:

Programming tools require a method through which messages can be displayed to the user on the VDU screen.

DBMS_OUTPUT is a package that includes a number of procedure and functions that accumulate information in a buffer so that it can be retrieved later. These functions can also be used to display messages to the user.

PUT_LINE: Put a piece of information in the package buffer followed by an end-of-line marker. It can also be used to display message to the user. Put_line expects a single parameter of character data type. If used to display a message, it is the message 'string'.

To display messages to the user the **SERVEROUTPUT** should be set to **ON**. SERVEROUTPUT is a SQL*PLUS environment parameter that displays the information passed as a parameter to the PUT_LINE function.

<u>Syntax:</u>
        SET SERVEROUTPUT [ON/OFF]

Comments:

A comment can have two forms:

- The comment line begins with a double hyphen (--). The entire line will be treated as a comment.
- The comment line begins with a slash followed by an asterisk (/*) till the occurrence of an asterisk followed by a slash (*/). All lines within are treated as comments. This form of specifying comments can be used to span across multiple lines. This technique can also be used to enclose a section of a PL/SQL block that temporarily needs to be isolated and ignored.

Conditional control in PL/SQL:

PL/SQL allows the use of IF statement to control the execution of a block of code. In PL/SQL, the IF - THEN - ELSIF - ELSE - END IF construct in code blocks allow specifying certain conditions under which a specific block of code should be executed.

<u>Syntax</u>:   **IF** <*Condition*> **THEN**
                    <Action>
       ELSIF <*Condition*> **THEN**
                    <Action>
       ELSE
                    <Action>
       END IF;

<u>Example:</u>
Write a PL/SQL code block that will accept an account number from the user and debit an amount of Rs. 2000 from the account if the account has a minimum balance of 500 after the amount is debited. The process is to be fired on the Accounts table.

Table name: Accounts

Account_Id	Name	Bal
AC001	Anuj	5000
AC002	Robert	10000
AC003	Mita	5000
AC004	Sunita	15000
AC005	Melba	10000

```
DECLARE
      /* Declaration of memory variables and constants to be used in the
         Execution section. */
      acct_balance  number(11,2);
      acct_no varchar2(6);
      debit_amt number(5) := 2000;
      min_bal constant number(5,2) := 500.00;
BEGIN
      /* Accept an account_no from the user*/
      acct_no := &acct_no;

      /* retrieving the balance from the accounts table where the account_no
      in the table is equal to the account_no entered by the user. */
      SELECT bal INTO acct_balance
            FROM accounts
            WHERE account_id = acct_no;

      /*substract an amount of Rs 2000 from the balance retrieved from the
      table*/
      acct_balance := acct_balance - debit_amt;

      /*checking if the resultant balance is greater than or equal to the
      minimum balance of Rs.500. If the condition is satisfied an amount of
      Rs.2000 is substracted from the balance of the corresponding
      account_no. */.
      IF acct_balance >= MIN_BAL THEN
            UPDATE accounts SET bal = bal - debit_amt
            WHERE account_id = acct_no;
      END IF;
END;
```

When the account_id entered is 'AC003',

- The SELECT statement will retrieve the balance amount from the *accounts* table that is related to account no 'AC003'.
- It will then debit an amount of Rs.2000 from this balance.

- The Oracle Engine then checks whether the resultant is greater than or equal to Rs. 500.

- If so the amount of Rs. 2000 will be debited from account_no 'AC003' and the result made permanent in the *accounts* table.

The data in the accounts table after the execution of the PL/SQL block of code will be as follows:

Table name: Accounts

Account_Id	Name	Bal
AC001	Anuj	5000
AC002	Robert	10000
AC003	*Mita*	*3000*
AC004	Sunita	15000
AC005	Melba	10000

Iterative Control:

Iterative control indicates the ability to repeat or skip sections of a code block. A *loop* marks a sequence of statements that has to be repeated. The keyword <u>loop</u> has to be placed before the first statement in the sequence of statements to be repeated, while the keyword <u>end loop</u> is placed immediately after the last statement in the sequence. Once a loop begins to execute, it will go on forever. Hence a conditional statement-that controls the number of times a loop is executed always accompanies loops.

PL/SQL supports the following structures for iterative control:

The *WHILE* loop:

Syntax:

        WHILE *<Condition>*
        LOOP
            <Action>
        END LOOP;

Example:

Write a PL/SQL code block to calculate the area of a circle for a value of radius varying from 3 to 7. Store the radius and the corresponding values of calculated area in a table, *Areas*

Table Name: Areas

Radius	Area

```
DECLARE
        /* Declaration of memory variables and constants to be used in the
            Execution section. */
        pi constant number(4,2) := 3.14 ;
        radius number(5);
        area number(14,2);
BEGIN
        /* Initialize the radius to 3, since calculations are required
        for radius 3 to 7 */
        radius := 3;

        /* Set a loop so that it fires till the radius value reaches 7 */
        WHILE radius <= 7
        LOOP
                /* Area calculation for a circle */
                area := pi * power(radius,2);

                /* Insert the value for the radius and its corresponding area
                    calculated in the table */
                INSERT INTO areas
                        VALUES (radius, area);

                /* Increment the value of the variable radius by 1 */
                radius := radius + 1;
        END LOOP;
END;
```

The above PL/SQL code block initializes a variable *radius* to hold the value of 3. The area calculations are required for the radii between 3 and 7. The value for area is calculated first with radius 3, and the radius and area are inserted into the table *Areas*. Now, the variable holding the value of radius is incremented by 1, i.e. it now holds the value 4. Since the code is held within a loop structure, the code continues to fire till the radius value reaches 7. Each time the value of radius and area is inserted into the areas table. After the loop is completed the table will now hold the following:

Table name: Areas

Radius	Area
3	28.26
4	50.24
5	78.5
6	113.04
7	153.86

The *FOR* Loop:

Syntax:

> **FOR** *variable* **IN [REVERSE] start..end**
> **LOOP**
> > *<Action>*
> **END LOOP;**

Note

The *variable* in the For Loop need not be declared. Also the increment value cannot be specified. The For Loop variable is always incremented by 1.

Example:
Write a PL/SQL block of code for inverting a number 5639 to 9365.

```
DECLARE
        /* Declaration of memory variables and constants to be used in the
                Execution section. */
        given_number varchar(5) := '5639';
        str_length number(2);
        inverted_number varchar(5);
BEGIN
        /* Store the length of the given number  */
        str_length := length(given_number);
        /* Initialize the loop such that it repeats for the number of times equal to the
        length of the given number. Also, since the number is required to be inverted, the
        loop should consider the last number first and store it i.e. in reverse order */
```

FOR *cntr* IN REVERSE 1..str_length
/ variables used as counter in for loop need not be declared i.e. cntr*
declaration is not required/*

LOOP
/ The last digit of the number is obtained using the **substr** function, and*
stored in a variable, while retaining the previous digit stored in the
variable/*
        inverted_number := inverted_number || substr(given_number, cntr, 1);
END LOOP;
/ Display the initial number, as well as the inverted number, which*
*is stored in the variable on screen */*
        dbms_output.put_line ('The Given number is ' || given_number);
        dbms_output.put_line ('The Inverted number is ' || inverted_number);
END;

The above PL/SQL code block stores the given number as well its length in two variables. Since the FOR loop is set to repeat till the length of the number is reached and in reverse order, the loop will fire 4 times beginning from the last digit i.e. **9**. This digit is obtained using the function SUBSTR, and stored in a variable. The loop now fires again to fetch and store the second last digit of the given number, in addition to the last digit stored previously. This repeats till each digit of the number is obtained and stored. The resultant display after execution of the PL/SQL code will be:

Output:
        The Given number is 5639
        The Inverted number is 9365

        PL/SQL procedure successfully completed.

The *GOTO* Statement:

The *GOTO* statement change of the *flow of control* within a PL/SQL block. This statement allows execution of a section of code, which is not in the normal flow of control. The entry point into such a block of code is marked using the tags *<<userdefined name>>*. The *GOTO* statement can then make use of this user-defined name to jump into that block of code for execution.
Syntax:
        GOTO *<codeblock name>*;

Example:
Write PL/SQL block of code to achieve the following: If the price of product 'P00001' is less than 4000, then change the price to 4000. The price change is to be recorded in the old_price_table along with product_no and the date on which the price was last changed.

Table Name: product_master

Product_No	Sell_Price
P00001	3200
P00002	4000
P00003	6000
P00004	9000
P00005	2800

Table Name: old_price_table

Product_No	Date_change	Old_Price

DECLARE

> /* Declaration of memory variables and constants to be used in the
> Execution section.*/
> Selling_price number(10,2) ;

BEGIN

> /* Fetch the sell_price of product_no 'P00001' into a variable */
> **SELECT** sell_price into selling_price
> > **FROM** product_master
> > **WHERE** product_no = 'P00001';

> /* If the sell_price is less than 4000, pass the execution control to a user labelled
> section of code, labelled as **add_old_price** in our example. If the price is equal to
> or greator than 4000, display a message giving the current sell_price of the
> product*/

> **IF** selling_price < 4000 **THEN**
> > **GOTO** add_old_price;
> **ELSE**
> > dbms_output.put_line('Current Price of P00001 is ' || selling_price);
> **END IF**;
> /* A labelled section of code which updates the sell_price of product 'P00001' to
> 4000. The product_no, current date and the old_price are inserted in to the table
> **old_price_table** and a message displaying the new price is displayed. */

> << add_old_price >>
> > **UPDATE** product_master
> > > **SET** sell_price = 4000
> > > **WHERE** product_no = 'P00001';
> > **INSERT INTO** old_price_table

```
                    (product_no, date_change, old_price )
            VALUES ( 'P00001', sysdate, selling_price) ;
         dbms_output.put_line('The new Price of P00001 is 4000' );
END;
```

The PL/SQL code first fetches the sell_price of the product_no 'P00001' into a variable *selling_price*. It then checks whether the value that is held in the variable *selling_price* it is less than 4000. If so, the control is passed to a different section of code, labelled as *add_old_price*. In this block of code, the value of sell_price for product_no 'P00001' in the product_master table is updated to 4000. Also, the product_no, the current date and the old_price are inserted into the old_price_table that keeps an audit trail of the change made to the product_master table.

In case the sell_price for product_no 'P00001' in the product_master table is already equal or greater than 4000, a message stating the current price of the product 'P00001' is displayed.

The table structures after the execution of the PL/SQL code will be as follows:

Table Name: product_master

Product_No	Sell_Price
P00001	*4000*
P00002	4000
P00003	6000
P00004	9000
P00005	2800

Table Name: old_price_table

Product_No	Date_change	Old_Price
P00001	18-MAR-98	3200

SELF REVIEW QUESTIONS

1. What are the components of a PL/SQL code block?

2. What is the maximum value that can be stored in a variable declared as NUMBER (6,2)?

3. What is the variable attribute used to create a variable bound to a table column?

4. Evaluate if the following declaration is valid or not? If invalid, correct it.

   Declare
   Emp_last_name   %type;

   Table Name: Emp

Emp_No	Emp_Name	Sal
E001	Harry	5000
E002	Blake	1000
E003	Jack	5000
E004	Clark	1000

5. What statement/s allow processing of a loop to be aborted?

TRUE OR FALSE

6. A PL/SQL block consists of several sections, the minimum being Declare, Begin and End, encompassing an Exception section.

   A) True   B) False

7. Delimiters are symbols that have a special meaning to PL/SQL.

   A) True   B) False

8. PL/SQL has a variety of control structures that allow a programmer to control the behavior of the PL/SQL block as it executes.

   A) True   B) False

9. The put_line function is available in the IO package in Oracle.

    A) True   B) False

10. The correct syntax for if is IF <condition> THEN <action> ELSEIF <condition> THEN <action> ELSE <action> END IF.

    A) True   B) False

11. The Step verb is used to specify the increments in a For Loop.

    A) True   B) False

12. The variable used in the For Loop must be declared in the Declare Section of the PL/SQL code block.

    A) True   B) False

FILL IN THE BLANKS

13. _____ is used to pick up data type and length for the variables that are defined in a PL/SQL block.

14. Comments in PL/SQL can be specified by using _____ and _____ characters.

15. The values that a Boolean variable can take are

    _____

    _____

    _____

16. _____ operator is used to check for NULL values in a PL/SQL block.

17. Constants can be declared by using the _____ verb in the declaration.

18. _____ is used to display messages to the user.

19. PL/SQL stands for _____

A QUICK REVIEW

➢ **Introduction to PL/SQL**
- Differences between SQL & PL/SQL

➢ **The generic PL/SQL code block.**
- Declare
- Begin
- Exception
- End

➢ **The PL/SQL execution environment.**

➢ **The PL/SQL syntax**
- Character set
- Literals
- Data types
  - Variables
  - Constants

➢ **Displaying user Messages on the VDU.**

➢ **Conditional Controls**
- If.. Then..Elsif..Then...Else ....End if

➢ **Iterative Controls**
- For Loop
- While Loop
- Goto Statements

More on PL/SQL

IN THIS CHAPTER

7. MORE ON PL / SQL

ORACLE TRANSACTIONS

A series of one or more SQL statements that are logically related, or a series of operations performed on Oracle table data is termed as a *Transaction*. Oracle treats this logical unit as a single entity. Oracle treats changes to table data as a two-step process. First, the changes requested are done. To make these changes permanent a COMMIT statement has to be given at the SQL prompt. A ROLLBACK statement given at the SQL prompt can be used to undo a part of or the entire transaction.

A transaction begins with the first executable SQL statement after a *commit, rollback* or *connection* made to the Oracle engine. All changes made to an Oracle table data via unit a transaction are made or undone at one instance.

Specifically, a transaction is a group of events that occurs between any of the following events:
- Connecting to Oracle.
- Disconnecting from Oracle.
- Committing changes to the database table
- Rollback.

Closing Transactions:

A transaction can be closed by using either a *commit* or a *rollback* statement. By using these statements, table data can be changed or all the changes made to the table data undone.

Using **COMMIT**:
A **COMMIT** ends the current transaction and makes permanent any changes made during the transaction. All transactional locks acquired on tables are released.

Syntax:
        COMMIT;

Using **ROLLBACK**:
A **ROLLBACK** does exactly the opposite of *COMMIT*. It ends the transaction but undoes any changes made during the transaction. All transactional locks acquired on tables are released.

Syntax:
        ROLLBACK [WORK] [TO [SAVEPOINT] savepoint]

Where:

WORK	:	is optional and is provided for ANSI compatibility.
SAVEPOINT	:	is optional and is used to rollback a partial transaction, as far as the specified savepoint.
savepoint	:	is a savepoint created during the current transaction.

Creating **SAVEPOINT**:

SAVEPOINT marks and saves the current point in the processing of a transaction. When a SAVEPOINT is used with a *ROLLBACK* statement, parts of a transaction can be undone. An active savepoint is one that is specified since the last COMMIT or ROLLBACK.

Syntax:

SAVEPOINT *savepointname*;

ROLLBACK can be fired from the SQL prompt *with or without* the SAVEPOINT clause. The implication of each is described below:

A ROLLBACK operation performed *without* the SAVEPOINT clause amounts to the following:

- Ends the transaction.
- Undoes all the changes in the current transaction.
- Erases all savepoints in that transaction.
- Releases the transactional locks.

A ROLLBACK operation performed *with* the TO SAVEPOINT clause amounts to the following:

- A predetermined portion of the transaction is rolled back.
- Retains the save point rolled back to, but loses those created after the named savepoint.
- Releases all transactional locks that were acquired since the savepoint was taken.

Example:

Write a PL/SQL block of code that first inserts a record in an 'Emp' table. Update the salaries of Blake and Clark by Rs. 2000 and Rs. 1500. Then check to see that the total salary does not exceed 20000. If the total salary is greater than 20000 then undo the updates made to the salaries of Blake and Clark.

Table Name: Emp

Emp_No	Emp_Name	Sal
E001	Harry	5000
E002	Blake	1000
E003	Jack	5000
E004	Clark	1000

```
DECLARE
        total_sal number(9);
BEGIN

        /* Insertion of a record in the 'Emp' table */
        INSERT INTO emp
                VALUES('E005', 'John', 1000);

        /*Defining a savepoint */
        SAVEPOINT no_update;

        /*Updation of the salaries of Blake and Clark in the 'Emp' table. */
        UPDATE emp SET  sal = sal + 2000
                WHERE emp_name = 'Blake';
        UPDATE emp SET sal = sal + 1500
                WHERE emp_name = 'Clark';

        /*Selecting the total salary from the 'Emp' table into a variable. If the total
           salary exceeds 20000, then undo the changes made to the 'Emp' table, else
           make the changes permanent. */

        SELECT sum(sal)  INTO total_sal
                FROM emp;
        IF total_sal > 20000 THEN
                ROLLBACK To Savepoint no_update;
        END IF;

        COMMIT;
END;
```

The above PL/SQL block first inserts a record in the *Emp* table. It then marks and saves the current position in the transaction i.e. it defines a *savepoint* called *no_update*. The salaries of Clark and Blake are updated next. Now, to check whether the total company salary exceeds 20000, the sum of all the salaries from the *Emp* table is fetched into a variable. If the content of this variable is greater than 20000, the transaction is rolled back to the savepoint *no_update* i.e. the updates made to the salaries of Blake and Clark are undone, whereas the record which was inserted during the transaction is made permanent in the table.

PROCESSING A PL/SQL BLOCK

A PL/SQL block can be run in one of two modes:

- Batch processing wherein records are gathered in a table and at regular intervals manipulated.
- Real Time processing wherein records are manipulated as they are created.

Batch Processing is a PL/SQL block run at the SQL prompt at regular intervals to process table data.

A technique that Oracle provides for manipulating table data in batch processing mode is the use of *Cursors*.

Oracle and the processing of SQL statements:

Whenever an SQL statement is executed, Oracle engine performs the following tasks:

- Reserves a private SQL area in memory
- Populates this area with the data requested in the SQL sentence.
- Processes the data in this memory area as required.
- Frees the memory area when the processing of data is complete.

Table Name: Employee

Column name	Data Type	Size	Attributes
Emp_code	varchar2	6	Primary Key
Emp_name	Varchar2	25	
Job	Varchar2	25	
Salary	Number	8,2	
Deptno	Varchar2	6	Foreign Key references deptno from the deptmast table.

An SQL statement that will display the *employee code, employee name, job* and *salary* from *employee* table in the ascending order of employee name will be as follows:

  SELECT *emp_code, emp_name, job, salary*
   FROM *employee*
   ORDER BY *emp_name;*

To execute the above statement, Oracle will reserve an area in memory and populate it with the records from *employee* table. These records are then sorted in the ascending order of *employee name* and displayed to the user. When all the records from the *employee* table are displayed, Oracle will free the memory area used for retrieving and sorting the data.

WHAT IS A CURSOR?

The Oracle Engine uses a work area for its internal processing in order to execute an SQL statement. This work area is private to SQL's operations and is called a **Cursor**.

The data that is stored in the cursor is called the **Active Data Set**. Conceptually, the size of the cursor in memory is the size required to hold the number of rows in the Active Data Set. The actual size however, is determined by the Oracle engine's built in memory management capabilities and the amount of RAM available. Oracle has a pre-defined area in main memory set aside, within cursors are opened. Hence the cursor's size will be limited by the size of this pre-defined area.

The values retrieved from the table are held in a cursor opened in memory on the Oracle Engine. This data is then transferred to the client machine via the network. In order to hold this data, a cursor is opened at the client end. If the number of rows returned by the Oracle engine is more than the area available in the cursor opened on the client, the cursor data and the retrieved data is swapped between WIN95 swap area and RAM under the control of the client's operating system.

Example:
When a user fires a select statement as,
      SELECT *empno, ename, job, salary* **FROM** *employee* **WHERE** *deptno = 20;*

the resultant data set in the cursor opened at the Server end will be as displayed as under:

SERVER			
SERVER RAM			
Active Data Set			
3456	IVAN	MANAGER	10000
3459	PRADEEP	ANALYST	7000
3446	MITA	PROGRMR	4000
3463	VIJAY	CLERK	2000
3450	ALDRIN	ACCTANT	3000

Diagram 7.1 : Contents of a cursor.

When a cursor is loaded with multiple rows via a query the Oracle engine opens and maintains a *row pointer*. Depending on user requests to view data the row pointer will be relocated within the cursor's Active Data Set. Additionally Oracle also maintains multiple cursor variables. The values held in these variables indicate the status of the processing being done by the cursor.

Types of Cursors:

Cursors are classified depending on the circumstances under which they are opened. If the Oracle Engine for its internal processing has opened a cursor they are known as *Implicit Cursors*. A user can also open a cursor for processing data as required. Such user-defined cursors are known as *Explicit Cursors*.

General Cursor attributes:

When the Oracle engine creates an Implicit or Explicit cursor, cursor control variables are also created to control the execution of the cursor. Whenever any cursor is opened and used, the Oracle engine creates a set of four system variables which keeps track of the 'Current' status of a cursor. These cursor variables can be accessed and used in a PL/SQL code block. Both *Implicit* and *Explicit* cursors have four attributes. They are described below:

Attribute Name	Description
%ISOPEN	Returns TRUE if cursor is open, FALSE otherwise.
%FOUND	Returns TRUE if record *was fetched* successfully, FALSE otherwise.
%NOTFOUND	Returns TRUE if record *was not fetched* successfully, FALSE otherwise.
%ROWCOUNT	Returns number of records processed from the cursor.

Implicit Cursor:

The Oracle engine implicitly opens a cursor on the Server to process each SQL statement. Since the implicit cursor is opened and managed by the Oracle engine internally, the function of reserving an area in memory, populating this area with appropriate data, processing the data in the memory area, releasing the memory area when the processing is complete is taken care of by the Oracle engine. The resultant data is then passed to the client machine via the network. A cursor is then opened in memory on the client machine to hold the rows returned by the Oracle engine. The number of rows held in the cursor on the client is managed by the RAM and the Win 95 swap area.

Implicit cursor attributes can be used to access information about the status of last *insert*, *update*, *delete* or single-row *select* statements. This can be done by preceding the implicit cursor attribute with the cursor name (i.e. SQL). The values of the cursor attributes always refer to the most recently executed SQL statement, wherever the statement appears. If an attribute value is to be saved for later use, it must be assigned to a *(boolean)* memory variable.

Implicit Cursor Processing in Client Server Environment:

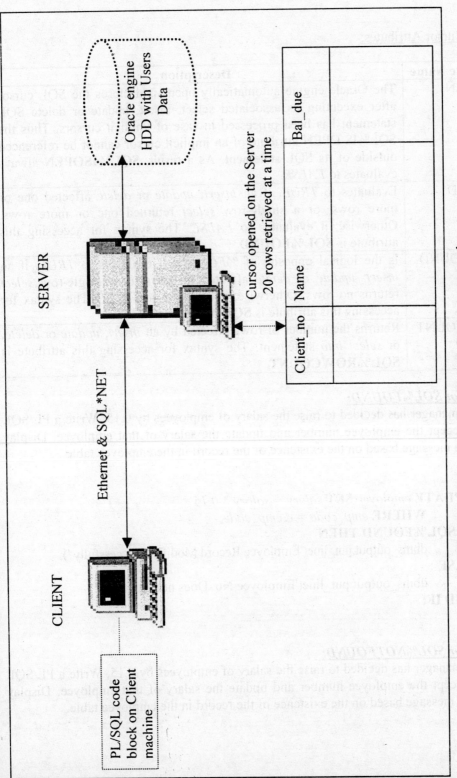

Diagram 7.2 : Client Server and Cursor processing

Implicit Cursor Attributes:

Attribute Name	Description
%ISOPEN	The Oracle engine automatically opens and closes the SQL cursor after executing its associated select, insert, update or delete SQL statement has been processed in case of implicit cursors. Thus the SQL%IS OPEN attribute of an implicit cursor cannot be referenced outside of its SQL statement. As a result, **SQL%ISOPEN** always evaluates to *FALSE*.
%FOUND	Evaluates to *TRUE*, if an *insert*, *update* or *delete* affected one or more rows, or a single-row *select* returned one or more rows. Otherwise, it evaluates to *FALSE*. The syntax for accessing this attribute is **SQL%FOUND**
%NOTFOUND	Is the logical opposite of *%FOUND*. It evaluates to *TRUE*, if an *insert, update* or *delete* affected no rows, or a single-row *select* returns no rows. Otherwise, it evaluates to *FALSE*. The syntax for accessing this attribute is **SQL%NOTFOUND**
%ROWCOUNT	Returns the number of rows affected by an *insert, update* or *delete*, or *select into* statement. The syntax for accessing this attribute is **SQL%ROWCOUNT**

__Example for SQL%FOUND:__
The HRD manager has decided to raise the salary of employees by 0.15. Write a PL/SQL block to accept the employee number and update the salary of that employee. Display appropriate message based on the existence of the record in the employee table.

```
BEGIN
        UPDATE employee SET salary = salary * 0.15
            WHERE emp_code = &emp_code;
        IF SQL%FOUND THEN
            dbms_output.put_line('Employee Record Modified Successfully ');
        ELSE
            dbms_output.put_line('Employee No. Does not Exist');
        END IF;
END;
```

__Example for SQL%NOTFOUND:__
The HRD manager has decided to raise the salary of employees by 0.15. Write a PL/SQL block to accept the employee number and update the salary of that employee. Display appropriate message based on the existence of the record in the employee table.

```
BEGIN
        UPDATE employee SET salary = salary * 0.15
                WHERE emp_code = &emp_code;
        IF SQL%NOTFOUND THEN
                dbms_output.put_line('Employee No. Does not Exist');
        ELSE
                dbms_output.put_line('Employee Record  Modified Successfully ');
        END IF;
END;
```

Note

Both SQL%FOUND and SQL%NOTFOUND attributes evaluate to *NULL* until they are set by an implicit or explicit cursor operation.

Example for SQL%ROWCOUNT:

The HRD manager has decided to raise the salary of employees working as 'Programmers' by 0.15. Write a PL/SQL block to accept the employee number and update the salary of that employee. Display appropriate message based on the existence of the record in the employee table.

```
DECLARE
        rows_affected char(4);
BEGIN
        UPDATE employee SET salary = salary * 0.15
                WHERE job = 'Programmers';
        rows_affected := to_char(sql%rowcount) ;
        IF SQL%ROWCOUNT > 0 THEN
            dbms_output.put_line(rows_affected || 'Employee Records Modified Successfully ') ;
        ELSE
            dbms_output.put_line('There are no Employees working as Programmers');
        END IF;
END;
```

Explicit Cursor:

When individual records in a table have to be processed inside a PL/SQL code block a *cursor* is used. This cursor will be declared and mapped to an SQL query in the Declare Section of the PL/SQL block and used within the Executable Section. A cursor thus created and used is known as an *Explicit Cursor*.

Explicit Cursor Management:

The steps involved in using an explicit cursor and manipulating data in its active set are:
- Declare a cursor mapped to a SQL select statement that retrieves data for processing.
- Open the cursor.
- Fetch data from the cursor one row at a time into memory variables.
- Process the data held in the memory variables as required using a loop.
- Exit from the loop after processing is complete.
- Close the cursor.

Cursor Declaration:

A cursor is defined in the declarative part of a PL/SQL block. This is done by naming the cursor and mapping it to a query. When a cursor is declared, the Oracle engine is informed that a cursor of the said name needs to be opened. The declaration is only an intimation. There is no memory allocation at this point in time. The three commands used to control the cursor subsequently are *open, fetch* and *close*.

The Functionality of *Open, Fetch* and *Close* Commands:

Initialization of a cursor takes place via the *open* statement, this
- defines a private SQL area named after the cursor name
- executes a query associated with the cursor which
- retrieves table data and populates the named private SQL area in memory i.e. creates the **Active Data Set**.
- Sets the cursor row pointer in the Active Data Set to the first record.

A *fetch* statement then moves the data held in the Active Data Set into memory variables. Data held in the memory variables can be processed as desired.

The *fetch* statement is placed inside a *Loop ... End Loop* construct, which causes the data to be fetched into the memory variables and processed until all the rows in the Active Data Set are processed. The *fetch* loop then exits. The exiting of the fetch loop is user controlled.

After the fetch loop exits, the cursor must be closed with the *close* statement. This will release the memory occupied by the cursor and its Active Data Set. A PL/SQL block is necessary to declare a cursor and create an Active Data Set. The cursor name is used to reference the Active Data Set.

Syntax:
>   **CURSOR** *cursorname* **IS**
>   *SQL Select statement*;

Opening a Cursor:
*Open*ing a cursor executes the query and creates the active set that contains all rows, which meet the query search criteria. An *open* statement retrieves records from a database table and places the records in the cursor (i.e. named private SQL area in memory). A cursor is opened in the Server's memory.

Syntax:
>   **OPEN** *cursorname*;

The working of the Client Tool and Oracle Engine when an explicit cursor is opened using the OPEN command is represented diagrammatically below:

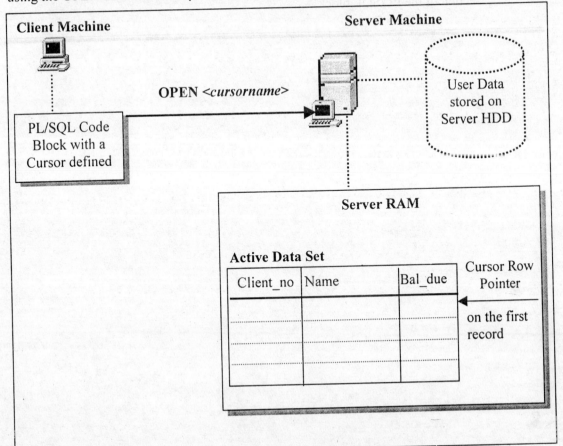

Diagram 7.3 : Processing of OPEN CURSOR command in the Oracle Engine

<u>Fetching a record from the Cursor:</u>

The *fetch* statement retrieves the rows from the active set opened in the Server into memory variables declared in the PL/SQL code block on the client one row at a time. The memory variables are opened on the client machine. Each time a *fetch* is executed, the cursor pointer is advanced to the next row in the Active Data Set.

A standard loop structure (Loop-End Loop) is used to fetch records from the cursor into memory variables one row at a time.

<u>Syntax:</u>

      FETCH *cursorname* **INTO** *variable1, variable2, ...;*

Note

     There must be a memory variable for each column value of the Active data set. Data types must match. These variables will be declared in the DECLARE section of the PL/SQL block.

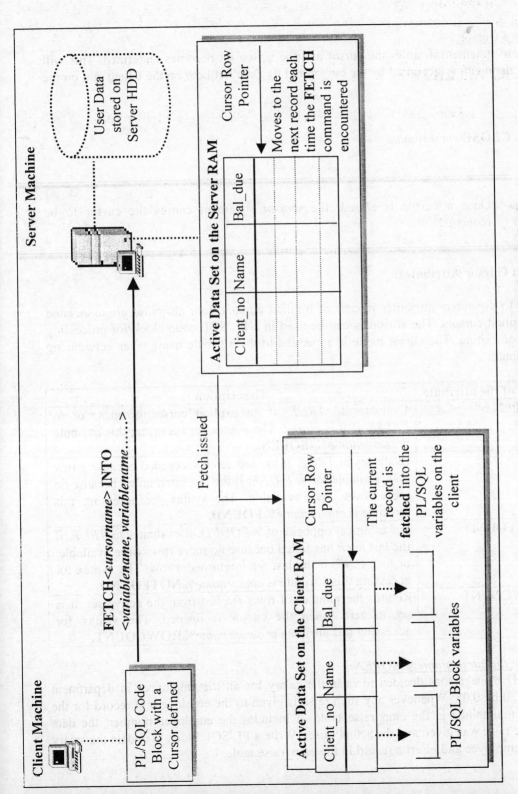

Diagram 7.4 : Processing of FETCH command in the Oracle Engine

Within the image:

Client Machine

Server Machine

User Data stored on Server HDD

Cursor Row Pointer

Moves to the next record each time the FETCH command is encountered

Active Data Set on the Server RAM

Client_no	Name	Bal_due

FETCH <cursorname> INTO <variablename, variablename……>

Fetch issued

Cursor Row Pointer

The current record is fetched into the PL/SQL variables on the client

Active Data Set on the Client RAM

Client_no	Name	Bal_due

PL/SQL Block variables

PL/SQL Code Block with a Cursor defined

Closing a Cursor:
The *close* statement disables the cursor and the active set becomes undefined. This will release the memory occupied by the cursor and its Data Set both on the Client and on the Server.

Syntax:
    CLOSE *cursorname*;

Note

Once a cursor is *close*d, the re*open* statement causes the cursor to be reopened.

Explicit Cursor Attributes:

Similar to the cursor attributes in case of implicit cursors, four attributes are associated with explicit cursors. The attributes can be used in a PL/SQL code block for processing of data or exiting. The cursor name is appended to the attribute name when referencing the attribute.

Name of the attribute	Description
%ISOPEN	Evaluates to *TRUE*, if an explicit cursor is *open;* or to *FALSE*, if it is *close*d. The syntax for accessing this attribute is *cursorname*%**ISOPEN.**
%FOUND	Evaluates to *TRUE*, if the last fetch succeeded because a row was available; or to *FALSE*, if the last fetch failed because no more rows were available. The syntax for accessing this attribute is *cursorname*%**FOUND.**
%NOTFOUND	Is the logical opposite of *%FOUND*. It evaluates to *TRUE*, if the last *fetch* has failed because no more rows were available; or to *FALSE*, if the last *fetch* returned a row. The syntax for accessing this attribute is *cursorname*%**NOTFOUND.**
%ROWCOUNT	Returns the number of rows *fetch*ed from the active set. It is set to zero when the cursor is *open*ed. The syntax for accessing this attribute is *cursorname*%**ROWCOUNT.**

Example for cursorname%ISOPEN:
The HRD manager has decided to raise the salary for all the employees in department number 20 by 0.05. Whenever any such raise is given to the employees, a record for the same is maintained in the emp_raise table. It includes the employee number, the date when the raise was given and the actual raise. Write a PL/SQL block to update the salary of each employee and insert a record in the emp_raise table.

```
DECLARE
        CURSOR c_emp IS SELECT emp_code, salary FROM employee
                        WHERE deptno = 20;
        str_emp_code employee.emp_code%type;
        num_salary employee.salary%type;
BEGIN
        OPEN c_emp;
        /* If the cursor is open continue with the data processing else display an
        appropriate error message */

        IF c_emp%ISOPEN THEN
         LOOP
            FETCH c_emp INTO str_emp_code, num_salary;
            exit when c_emp%NOTFOUND ;
            UPDATE employee SET salary = num_salary + (num_salary * .05)
                WHERE emp_code = str_emp_code ;
            INSERT INTO emp_raise VALUES (str_emp_code, sysdate, num_salary * 0.05);
         END LOOP;
         COMMIT;
         CLOSE c_emp;
         ELSE
                dbms_output.put_line ('Unable to open Cursor ');

        END IF;
END;
```

Example for cursorname%FOUND:

The HRD manager has decided to raise the salary for all the employees in department number 20 by 0.05. Whenever any such raise is given to the employees, a record for the same is maintained in the emp_raise table. It includes the employee number, the date when the raise was given and the actual raise. Write a PL/SQL block to update the salary of each employee and insert a record in the emp_raise table.

```
DECLARE
        CURSOR c_emp IS SELECT emp_code, salary FROM employee
                        WHERE deptno = 20;
        str_emp_code employee.emp_code%type;
        num_salary employee.salary%type;
BEGIN
        OPEN c_emp;
        LOOP
         FETCH c_emp INTO str_emp_code, num_salary;
         /* If no. of records retrieved > 0 then process the data else exit the loop. */
         IF c_emp%FOUND THEN
            UPDATE employee SET salary = num_salary + (num_salary * .05)
                WHERE emp_code = str_emp_code ;
            INSERT INTO emp_raise VALUES (str_emp_code, sysdate, num_salary * 0.05) ;
         ELSE
            exit;
         END IF;
         END LOOP;
         COMMIT;
         CLOSE c_emp;
END;
```

Example for cursorname%NOTFOUND:

The HRD manager has decided to raise the salary for all the employees in department number 20 by 0.05. Whenever any such raise is given to the employees, a record for the same is maintained in the emp_raise table. It includes the employee number, the date when the raise was given and the actual raise. Write a PL/SQL block to update the salary of each employee and insert a record in the emp_raise table.

```
DECLARE
        CURSOR c_emp IS SELECT emp_code, salary FROM employee
                                WHERE deptno = 20;
        str_emp_code employee.emp_code%type;
        num_salary employee.salary%type;
BEGIN
        OPEN c_emp;
        LOOP
            FETCH c_emp INTO str_emp_code, num_salary;
        /* If number of records retrieved is 0 or if all the records are fetched then exit
            the loop. */
                exit when c_emp%NOTFOUND ;
                UPDATE employee SET salary = num_salary + (num_salary * .05)
                        WHERE emp_code = str_emp_code ;
                INSERT INTO emp_raise VALUES (str_emp_code, sysdate, num_salary * 0.05) ;
        END LOOP;
        COMMIT ;
        CLOSE c_emp;
END;
```

Example for cursorname%ROWCOUNT:

Write a PL/SQL block that will display the name, department and salary of the first 10 employees getting the highest salary.

```
DECLARE
        CURSOR c_emp IS
                SELECT emp_name, deptno, salary FROM employee, deptmaster
                WHERE deptmaster.deptno = employee.deptno
                ORDER BY salary desc ;
        str_ename employee.emp_name%type ;
        num_deptno employee.deptno%type ;
        num_salary employee.salary%type ;
BEGIN
        OPEN c_emp;
        dbms_output.Put_line ('Name            Department        Salary');
        dbms_output.Put_line ('--------        ---------------   ---------');
        LOOP
                FETCH c_emp INTO str_ename, num_deptno, num_salary;
                exit when c_emp%ROWCOUNT = 10 or c_emp%NOTFOUND ;
                dbms_output.Put_line (str_ename || '      ' || num_deptno || '            ' ||
                num_salary);
        END LOOP;
END ;
```

Example:
A HRD manager has decided to raise the salary for all the employees in department number 20 by 0.05. Whenever any such raise is given to the employees, an audit trail of the same is maintained in the *emp_raise* table. The *emp_raise* table holds the employee number, the date when the raise was given and the raise amount. Write a PL/SQL block to update the salary of each employee of dept_no 20 appropriately and insert a record in the *emp_raise* table as well.

Table name: employee

Column name	Data Type	Size	Attributes
emp_code	varchar	10	Primary Key, via which we shall seek data in the table
ename	varchar	20	The first name of the candidate.
deptno	Number	5	The department number.
Job	varchar	20	Employee job details.
salary	number	8,2	The current salary of the employee.

Table name: emp_raise

Column name	Data Type	Size	Attributes
emp_code	varchar	10	is the part of a composite key via which we shall seek data in the table
raise_date	date		The date on which the raise was given
raise_amt	number	8,2	The raise given to the employee.

Emp_code and raise_date together form a composite primary key.

```
DECLARE
        /* Declaration of the cursor named c_emp
        The active data set will include the names, department numbers
        and salaries of all the employees belonging to  department 20 */
        CURSOR c_emp IS
                SELECT emp_code, salary FROM employee
                        WHERE deptno = 20;

        /* Declaration of memory variable that holds data fetched from
           the cursor */
        str_emp_code            employee.emp_code%type;
        num_salary              employee.salary%type;

BEGIN

        /* Opening cursor c_emp */
        OPEN c_emp;
        /* infinite loop to fetch data from cursor c_emp one row
           at a time */

        LOOP
            FETCH c_emp INTO str_emp_code, num_salary;
            EXIT when c_emp%NOTFOUND;
        /* Updating the salary in the employee table as current salary + raise */

            UPDATE employee SET salary = num_salary + (num_salary * .05)
                WHERE emp_code = str_emp_code;
        /* Insert a record in the emp_raise table */

            INSERT INTO emp_raise
                VALUES (str_emp_code, sysdate, num_salary * 0.05);
        END LOOP;
        COMMIT ;
        /* Close cursor c_emp */
        CLOSE c_emp;
END;
```

CURSOR *FOR* LOOPS:

Another technique commonly used to control the Loop...End Loop within a PL/SQL block is the **FOR** *variable* **IN** *value* construct. This is an example of a machine defined loop exit i.e. when all the *values* in the **FOR** construct are exhausted looping stops.

Syntax:

> **FOR** *memory variable* **IN** *cursorname*

Here, the verb **FOR** automatically creates the *memory variable* of the *%rowtype*. Each record in the opened cursor becomes a value for the *memory variable* of the *%rowtype*. The **FOR** verb ensures that a row from the cursor is loaded in the declared *memory variable* and the loop executes once. This goes on until all the rows of the cursor have been loaded into the *memory variable*. After this the loop stops.

A cursor for loop automatically does the following:
- implicitly declares its loop index as a *%rowtype* record
- opens a cursor
- fetches a row from the cursor for each loop iteration.
- closes the cursor when all rows have been processed.

Cursor can be closed even when an *exit* or a *goto* statement is used to leave the loop prematurely, or if an *exception* is raised inside the loop.

Example:

The HRD manager has decided to raise the salary for all the employees in department number 20 by 0.05. Whenever any such raise is given to the employees, a record for the same is maintained in the *emp_raise* table. It includes the employee number, the date when the raise was given and the actual raise. Write a PL/SQL block to update the salary of each employee and insert a record in the *emp_raise* table.

Table Name: Emp

Emp_No	Dept_no	Sal
E001	20	5000
E002	10	1000
E003	20	1000
E004	20	5000
E005	10	5000
E006	20	1000

Table Name: Emp_Raise

Emp_No	Change_Date	Salary

```
DECLARE
        /* Declaration of a cursor which fetches the records having dept_no 20 */
        CURSOR c_emp IS
                SELECT emp_code, salary
                FROM employee
                WHERE deptno = 20;
BEGIN
        /* Use of a cursor FOR loop */
        FOR emp_rec in c_emp
        LOOP

        /* Updation of the salaries (raise by 5%) and insertion of each record into the
           new table keeping track of the date of change of salary and the raise in salary */

                UPDATE employee
                        SET salary = emp_rec.salary + (emp_rec.salary * .05)
                        WHERE emp_code = emp_rec.emp_code;
                INSERT INTO emp_raise
                        VALUES (emp_rec.emp_code, sysdate, emp_rec.salary * .05);
        END LOOP;
        COMMIT ;
END;
```

The above PL/SQL code block will function as follows:

- The block implicitly declares *emp_rec* as belonging to type *c_emp%rowtype* and retrieves all the records having dept_no 20, as declared in the cursor *c_emp*
- The sequence of statements inside the loop is executed once for every row that is fetched i.e. the salary for every record will be updated as required one by one and loaded into *emp_rec* by the **FOR** verb. At the same time, information like the emp_no, date of salary change and the raise in salary is inserted into a table *emp_raise*.
- The cursor closes automatically when all the records in the cursor have been processed. This is because there are no more rows left to load into *emp_rec*. This situation is sensed by the **FOR** verb which, causes the loop to exit.

The data in the tables *employee* and *emp_raise* after the execution of the PL/SQL code will be as follows:

Table Name: Emp

Emp_No	Dept_no	Salary
E001	20	5250
E002	10	1050
E003	20	1050
E004	20	5250
E005	10	5000
E006	20	1050

Table Name: Emp_Raise

Emp_No	Change_Date	Salary
E001	25-MAR-97	250
E003	25-MAR-97	50
E004	25-MAR-97	250
E006	25-MAR-97	50

PARAMETERIZED CURSORS

Till now, all the cursors that have been that have been declared and used fetch a pre-determined set of records. Records, which satisfy conditions, set in the where condition of the SELECT statement mapped to the cursor. In other words, the criteria on which the Active Data set is determined is hard coded and never changes.

Commercial applications require that the query, which, defines the cursor, be generic and the data that is retrieved from the table be allowed to change according to need.

Oracle recognizes this and permits the creation of a parameterized cursor prior opening. Hence the contents of the opened cursor will constantly change depending upon a value passed.

Since the cursor accepts values or Parameters it is called as *Parameterized Cursor*. The parameters can be either a constant or a variable.

Declaring a Parameterized Cursor:

<u>Syntax:</u>

> **CURSOR** *cursor_name* (*variable_name datatype*) **IS**
> < **SELECT** *statement...* >

Opening a Parameterized cursor and passing values to the cursor:

<u>Syntax</u>:

      OPEN *cursor_name (value / variable / expression)*

Note

> The scope of cursor parameters is local to that cursor, which means that they can be referenced only within the query declared in the cursor declaration. Each parameter in the declaration must have a corresponding value in the *open* statement.

<u>Example:</u>

Write a PL/SQL block of code that would update the *bal_stock* in the *item_*master table each time a transaction takes place in the *item_transaction* table. The change in the *item_master* table depends on the *itemid*. If the *itemid* is already present in the *item_master* table then an update operation is performed to decrease the *bal_stock* by the *quantity* specified in the *item_transaction* table. In case the *itemid* is not present in the *item_master* table then the record is inserted into the *item_master* table.

Table name: Item_master

Column name	Data Type	Size	Attributes
Itemid	number	4	Primary Key
Description	varchar	20	Item description
Bal_stock	number	3	Balance stock for an item

Table name: Item_Transaction

Column name	Data Type	Size	Attributes
Itemid	number	4	
Description	varchar	20	Item description
Quantity	number	3	Qty sold

```
DECLARE
        /* Cursor c_item_tran retrieves all the records of table item_transaction  */

        CURSOR c_item_tran IS
                SELECT itemid, description, quantity FROM item_transaction;

        /* Cursor c_itemchk accepts the value of itemid from the current row of cursor
          c_item_tran */
```

```
       CURSOR  c_itemchk (mastitemid number) IS
              SELECT itemid
              FROM item_master
              WHERE itemid = mastitemid;


       /* variables that hold data from the cursor c_item_tran */
       itemidno number(4);
       descrip varchar2(30);
       quantity number(3);

       /* variable that hold data from the cursor c_itemchk */

       mast_ins_uptd number(4);

BEGIN
       /* open the c_item_tran cursor */

       OPEN c_item_tran;
       LOOP
              /* Fetch the records from the c_item_tran cursor */

              FETCH c_item_tran INTO itemidno, descrip, quantity;
              EXIT WHEN c_item_tran%notfound;

              /* Open the c_itemchk cursor
                Note that the value of variable passed to the c_itemchk cursor
                is set to the value of item id in the current row of cursor c_item_tran */

              OPEN c_itemchk (itemidno);
              FETCH c_itemchk INTO mast_ins_uptd;

              /* if the record is found then update quantity
                      else insert a record in the item_master table */

              IF c_itemchk%found THEN
                      UPDATE item_master
                              SET bal_stock = bal_stock - quantity
                              WHERE itemid = itemidno;
              ELSE
                      INSERT INTO item_master(itemid, description, bal_stock)
                              VALUES(itemidno, descrip, quantity);
              END IF;
              CLOSE c_itemchk;
       END LOOP;
```

            CLOSE c_item_tran;
            COMMIT;
END;

The above PL/SQL block uses two cursors
- *c_item_tran*, which retrieves all the records of table *item_transaction*
- *c_itemchk*, a parameterized cursor which fetches records based on the value passed by the *c_item_tran* cursor.

The functionality of the PL/SQL block of code will be as follows:

The cursor *c_item_tran* holds all the records of the *item_transacation* table as the active data set. The fetch command holds the values of itemid, description and quantity into the variables *itemidno, descrip, quantity* respectively for the first record in the cursor *c_item_tran*. The value held in the variable *itemidno* indicates the *itemid* for which, the stock has to be updated in the *item_master* table.

This *itemidno* value is then passed as a parameter to the second cursor, which has to fetch the corresponding record to be updated from the *item_master* table. The WHERE condition of the select statement that defines the cursor *c_itemchk* gets its value from the variable *itemidno*.

Now, if the select statement retrieves a record from the *item_master* table i.e. the corresponding *itemid* is present in the *item_master* table, an update operation is performed on that record and the *bal_stock* is updated. If the select retrieves no record i.e. the *itemid* does not exist in the *item_master* table, a new record is inserted into the *item_master* table.

The above process continues till all the records in the cursor, *c_item_tran* are processed. When all the records have been processed the PL/SQL block exists the loop and the all the transactions are completed with the COMMIT statement.

SELF REVIEW QUESTIONS

1. How is a transaction ended?

2. Where is the cursor pointer when the cursor is first opened?

3. What are cursors opened and managed by the Oracle engine called?

4. When is an Explicit cursor used?

5. What are the basic steps to be followed while using Explicit Cursors?

6. Can the steps in the use of Explicit Cursors be reduced? If so, explain how this can be achieved?

7. Write a PL/SQL code block that determines the top *three* highest paid employees from the employee table. Use appropriate cursor attributes for the same. Display the name and the salary of these employees.

    Table Name: Emp

Emp_No	Emp_Name	Salary
E001	Mita	10000
E002	Vaishali	1000
E003	Lakshmi	3500
E004	Praveen	4000
E005	Aditya	2500
E006	Ajay	2500
E007	Sunita	2000
E008	Melba	2100

TRUE OR FALSE

8. The cursor system variables that are associated with a user defined cursor are SQL%IsOpen, SQL%Found, SQL%NotFound, SQL%RowCount.

    A) True   B) False

9. Commit can be fired upto a savepoint.

    A) True   B) False

10. A cursor can display information from a single table only.

    A) True   B) False

11. We need to declare the variable of type record if we want to use a Cursor For Loop.

    A) True   B) False

12. Fetch statement is used to get the data from the table into the cursor.

    A) True   B) False

13. Only constant values can be passed as parameters to parametrised cursors.

    A) True   B) False

FILL IN THE BLANKS

14. The data that is stored in a cursor is called _____.

15. Cursors defined by the users are called _____.

16. _____ is always evaluated to false in case of implicit cursors.

17. All LOOP statements must end with an _____ statement.

18. _____ allows passing values dynamically to a cursor while opening a cursor.

A QUICK REVIEW

➤ **Oracle Transactions**
  ▪ *Using Commit to end transactions*
  ▪ *Using Rollback to end transactions*
    - A complete Rollback
    - Rollback to a Savepoint

➤ **Implicit Cursors**
  ▪ *Implicit Cursor Attributes*
    - SQL%ISFOUND
    - SQL%NOTFOUND
    - SQL%ISOPEN
    - SQL%ROWCOUNT

➤ **Explicit Cursors**
  ▪ *Use of Explicit Cursors*
    - Declaring a Cursor
    - Opening a Cursor
    - Fetching values of cursor into variables
    - Closing Cursors
  ▪ *Explicit Cursor Attributes*
    - Cursorname%ISFOUND
    - Cursorname%NOTFOUND
    - Cursorname%ISOPEN
    - Cursorname%ROWCOUNT

➤ **Cursor For Loops**

➤ **Parameterized cursors**

Improving On PL/SQL

IN THIS CHAPTER

➢ **Concurrency Control**
- Oracle's Implicit Locking Strategy
- Explicit Locking

➢ **Error Handling**
- Named Exception Handlers
- User Defined Exception Handlers

8. IMPROVING ON PL / SQL

CONCURRENCY CONTROL IN ORACLE

Users manipulate Oracle table data via SQL or PL/SQL sentences. An Oracle transaction can be made up of a single SQL sentence or several SQL sentences. This gives rise to Single Query Transactions and Multiple Query Transactions i.e. SQT and MQT.

These transactions (whether SQT or MQT) access an Oracle table or tables. Since Oracle works on a multi-user platform, it is more than likely that several people will access data either for viewing or for manipulating (inserting, updating and deleting records) from the same tables at the same time via different SQL statements. The Oracle table is therefore a *global resource*, i.e. it is shared by several users.

Tables (i.e. global resource) contain valuable data on which business decisions are based. There is a definite need to ensure the integrity of data in a table is maintained each time that its data is accessed. The Oracle Engine has to allow simultaneous access to table data without causing damage to the data.

The technique employed by the Oracle engine to protect table data when several people are accessing it is called *Concurrency Control.*

Oracle uses a method called **Locking** to implement concurrency control when multiple users access a table to manipulate its data at the same time.

LOCKS

Locks are mechanisms used to ensure data integrity while allowing maximum concurrent access to data. Oracle's locking is fully automatic and requires no user intervention. The Oracle engine automatically locks table data while executing SQL statements. This type of locking is called *Implicit* Locking.

Oracle's Default Locking Strategy – Implicit Locking:

Since the Oracle engine has a fully automatic locking strategy, it has to decide on two issues:
- Type of Lock to be applied
- Level of Lock to be applied

Types of Locks:

The type of lock to be placed on a resource depends on the operation being performed on that resource. Operations on tables can be distinctly grouped into two categories:
- Read Operations : SELECT statements
- Write Operations: INSERT, UPDATE, DELETE statements

Since Read operations make no changes to data in a table and are meant only for viewing purposes, simultaneous *read* operations can be performed on a table without any danger to the table's data. Hence, the Oracle engine places a 'Shared' lock on a table when its data is being viewed.

On the other hand, *write* operations cause a change in table data i.e. any insert, update or delete statement affects table data directly and hence, simultaneous write operations can adversely affect table data integrity. Simultaneous write operation will cause 'Loss of data consistency' in the table. Hence, the Oracle engine places an 'Exclusive' lock on a table or specific sections of the table's resources when data is being 'written' to a table.

The rules of locking can be summarized as:
- DATA being CHANGED cannot be READ
- Writers wait for other writers, *if* they attempt to update <u>the same rows at the same time.</u>

The two *Types* of locks supported by Oracle are:

<u>Shared locks:</u>
- Shared locks are placed on resources whenever a *Read* operation (SELECT) is performed.
- Multiple shared locks can be simultaneously set on a resource.

<u>Exclusive locks:</u>
- Exclusive locks are placed on resources whenever *Write* operations (INSERT, UPDATE and DELETE) are performed.
- Only **one** exclusive lock can be placed on a resource at a time i.e. the first user who acquires an exclusive lock will continue to have the sole ownership of the resource, and **no other user can acquire an exclusive lock** on that resource.

Note

In the absence of explicit user defined locking being defined to the Oracle engine, if a default 'Exclusive' lock is taken on a table a 'Shared' lock on the very same data is permitted.

Automatic application of locks on resources by the Oracle engine results in a high degree of data consistency.

Levels of Locks:

A table can be decomposed into rows and a row can be further decomposed into fields. Hence, if an automatic locking system is designed so as to be able to lock the fields of a record, it will be the most flexible locking system available.

It would mean that more than one user can be working on a single record in a table i.e. each on a different field of the same record in the same table. *Oracle does not provide a field level lock.*

Oracle provides the following three levels of locking:
- Row level.
- Page level
- Table level

The Oracle engine decides on the level to be used by the *presence* or *absence* of a *where* condition in the SQL sentence.
- If the WHERE clause evaluates to only one row in the table, a **row level** lock is used.
- If the WHERE clause evaluates to a set of data, a **page level** lock is used.
- If there is no WHERE clause, (i.e. the query accesses the entire table,) a **table level** lock is used.

Although the Oracle engine, has a default locking strategy in commercial application, explicit user defined locking is often required. Consider the example below:

If two client computers (Client A and Client B) are entering sales orders, each time a sales-order is prepared the qty on hand of the product for which the order is being generated needs to be updated in the Product_master table.

Now, if Client A fires an update command on a record in the Product_master table, then Oracle will implicitly lock the record so that no further data manipulation can be done by any other user till the lock is released. The lock will be released only when Client A fires a commit or rollback.

In the meantime, if Client B tries to view the same record, the Oracle engine will display the old set for values for the record as the transaction for that record has not been completed by Client A. *This leads to wrong information being displayed to Client B.*

In such cases, Client A must explicitly lock the record such that, no other user can access the record even for viewing purposes till Client A's transaction is completed.

A Lock so defined is called Explicit Lock. User defined explicit locking always overrides Oracle's default locking strategy.

Explicit Locking:

The technique of lock taken on a table or its resources by a user is called Explicit Locking.

Who can explicitly lock?
- Users can lock tables they own or any tables on which they have been granted table privileges (such as *select*, *insert*, *update*, *delete*).

Oracle provides facilities by which the default locking strategy can be overridden. Table(s) or row(s) can be explicitly locked by using either the *select...for update* statement, or *lock table* statement.

The Select...For Update statement:

It is used for acquiring exclusive row level locks in anticipation of performing updates on records. This clause is generally used to signal the Oracle engine that data currently being used needs to be updated. It is often followed by one or more *update* statements with a *where* clause.

Example:
- Two client machines Client A and Client B are generating sales_orders simultaneously
- Client A fires the following select statement

Client A> SELECT * FROM *sales_order*
        WHERE *order_no = 'O00001'* **FOR UPDATE;**

When the above select statement is fired, the Oracle engine locks the record O00001. This lock is released when a commit or rollback is fired by Client A.

Now Client B fires a Select statement which points to record O00001, which has already been locked by Client A

Client B> SELECT * FROM *sales_order*
        WHERE *order_no = 'O00001'* **FOR UPDATE;**

The Oracle engine will ensure that Client B's SQL statement waits for the lock to be released on sales_order by a *commit* or *rollback* statement fired by Client A **forever**.

In order to avoid unnecessary waiting time, a **NOWAIT** option can be used to inform the Oracle engine to terminate the SQL statement if the record has already been locked. If this happens the Oracle engine terminates the running DML and comes up with a message indicating that the _resource is busy_.

If Client B fires the following select statement now with a **NOWAIT** clause
Client B> SELECT * FROM _sales_order_
              WHERE _order_no_ = _'O00001'_ **FOR UPDATE NOWAIT;**

Output:
Since Client A has already locked the record O00001 when Client B tries to acquire a shared lock on the same record the Oracle Engine displays the following message:

    SQL> 00054: resource busy and acquire with nowait specified.

The _select... for update_ cannot be used with the following:
- _distinct_ and the _group by_ clause
- _set_ operators and _group_ functions

Using lock table statement:

To manually override Oracle's default locking strategy by creating a data lock in a specific mode.

Syntax:
    LOCK TABLE _tablename [,tablename]..._
    IN _{ROW SHARE|ROW EXCLUSIVE|SHARE UPDATE|_
    SHARE|SHARE ROW EXCLUSIVE|EXCLUSIVE }
    [NOWAIT]

where,
tablename: indicates the name of table(s), view(s) to be locked. In case of views, the lock
        is placed on underlying tables.

IN   : decides what other locks on the same resource can exist simultaneously. For
        example, if there is exclusive lock on the table no user can update rows in the
        table. It can have any of the following values:

    Exclusive   : They allow query on the locked resource but prohibit
                    any other activity.

    Share   : It allows queries but prohibits updates to a table.

    Row Exclusive   : Row exclusive locks are the same as row share locks,
                     also prohibit locking in shared mode. These locks are
                     acquired when updating, inserting or deleting.

Share RowExclusive: They are used to look at a whole table, to selective updates and to allow other users to look at rows in the table but not lock the table in share mode or to update rows.

NOWAIT : indicates that the Oracle engine should immediately return to the user with a message, if the resources are busy. If omitted, the Oracle engine will wait till resources are available forever.

Example:
Table Name: Emp

Emp_code	Emp_name	Dept_code	Salary
E0001	Lakshmi	30	6000
E0002	Vaishali	30	5000
E0003	Mita	10	6500
E0004	Praveen	20	5500
E0005	Aditya	20	5200

Focus:
Two client machines Client A and Client B are performing data manipulation on the table *emp*.

❑ Client A has locked the table in exclusive mode

❑ (i.e. only querying of records is allowed on the *emp* table by Client B).
Syntax:
Client A> LOCK TABLE *emp*
         IN *Exclusive Mode*
         NOWAIT;
Output:
      Table(s) Locked.

❑ Client A performs an insert operation but does not commit the transaction.
Syntax:
Client A> INSERT INTO *emp* **VALUES** *('E0006', 'Ajay',10, 5400);*

Output:
      1 row created.

❑ Client B performs a view operation.

<u>Syntax:</u>
Client B> SELECT *emp_code, emp_name* **FROM** *emp*;

<u>Output:</u>

Emp_code	Emp_name
E0001	Lakshmi
E0002	Vaishali
E0003	Mita
E0004	Praveen
E0005	Aditya

❏ Client B performs an insert operation

<u>Syntax:</u>
Client B> INSERT INTO *emp* **VALUES** *('E0007', 'Sunita',10, 5400);*

<u>Output:</u>
Client B's SQL DML enters into a wait state waiting for Client A to release the locked resource by using a 'Commit' or 'Rollback' statement.

Inferences:

❏ *When Client A locks the table emp in exclusive mode the table is available only for querying to other users. No other data manipulation (i.e. Insert, Update and Delete operation) can be performed on the emp table by other users.*

❏ *Since Client A has inserted a record in the emp table and not committed the changes when Client B fires a select statement the newly inserted record is not visible to Client B.*

❏ *As the emp table has been locked when Client B tries to insert a record, the system enters into an indefinite wait period till all locks are released by Client A taken on emp table.*

Releasing Locks:

Locks are released under the following circumstances:
- The transaction is committed successfully using the '*Commit*' verb.
- A *rollback* is performed.
- A *rollback to a savepoint* will release locks set after the specified *savepoint*.

Note

- All locks are released on *commit* or *unqualified Rollback*.
- Table locks are released by rolling back to a savepoint.
- Row-level locks are not released by rolling back to a savepoint.

Explicit Locking using SQL and the Behavior of the Oracle Engine:

The locking characteristics for the *insert, update, delete* SQL statements in a multi user environment where real time processing takes place, is explained by taking an example of two client computers (Client A and Client B in our example) talking to the same *client_master* table via the Oracle Engine.

Table name: Client_master

Client_no	Name	City	Pincode	State	Bal_Due
C00001	Ivan Bayross	Bombay	400054	Maharashtra	15000
C00002	Vandana Saitwal	Madras	780001	Tamil Nadu	0
C00003	Pramada Jaguste	Bombay	400057	Maharashtra	5000
C00004	Basu Navindgi	Bombay	400056	Maharashtra	0
C00005	Ravi Sreedharan	Delhi	100001		2000
C00006	Rukmini	Bombay	400050	Maharashtra	0

An **INSERT** Operation:

Focus: To check the behavior of the Oracle Engine in multi-user environment when an insert operation is performed.

1. In a scenario, where

- Client A performs an insert operation on the client_master table.
  Syntax:
  Client A> INSERT INTO *client_master*
  VALUES(*'C00007', 'Ravi Shankar', 'Bombay', '400022', 'Maharashtra', 0);*

- Client A fires a *select* statement on the client_master table
  Syntax:
  Client A> SELECT *client_no, name, bal_due* **FROM** *client_master;*

  Output:

Client_no	Name	Bal_Due
C00001	Ivan Bayross	15000
C00002	Vandana Saitwal	0
C00003	Pramada Jaguste	5000
C00004	Basu Navindgi	0
C00005	Ravi Sreedharan	2000
C00006	Rukmini	0
C00007	*Ravi Shankar*	*0*

- Client B fires a *select* statement on the client_master table

  Syntax:

  SELECT *client_no, name. bal_due* **FROM** *client_master;*

  Output:

Client_no	Name	Bal_Due
C00001	Ivan Bayross	15000
C00002	Vandana Saitwal	0
C00003	Pramada Jaguste	5000
C00004	Basu Navindgi	0
C00005	Ravi Sreedharan	2000
C00006	Rukmini	0

Observation:

- Client A can see the newly inserted record 'C00007'.
- Client B cannot see the newly inserted record, as Client A has not committed it.

Inferences:

- *Since Client A has not fired a commit statement for permanently saving the newly inserted record in the client_master table, Client B cannot access the newly inserted record or manipulate it any way.*

Note

Client A can *view*, *update* or *delete* the newly inserted record since it exists in the in buffer on the Client A's computer. However, this record does not exist in the Server's table, because Client A has not committed the transaction.

An **UPDATE** Operation:

Focus: To check the behavior of the Oracle Engine in multi-user environment when an update operation is performed.

1. In a scenario, where

- Client A performs an *update* operation on client_no 'C00002' in the client_master table

  Syntax:

  Client A> UPDATE *client_master*
  SET *bal_due* = 10000
  WHERE *client_no* = *'C00002';*

- Client A fires a *select* statement on the client_master table

Syntax:
Client A> SELECT *client_no, name, bal_due* **FROM** *client_master;*

Output:

Client_no	Name	Bal_Due
C00001	Ivan Bayross	15000
C00002	*Vandana Saitwal*	*10000*
C00003	Pramada Jaguste	5000
C00004	Basu Navindgi	0
C00005	Ravi Sreedharan	2000
C00006	Rukmini	0

- Client B fires a *select* statement on the client_master table

Syntax:
Client B> SELECT *client_no, name, bal_due* **FROM** *client_master;*

Output:

Client_no	Name	Bal_Due
C00001	Ivan Bayross	15000
C00002	*Vandana Saitwal*	*0*
C00003	Pramada Jaguste	5000
C00004	Basu Navindgi	0
C00005	Ravi Sreedharan	2000
C00006	Rukmini	0

Observation:
- Client A can see the changes made to the record 'C00002' that was updated
- Client B continues to see the old values of the updated record, as Client A has not committed the transaction.

Inferences:

❑ Client A has updated the record 'C00002' and not committed it. Hence, when Client B fires a select statement, Client B cannot see the changes made to record 'C00002'.

2. In a scenario, where
   - Client A *selects* all the records from the client_master table with the *for update* clause.

   Syntax:
   Client A> SELECT *client_no, name, bal_due*
                      FROM *client_master* **FOR UPDATE;**

- Client A performs an update operation on the record 'C00002' in the client_master table.

Syntax:

Client A> UPDATE *client_master*
SET *bal_due = 10000*
WHERE *client_no = 'C00002';*

- Client A fires a *select* statement on the client_master table

Syntax:

Client A> SELECT *client_no, name, bal_due* **FROM** *client_master;*

Output:

Client_no	Name	Bal_Due
C00001	Ivan Bayross	15000
C00002	*Vandana Saitwal*	*10000*
C00003	Pramada Jaguste	5000
C00004	Basu Navindgi	0
C00005	Ravi Sreedharan	2000
C00006	Rukmini	0

- Client B fires a *select* statement with a *for update* clause on the client_master table

Syntax:

Client B> SELECT *client_no, name, bal_due* **FROM** *client_master for update;*

Output:

Client B's SQL DML enters into an indefinite wait state waiting for Client A to release the locked resource by using a 'Commit' or 'Rollback' statement.

Observation:

- Client A can see the changes made to the record 'C00002' that was updated
- When Client B fires a *select* command with for update clause, Oracle enters a **wait** state till Client A releases the locks on the client_master table.

Inferences:

❑ *The select for update fired by Client A acquires an exclusive lock on the records of the client_master table.*

❑ *Client A has not committed the record 'C00002' that was updated.*

❑ *The select statement fired by Client B tries to acquire a lock on all the records of the client_master table.*

❏ *Since these records are already locked by Client A, Client B enters into a Wait state.*

❏ *When Client A fires a Commit or Rollback, all locks are released by Client A. The records are now available to Client B for locking.*

❏ *The select statement processing executed by Client B will now be completed as Client B would see all the records and lock them.*

3. In a scenario, where
- Client A *selects* a record from the client_master table with the *for update* clause.
  Syntax:
  Client A> SELECT *client_no, name, bal_due*
          FROM *client_master* **FOR UPDATE;**

- Client A performs an *update* operation on the record 'C00002' in the client_master table
  Syntax:
  Client A> UPDATE *client_master*
          SET *bal_due* = 10000
          WHERE *client_no* = 'C00002';

- Client A fires a *select* statement in the client_master table
  Syntax:
  Client A> SELECT *client_no, name, bal_due* **FROM** *client_master;*

  Output:

Client_no	Name	Bal_Due
C00001	Ivan Bayross	15000
C00002	*Vandana Saitwal*	*10000*
C00003	Pramada Jaguste	5000
C00004	Basu Navindgi	0
C00005	Ravi Sreedharan	2000
C00006	Rukmini	0

- Client B fires a *select* command also with a *for update* and *nowait* clause on the client_master table
  Syntax:
  Client B> SELECT *client_no, name, bal_due*
          FROM *client_master* **FOR UPDATE**
          NOWAIT;
  Output:
        SQL> 00054: resource busy and acquire with nowait specified.
        no rows selected

Observation:
- Client A can see the changes made to the record 'C00002' that was updated
- When Client B fires a *select* command, Oracle checks to find if the record 'C00002' is available for a lock to be taken. Since the record has already been locked by Client A the Oracle engine displays an appropriate error message

Inferences:

❑ *The select 'for update' fired by Client A acquires an exclusive lock on all the records the client_master table.*

❑ *Since Client A has not committed the record 'C00002' that was updated. Hence, when Client B fires a select statement 'for update' and 'nowait' clause, the Oracle engine returns a message that the resource is in use by another user and terminates Client B's SQL sentence.*

❑ *The SQL prompt returns on Client B's VDU.*

❑ *Only when Client A fires a Commit or a Rollback, will all locks taken be released and the records available to Client B.*

A **DELETE** Operation:

Focus: To check the behavior of the Oracle Engine in multi-user environment when a delete operation is performed.

1. In a scenario, where

- Client A performs a *delete* operation on a record 'C00002' in the client_master table
  Syntax:
  Client A> DELETE FROM *client_master*
  WHERE *client_no = 'C00002'*;

- Client A fires a *select* statement on the client_master table
  Syntax:
  Client A> SELECT *client_no, name, bal_due* **FROM** *client_master;*
  Output:

Client_no	Name	Bal_Due
C00001	Ivan Bayross	15000
C00003	Pramada Jaguste	5000
C00004	Basu Navindgi	0
C00005	Ravi Sreedharan	2000
C00006	Rukmini	0

- Client B fires a *select* statement on the client_master table

  Syntax:

  Client B> SELECT *client_no, name, bal_due* **FROM** *client_master;*

  Output:

Client_no	Name	Bal_Due
C00001	Ivan Bayross	15000
C00002	Vandana Saitwal	10000
C00003	Pramada Jaguste	5000
C00004	Basu Navindgi	0
C00005	Ravi Sreedharan	2000
C00006	Rukmini	0

Observation:

- Client A does not see the record 'C00002' any more as it has been deleted.
- Client B continues to see the record 'C00002', as Client A has not committed the deletion operation.

Inferences:

- *Client A has deleted the record 'C00002' and not committed the same.*
- *Hence when Client B fires a select statement, Client B can still see record 'C00002'.*

2. In a scenario, where

- Client A *selects* a record from the client_master table with the *for update* clause.

  Syntax:

  Client A> SELECT *client_no, name, bal_due*

             FROM *client_master* **FOR UPDATE;**

- Client A performs a *delete* operation on the record 'C00002' in the client_master table.

  Syntax:

  Client A> DELETE FROM *client_master*

             WHERE *client_no* = 'C00002';

- Client A fires a *select* on the client_master table

  Syntax:

  Client A> SELECT *client_no, name, bal_due* **FROM** *client_master;*

Output:

Client_no	Name	Bal_Due
C00001	Ivan Bayross	15000
C00003	Pramada Jaguste	5000
C00004	Basu Navindgi	0
C00005	Ravi Sreedharan	2000
C00006	Rukmini	0

- Client B fires a *select* command with for update clause on the client_master table

Syntax:

Client B> SELECT *client_no, name, bal_due* **FROM** *client_master*
      FOR UPDATE;

Output:

Client B's SQL DML enters into a wait state waiting for Client A to release the locked resource by using a 'Commit' or 'Rollback' statement.

Observation:

- Client A can no longer see the record as it has been deleted.
- When Client B fires a *select* command, Oracle enters a *wait* state till Client A releases the lock on the record.

Inferences:

- Since Client A has fired a select statement with a 'for update' clause, all the records of the client_master table has been exclusively locked by Client A.
- The record 'C00002' is deleted by Client A, no locks have been released.
- When Client B fires a select statement and tries to acquire a lock on all the records of client_master table, Client B enters into a Wait stage.
- Only when Client A fires a Commit or a Rollback, will all locks on the records be released and the records will be available to Client B for locking.
- The select statement processing executed by Client B will now be completed as Client B would see all the records and lock them.

3. In a scenario, where,
   - Client A selects a record 'C00002' from the client_master table with the *for update* clause.

     Syntax:

     Client A> SELECT *client_no, name, bal_due*
                    FROM *client_master* **FOR UPDATE;**

   - Client A performs a *delete* operation on the record in the client_master table

     Syntax:

     Client A> DELETE FROM *client_master*
                   WHERE *client_no = 'C00002';*

   - Client A fires a *select* statement on the client_master table

     Syntax:

     Client A> SELECT *client_no, name, bal_due* **FROM** *client_master;*

     Output:

Client_no	Name	Bal_Due
C00001	Ivan Bayross	15000
C00003	Pramada Jaguste	5000
C00004	Basu Navindgi	0
C00005	Ravi Sreedharan	2000
C00006	Rukmini	0

   - Client B fires a *select* statement on the client_master table

     Syntax:

     Client B> SELECT client_no, name, bal_due
                   FROM client_master **FOR UPDATE**
                   NOWAIT;

     Output:

           SQL> 00054: resource busy and acquire with nowait specified.

           no rows selected

Observation:
- Client A can no longer see the record 'C00002' as it has been deleted.
- When Client B fires a *select* command, Oracle checks to find if the record 'C00002' is available for a lock to be taken. Since Client A has already locked the record the Oracle engine displays an appropriate message.

Inferences:

☐ *The select for update fired by Client A acquires an exclusive lock on all the records of the client_master table.*

☐ *Client A has not committed the record 'C00002' that was deleted*

☐ *When Client B fires a select for update and nowait clause, the Oracle engine displays the message that the resource is in use by another user and returns Client B to the SQL prompt.*

☐ *Only when Client A fires a Commit or a Rollback, will all locks on the records be released*

Explicit Locking using PL/SQL and the Oracle Engine:

The manner in which explicit locking can be used in a PL/SQL block of code and functionality of the Oracle engine in processing the code block in a multi-user environment is explained with the help of the following example:

Example:
Write a PL/SQL code block that will accept:

- An account number, the type of transaction, the amount involved and whether the amount to be debited to or credited to an account number.
- The balance in the *account* table for the corresponding account number is updated.
- Before the update is fired, the record is viewed in the *for update nowait mode* so that a lock can be acquired on the record to be updated and no other user has access to the same record till the transaction is completed.

Table name: Accounts

Account_id	Name	Bal
AC001	Anuj	5000
AC002	Robert	10000
AC003	Mita	5000
AC004	Sunita	15000
AC005	Melba	10000

```
DECLARE
      /* Declaration of memory variables and constants to be used in the
          Execution section. */
      acct_balance  number (11,2);
      acct_no varchar2(6);
      trans_amt number(5) ;
      oper     char(1);
BEGIN
      /* Accept an acc_id,oper_type and the trans_amt from the user*/
      acct_no :=&acct_no;
      trans_amt:=&trans_amt;
      oper:=&oper;

      /* Retrieving the balance from the accounts table where the account_id
      in the table is equal to the acct_no entered by the user. Also the select is
      with a for update and nowait clause in order to acquire a lock on the
      record */
      SELECT bal INTO acct_balance
            FROM accounts
            WHERE account_id = acct_no FOR UPDATE NOWAIT;
```

/ Checking if the operation specified is debit or credit. If the operation specified is debit then the balance is reduced by the trans_amt. If the operation specified is credit then the balance is added by the trans_amt of the corresponding account_no. */*

```
IF oper= 'D' THEN
        UPDATE accounts SET bal = bal - trans_amt
            WHERE account_id = acct_no;
ELSIF  oper= 'C' THEN
        UPDATE accounts SET bal = bal + trans_amt
        WHERE account_id = acct_no;
    END IF;
END;
```

In a scenario, where two users Client A and Client B are accessing the accounts table and Client A first executes the PL/SQL block of code and enters 'AC003' as the *acct_no*, 1500 as the *trans_amt* and 'C' for *oper:*

* The SELECT statement will retrieve the balance amount of 5000 from the *accounts* table that is related to account no 'AC003'. The Oracle engine will also acquire a lock on the record 'AC003' as the SELECT statement is with the FOR UPDATE NOWAIT clause.

* The Oracle Engine then checks whether the *oper* entered is 'C' or 'D'.

* Since the *oper* entered is 'C' the trans_amt of Rs. 1500 will be added to *account_id* 'AC003'.

* At this point in time, if Client A fires a select sentence.

Syntax:
    SELECT * FROM *accounts*;

Output:

Account_Id	Name	Bal
AC001	Anuj	5000
AC002	Robert	10000
AC003	*Mita*	*6500*
AC004	Sunita	15000
AC005	Melba	10000

- Since Client A has not yet committed the record, the lock on the record still exists.

- Now if Client B fires the PL/SQL block of code for the same record 'AC003', the SELECT statement will fail to acquire the lock as Client A already locked the record. Since the NOWAIT clause has been specified in the SELECT sentence, the Oracle engine will come out of the PL/SQL block and display the following message:

```
DECLARE
*
ERROR at line 1:
ORA-00054: resource busy and acquire with NOWAIT specified
ORA-06512: at line 10
```

Thus, by exclusively locking the row just before the UPDATE is fired in a PL/SQL block of code, concurrency control can be maintained in a multi-user environment where multiple users would want to access the same resource at the same time.

ERROR HANDLING IN PL/SQL

Every PL/SQL block of code encountered by the Oracle engine is accepted as a client. Hence the Oracle engine will make an attempt to execute every SQL sentence within the PL/SQL block. However while executing the SQL sentences anything can go wrong and the SQL sentence can fail.

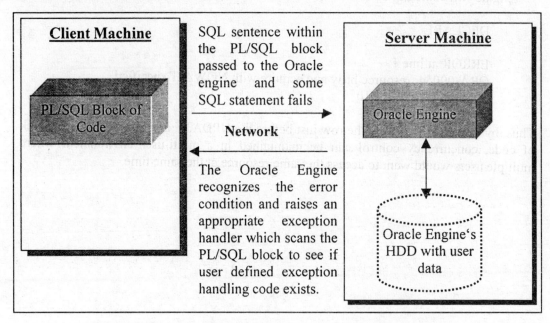

Diagram 8.1 : Exception Handling and the Oracle Engine.

When an SQL sentence fails the Oracle engine is the first to recognize this as an *Exception condition.* The Oracle engine immediately tries to handle the exception condition and resolve it. This is done by raising a built-in *Exception Handler*.

An *Exception Handler* is nothing but a code block in memory that will attempt to resolve the current exception condition. The Oracle engine can recognize every exception condition that occurs in memory. To handle very common and repetitive exception conditions the Oracle engine uses *Named Exception Handlers*. The Oracle engine has about *fifteen to twenty* **named** exception handlers. In addition to this the Oracle engine uses more than *twenty thousand* **numbered** exception handlers. These exception handlers are identified not by names but by four integers preceded by a hyphen (**i.e. –1414**). These exception handler names are actually a set of negative signed integers. Each Exception Handler, irrespective of how it is identified, (i.e. by Name or Number) has code attached that will attempt to resolve an exception condition. This is how Oracle's, *Default Exception-Handling* strategy works.

Oracle's default exception handling code can be overridden. When this is done Oracle's default exception handling code is not executed but the code block that takes care of the exception condition, in the exception section, of the PL/SQL block is executed. This is an example of a programmer giving explicit exception handling instructions to an Oracle exception handler.

This means that the Oracle engine's Exception Handler must establish whether to execute its own exception handling code or whether it has to execute user defined exception handling code.

As soon as the Oracle engine invokes an exception handler the exception handler goes back to the PL/SQL block from which the exception condition was raised. The exception handler scans the PL/SQL block for the existence of an **Exception section** within the PL/SQL block. If an exception section within the PL/SQL block exists the exception handler scans the first word, after the action word **When,** within this exception section.

If the first word after the action word **When,** is the exception handler's _name_ then the exception handler executes the code contained in the **Then** section of the construct as follows:

Exception
When {Exception Name}**Then**
      {User defined action to be carried out}

The first word that follows the action word **When** must be '_String_'. Hence this technique will work well for the fifteen to twenty '_named exception handlers_'. In addition to these the Oracle engine has twenty thousand, numbered exception handlers, which are raised automatically and appropriately when the Oracle engine recognizes and exception condition. User defined exception handling code must be permitted even for these (numbered) exception handlers.

ORACLE'S NAMED EXCEPTION HANDLERS

The Oracle engine has a set of pre-defined Oracle error handlers called _Named Exceptions_. These error handlers are referenced by their name. The following are some of the pre-defined Oracle named exception handlers:

Pre-determined internal PL/SQL exceptions:
- **DUP_VAL_ON_INDEX**: Raised when an _insert_ or _update_ attempts to create two rows with duplicate values in column/s constrained by a _unique_ index.
- **LOGIN_DENIED**: Raised when an invalid username/password was used to log onto Oracle.
- **NO_DATA_FOUND**: Raised when a _select_ statement returns zero rows.
- **NOT_LOGGED_ON**: Raised when PL/SQL issues an Oracle call without being logged onto Oracle.

- **PROGRAM_ERROR**: Raised when PL/SQL has an internal problem.
- **TIMEOUT_ON_RESOURCE**: Raised when Oracle has been waiting to access a resource beyond the user-defined timeout limit.
- **TOO_MANY_ROWS**: Raised when a *select* statement returns more than one row.
- **VALUE_ERROR**: Raised when the data type or data size is invalid.
- **OTHERS**: stands for all other exceptions not explicitly named.

Example:

The *salesman_master* table records the *salesman_no, name, rate_of_commission, ytd_sales*. The *commission_amount* and *date_of_payment* along with the *salesman_no* is calculated and recorded in *commission_payable* table.

Write a PL/SQL block of code such that depending upon the user entered *salesman_no*, the *commission_amount* is calculated and inserted into the *commission_payable* table. If the user enters a *salesman_no* that is not in the *salesman_master* table, then the PL/SQL block must display appropriate error message back to the user.

```
DECLARE
            sman_no     salesman_master.salesman_no%type ;
            sales_amt   salesman_master.ytd_sales %type;
            comm_rate   salesman_master.rate_of_commission%type;

BEGIN
            /*Retrieving records from the salesman_master table and assigning them
            to memory variables for the salesman_no entered by the user */
            SELECT salesman_no, rate_of_commission, ytd_sales
                INTO sman_no, comm_rate, sales_amt
                FROM salesman_master
                WHERE salesman_no  = &salesman_no;

            /*Calculating the commission_amount payable and inserting into the
            commission_payable table*/
            INSERT INTO commission_payable
                VALUES (sman_no, sysdate, sales_amt* comm_rate/ 100);

EXCEPTION
            /* Using the Oracle engine's named exception handler to handle the
            error condition that may occur if the user enters a salesman_no that is
            not present in the salesman_master table*/
            WHEN no_data_found THEN
                DBMS_OUTPUT.PUT_LINE('Salesman No ' || sman_no ||
                     ' is not present in the salesman_master table');

END;
```

USER-Named Exception Handlers

The technique that is used is to bind a numbered exception handler to a name using **'Pragma Exception_init( )'** This binding of a numbered exception handler, to a name (i.e. a String), is done in the Declare section of the PL/SQL block.

All objects declared in the Declare section of a PL/SQL block are **not created** until actually required within the PL/SQL block. However, the binding of a numbered exception handler to a name *must be done exactly when declared* **not** when the exception handler is invoked due to an exception condition.

The **Pragma** action word is a *call to a pre-compiler*, which immediately binds the numbered exception handler to a name when encountered.

The function **Exception_init( )** takes two parameters the *first* is the user defined exception name the *second* is the Oracle engine's exception number. These lines will be included in the **Declare** section of the PL/SQL block.

Note

The user defined exception name must be the statement that immediately precedes the Pragma Exception_init ( ) statement.

Syntax:
```
DECLARE
        exception_name EXCEPTION;
            PRAGMA EXCEPTION_INIT (exception_name, error_code_no);
    BEGIN
```

Using this technique it is possible to bind appropriate numbered exception handlers to names and use these names in the Exception section of a PL/SQL block. When this is done the default exception handling code of the exception handler is overridden and the user-defined exception handling code is executed.

Syntax:
```
DECLARE
        exception_name EXCEPTION;
            PRAGMA EXCEPTION_INIT (exception_name,error_code_no);
    BEGIN
        ............
        ............
    EXCEPTION
            WHEN exception_name THEN
                <action>
    END;
```

User Defined Exception Handlers (For I/O Validations)

The manner of defining and handling an exception in a PL/SQL block of code is shown in the following example.

Example:

Two client machines (Client A and Client B) are accessing the same *client_master* table using identical PL/SQL code blocks for updating the *bal_due* column of the table *client_master*.

Table Name: Client_master

Client_no	Bal_due
C00001	1000
C00002	5000
C00003	3800
C00004	1200
C00005	400
C00006	3000

```
DECLARE
        bal_amt number(10,2);
        trans_amt number(10,2);
        cl_no varchar2(6);
        trans_type char(1);


        /*Declaring a variable of the type exception and associating the variable to an
        Oracle error number */


        resource_busy EXCEPTION;
        PRAGMA EXCEPTION_INIT (resource_busy,-00054);
BEGIN
        /*Accepting values from the user at the SQL Prompt and assigning these values
        to the memory variables.*/


        trans_amt:=&trans_amt;
        cl_no:='&cl_no';
        trans_type:='&trans_type';


        /* Retrieving the value of bal_due for the client_no entered by the user from the
        client_master table*/


        SELECT bal_due INTO bal_amt FROM client_master
                WHERE client_no =cl_no FOR UPDATE NOWAIT;
```

/*Checking if the trans_type is debit or credit and updating the bal_due column accordingly for the client_no entered by the user*/

IF trans_type='D' **THEN**
        UPDATE client_master **SET** bal_due =bal_due-trans_amt
             WHERE client_no=cl_no;
ELSIF trans_type='C' **THEN**
        UPDATE client_master **SET** bal_due =bal_due+trans_amt
             WHERE client_no=cl_no;
END IF;

EXCEPTION
        WHEN resource_busy **THEN**
        DBMS_OUTPUT.PUT_LINE ('The row is in use');

END;

In a scenario where,

1. Client A has fired a select statement for viewing the record 'C00003' with a *for update nowait* clause i.e. Client A has acquired a lock on the record C00003' in the client_master table.

2. Client A has updated the record 'C00003' by debiting an amount of Rs.3000. Client A has not yet completed the transaction (i.e. *No commit or rollback statement has been fired by Client A*)

3. Now, if the second user i.e. Client B also fires the same PL/SQL block of code and enters the same client_no 'C00003', when Client A has locked the record with a SELECT FOR UPDATE clause then

Observation:
The Oracle engine instead of displaying its own error message, will now display a user-defined message as defined in the exception handling section of the PL/SQL block of code.

EXCEPTION
        WHEN resource_busy **THEN**
        DBMS_OUTPUT.PUT_LINE **('The row is in use by another');**

In case the above error condition was not handled by the user in the exception section then the Oracle engine will raise it's own error handler and display the following message to the user

```
DECLARE
*
ERROR at line 1:
ORA-00054: resource busy and acquire with NOWAIT specified
ORA-06512: at line 10
```

User Defined Exception Handling (For Business Rule Validations)

In commercial application data being manipulated needs to be validated against business rules. If the data violates a business rule, the entire record must be rejected. In such cases, the insert SQL DML actually runs successfully. It is the data values that the insert statement is placing in the table, which violates the business rule.

Since the SQL DML did not cause any system error, the Oracle engine cannot object to the erroneous data value being inserted into a table.

To trap business rules being violated the technique of *raising* user-defined exceptions and then *handling* them, is used.

All business rule exceptions are completely transparent to the Oracle engine and hence the skill of translating a business rule into appropriate PL/SQL user-defined exception handling code is vital to a programmer.

User-defined error conditions must be declared in the declarative part of any PL/SQL block. In the executable part, a check for the condition that needs special attention is made. If that condition exists, the call to the user-defined exception is made using a RAISE statement. The exception once raised is then handled in the Exception handling section of the PL/SQL code block.

<u>Syntax:</u>

```
DECLARE
        <Exceptionname> Exception
BEGIN
        SQL sentence;
        IF <condition> THEN
            RAISE <Exceptionname>;
        END IF;
EXCEPTION
        WHEN <Exceptionname>THEN
                {User defined action to be taken};
END;
```

Example:
The salesman_master table records the salesman_no, salesman_name, ytd_sales, rate_of_commission along with the minimum tgt_to_get. A salesman is eligible for commission only when a salesman achieves the target sales. When commission is paid the commission amount along with the salesman_no and the date_of_payment is recorded in commissison_payable table.

Table Name: Salesman_master

Salesman_no	Salesman_name	Rate_of_Commission	Tgt_To_Get	Ytd_Sales
S00001	Kiran	5	100	50
S00002	Manish	4	200	300
S00003	Ravi	3	200	350
S00004	Ashish	7	200	150

Table Name: Commission_Payable

Salesman_no	Date_of_Payment	Commisssion_amount

```
DECLARE
            less_than_target EXCEPTION;
            sman_no salesman_master.salesman_no%type ;
            tgt_sales salesman_master.tgt_to_get%type;
            act_sales salesman_master.ytd_sales%type;
            comm_rate salesman_master.rate_of_commission%type;
BEGIN
            SELECT salesman_no, rate_of_commission, tgt_to_get, ytd_sales
                    INTO sman_no, comm_rate, tgt_sales, act_sales
                    FROM salesman_master
                    WHERE salesman_no  = &sman_no;
            IF act_sales < tgt_sales THEN
                    RAISE less_than_target;
            ELSE
                    INSERT INTO commission_payable
                            VALUES (sman_no, sysdate, act_sales * comm_rate/100);
            END IF;
EXCEPTION
            WHEN less_than_target THEN
                            DBMS_OUTPUT.PUT_LINE ('Salesman No ' || sman_no ||
                                    ' is not entitled to get commission');
END;
```

SELF REVIEW QUESTIONS

1. What are Locks?

2. What is Explicit Locking? What are the statements used for Explicit Locking?

3. Two client machines Client A and Client B are performing a data manipulation operation on the *'employee'* table that has *emp_no* as the primary key. In a senario where,

   - Client A has performed an Insert operation

   Syntax:
   INSERT INTO *employee* **VALUES** (*'E00010', 'Lakshmi', 6000*);

   - Client A has not yet committed or rollbacked the record

   - Client B also performs a Insert operation

   Syntax:
   INSERT INTO *employee* **VALUES** (*'E00010', 'Vaishali', 5000*);

   What happens when Client B fires the insert statement?

4. What is the use of a NOWAIT clause?

5. What causes a table or record level lock to be released?

6. What are the types of locks that can be placed on a table? What determines the type of lock placed on a table?

7. Name at least four pre-defined exceptions?

FILL IN THE BLANKS

8. _____ is used for Error trapping in PL/SQL blocks

9. _____ is an exception raised when no information is retrieved from the table.

10. _____ function is used to connect an Oracle Error number to an exception name.

11. The _____ clause in an SQL statement determines the level of lock to be placed on the table.

12. The Oracle engine provides with the _____exception to trap all exceptions in case the user does not know what error to anticipate.

A QUICK REVIEW

➤ **Concurrency Control - Locks**
- ▪ *Oracle's default Locking Strategy (Implicit Locking)*
  - \- Types of Locks
    - Shared
    - Exclusive
  - \- Levels of Locks
    - Row level lock
    - Page level lock
    - Table level lock
- ▪ *Explicit Locking*
  - \- *Select For Update Statement*
  - \- *Lock Table Statement*

➤ **Error Handling In PL/SQL**
- ▪ *Named Exception Handlers*
- ▪ *User Defined Exception Handlers*
  - \- For i/o validations
  - \- For business rules

Database Objects

IN THIS CHAPTER

> Stored Procedure & Functions.

> Oracle Packages.

> Overloading Procedure & Functions.

> Database Triggers.

> Dynamic SQL using the DBMS_SQL built-in package.

9. DATABASE OBJECTS

STORED PROCEDURES AND FUNCTIONS

What are Procedures / Functions?

A Procedure or Function is a logically grouped set of SQL and PL/SQL statements that perform a specific task. A *stored procedure or function* is a named PL/SQL code block that have been compiled and stored in one of the Oracle engine's system tables.

To make a Procedure or Function dynamic either of them can be passed parameters before execution. A Procedure or Function can then change the way it works depending upon the parameters passed prior to its execution.

Procedures and Functions are made up of:
1. A declarative part,
2. An executable part, and
3. An optional exception-handling part.

Declarative part:

The declarative part may contain the declarations of cursors, constants, variables, exceptions and subprograms. These objects are local to the procedure or function. The objects become invalid once the user exits from the procedure or the function.

Executable part:

The executable part is a PL/SQL block consisting of SQL and PL/SQL statements that assign values control execution and manipulate data. The action that the procedure or function is expected to perform is coded here. The data that is to be returned back to the calling environment is also returned from here. Variables declared are put to use in this block.

Exception handling part:

This part contains code that performs required actions to deal with exceptions that may be raised during the execution of code in the *executable* part. An Oracle exception handler can be redirected to the exception handling section of the procedure or function where the procedure or function determines the actual action that must be carried out by Oracle's exception handler.

One cannot transfer the flow of execution from the Exception Handling part to the Executable part.

Where do Stored Procedures and Functions reside?

Procedures and Functions are stored in the Oracle database. They are invoked or called by any the PL/SQL block that appears within an application. Before the procedure or function is stored, the Oracle engine parses and compiles the procedure or function.

How the Oracle Engine creates a Procedure / Function?

When a procedure is created, the Oracle engine automatically performs the following steps:

1. Compiles the procedure or function.
2. Stores the procedure or function in the database.

The Oracle engine compiles the PL/SQL code block. If an error occurs when the procedure or function *an invalid procedure or function* is created. The Oracle engine displays a message after creation that the procedure or function was created with *compilation errors*.

It does not display the errors. These errors can be viewed using the *select* statement:

SELECT * FROM *user_errors*;

When the procedure or function is invoked, the Oracle engine loads the compiled procedure or function in the memory area called the System Global Area (SGA). This allows the code to be executed quickly. Once loaded in the SGA other users also access the same procedure or function if they have been granted permission to do so.

How the Oracle Engine executes Procedures / Functions?

The Oracle engine performs the following steps to execute a procedure or function

1. Verifies user access.
2. Verifies procedure or function validity.
3. Executes the procedure or function.

The Oracle engine checks if the user who called the procedure or function has the *execute* privilege for the procedure or function. If the user is invalid, then access is denied otherwise the Oracle engine proceeds to check whether the called procedure or function is valid or not. The status of a procedure or function is seen by using a *select* statement as follows:

> **SELECT** *object_name, object_type, status*
> **FROM** *user_objects*
> **WHERE** *object_type* = *'PROCEDURE'*;

Or

> **SELECT** *object_name, object_type, status*
> **FROM** *user_objects*
> **WHERE** *object_type* = *'FUNCTION'*;

Only if the status is *valid*, can a procedure or function be executed. Once found valid, the Oracle engine then loads a procedure or function into memory (i.e. if it is not currently present in memory) and executes it.

Advantages of using a Procedure or Function:

1. **Security**: Stored procedures and functions can help enforce data security. For e.g. by giving permission to a procedure or function that can query a table and granting the procedure or function to users, permissions to manipulate the table itself need not be granted to users.

2. **Performance**: It improves database performance in the following ways:
    *   Amount of information sent over a network is less.
    *   No compilation step is required to execute the code.
    *   Once the procedure or function is present in the shared pool of the SGA retrieval from disk is not required every time different users call the procedure or function i.e. reduction in disk i/o.

3. **Memory Allocation**: The amount of memory used reduces as stored procedures or functions have shared memory capabilities. Only one copy of procedure needs to be loaded for execution by multiple users. Once a copy of the procedure or function is opened in the Oracle engine's memory, other users who have permissions may access them when required.

4. **Productivity**: By writing procedures and functions redundant coding can be avoided, increasing productivity.

5. **Integrity**: A procedure or function needs to be tested only once to guarantee that it returns an accurate result. Since procedures and functions are stored in the Oracle engine 's they become a part of the engine's resource. Hence the responsibility of maintaining their integrity rests with the Oracle engine. The Oracle engine has high level of in-built security and hence integrity of procedures or functions can be safely left to the Oracle engine.

Procedures versus Functions:

The differences between Procedures and Functions can be listed as below:

❑ A function must return a value back to the caller. A function can return only one value to the calling PL/SQL code block.

❑ By defining multiple OUT parameters in a procedure, multiple values can be passed to the caller. The OUT variable being global by nature, its value is accessible by any PL/SQL code block including the calling PL/SQL block.

Syntax for creating Stored Procedure and Functions:

Syntax for Creating a Procedures:
>   **CREATE OR REPLACE PROCEDURE** *[schema.] procedurename*
>   *(argument* **{ IN, OUT, IN OUT}** *data type, ...)* **{IS, AS}**
>   *variable declarations ;*
>   *constant declarations ;*
>   BEGIN
>   *PL/SQL subprogram body ;*
>   EXCEPTION
>   *exception PL/SQL block ;*
>   END;

Keywords and Parameters:

The keywords and the parameters used for creating database procedures are explained below:

REPLACE | recreates the procedure if it already exists. This option is used to change the definition of an existing procedure without dropping, recreating and re-granting object privileges previously granted on it. If a procedure is redefined the Oracle engine recompiles it.

schema | is the schema to contain the procedure. The Oracle engine takes the default schema to be the current schema, if it is omitted.

procedure | is the name of the procedure to be created.

argument | is the name of an argument to the procedure. Parentheses can be omitted if no arguments are present.

IN | specifies that a value for the argument must be specified when calling the procedure.

| OUT | specifies that the procedure passes a value for this argument back to its calling environment after execution. |

| IN OUT | specifies that a value for the argument must be specified when calling the procedure and that the procedure passes a value for this argument back to its calling environment after execution. *By default it takes IN.* |

| Data type | is the data type of an argument. It supports any data type supported by PL/SQL. |

PL/SQL subprogram body is the definition of procedure consisting of PL/SQL statements.

<u>Syntax for Creating a Functions</u>:

CREATE OR REPLACE FUNCTION *[schema.] functionname*
    (argument **IN** *data type, ...)*
    RETURN *data type* {**IS, AS**}
    variable declarations;
    constant declarations;
    BEGIN
        PL/SQL subprogram body;
    EXCEPTION
        exception PL/SQL block ;
    END;

Keywords and Parameters:

The keywords and the parameters used for creating database functions are explained below:

| REPLACE | recreates the function if it already exists. This option is used to change the definition of an existing function without dropping, recreating and re-granting object privileges previously granted on it. If a function is redefined, Oracle recompiles it. |

| Schema | is the schema to contain the function. Oracle takes the default schema to be the current schema, if it is omitted. |

| function | is the name of the function to be created. |

| argument | is the name of an argument to the function. Parentheses can be omitted if no arguments are present. |

| IN | specifies that a value for the argument must be specified when calling the function. |

RETURN *data type*   is the data type of the function's return value. Because every function must return a value, *this clause is required*. It supports any data type supported by PL/SQL.

PL/SQL subprogram body is the definition of function consisting of PL/SQL statements.

Diagrammatic representation of the working of a Procedure in Server RAM:

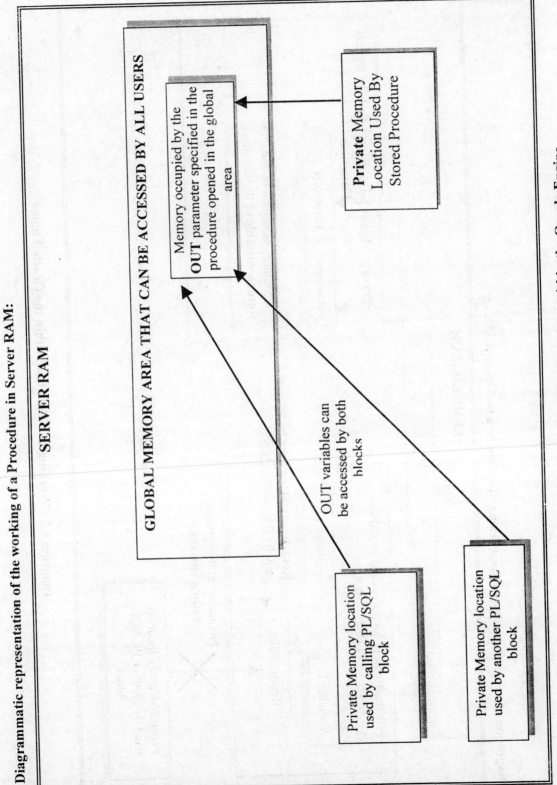

Diagram 9.1 : Working of a Procedure within the Oracle Engine

Diagrammatic representation of the working of a Function in Server RAM:

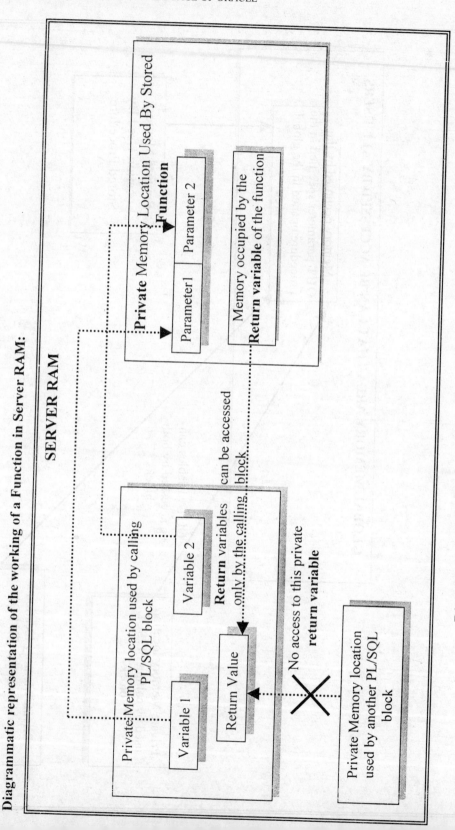

Diagram 9.2 : Working of a Function within the Oracle Engine

Example for using a function:

Focus:

Consider the tables item_master and item_transaction. Both the tables belong to an inventory system. The item_transaction table is used to register the inward movement of stock, as it happens. At regular intervals, as a batch process the stock value must be written to the item_master table.

Write a PL/SQL block of code that would update the *bal_stock* in the *item*_master table each time a transaction takes place in the *item_transaction* table. The change in the *item_master* table depends on the *itemid*. If the *itemid* is already present in the *item_master* table then an update operation is performed to increase the *bal_stock* by the *quantity* specified in the *item_transaction* table. In case the *itemid* is not present in the *item_master* table then the record is inserted into the *item_master* table.

Table name: item_master

Column name	Data Type	Size	Attributes
itemid	number	4	Primary Key
description	varchar	20	Item description
bal_stock	number	3	Balance stock for an item

Table name: item_transaction

Column name	Data Type	Size	Attributes
itemid	number	4	
description	varchar	20	Item description
quantity	number	3	Qty sold

To help simplify this process (of batch updating) a function called *f_itemidchk* has been created. The function checks for the existence of *itemid* in the table *item_master*. The function has one argument, which receives a value. The function will search for a matching value in the *item_master* table when a value is passed to it while calling it.

The function will return value '1' indicating that a match is found and a value '0' indicating that no match is found. This value returned by the function is used to make a decision to 'INSERT' or 'UPDATE' the *item_master* table.

Creating Function for use:

A stored function is created to perform the itemid check operation. *f_itemidchk* is the name of the function which accepts a variable *itemid* and returns a variable *valexists* to the host environment. The value of *valexists* changes from *0* (itemid does not exist) to *1* (itemid exists) depending on the records retrieved.

```
CREATE FUNCTION f_itemidchk(vitemidno IN number) RETURN number IS
    /* variable that hold data from the item_master table */

    dummyitem number(4);

BEGIN
    SELECT itemid INTO dummyitem
        FROM item_master WHERE itemid = vitemidno ;

        /* if the select statement retrieves data, valexists is set to 1 */

    RETURN 1;

EXCEPTION

    /* if the select statement does not retrieve data, valexists is set to 0 */

    WHEN NO_DATA_FOUND THEN
        RETURN 0;
END;
```

This function is then called in the PL/SQL block follows. The return value is then checked and appropriate action is taken.

Calling the Function *f_itemidchk* in a PL/SQL code block:

```
DECLARE
        /* Cursor scantable retrieves all the records of table itemtran */

        CURSOR scantable IS
                SELECT itemid, quantity, description FROM item_transaction;

        /* Variables that hold data from the cursor scantable */

        vitemidno item_transaction.itemid%type;
        vdescrip item_transaction.description%type;
        vquantity item_transaction.quantity%type;

        /* Variable that stores the value returned by the f_itemidchk function i.e. 1 or 0 */

        valexists number(1);
```

```
BEGIN
        OPEN scantable;
        LOOP
                FETCH scantable INTO vitemidno, vquantity,vdescrip;
                EXIT WHEN scantable%NOTFOUND;
                /* Call function f_itemidchk to check if itemid is present in
                 item_master table */

                valexists := f_itemidchk(vitemidno);

                /* if itemid does not exists insert a record in the item_master table */

                IF valexists = 0 THEN
                        INSERT INTO item_master(itemid, description, bal_stock)
                                VALUES (vitemidno, vdescrip, vquantity);

                /* if the record is found then update quantity in the item_master table */

                ELSIF valexists = 1 THEN
                        UPDATE item_master
                                SET bal_stock = bal_stock + vquantity
                                WHERE itemid = vitemidno;
                END IF;
        END LOOP;
        CLOSE scantable;
        COMMIT;
END;
```

The functionality of the PL/SQL block of code will be as follows:

A call is made to the function and the *itemidno* value is then passed as a parameter. The WHERE condition of the select statement of the function gets its value from the variable itemidno and depending on whether the value exists in the item_master table or not, a value of 0 or 1 is returned to the calling PL/SQL block.

If the select statement retrieves a record from the *item_master* table (i.e. the corresponding *itemid* is present in the *item_master* table) an update operation is performed on that record and the *bal_stock* is updated.

If the select retrieves no record i.e. the *itemid* does not exist in the *item_master* table, a new record is inserted into the *item_master* table.

The above process continues till all the records in the cursor, *scantable* are processed. When all the records have been processed the PL/SQL block exits the loop and the all the transactions are completed with the COMMIT statement.

Example for using a procedure:

Focus:

The current example deals with the Sales Order Processing system. The tables involved with this processing are product_master, sales_order, sales_order_details, challan_header and challan_details.

Each time a entry is made in the challan_details table, there is an actual reduction in inventory as goods are delivered to the customer. So, an entry needs to be made in the product_master table that will reduce the qty_in_hand by the quantity for which the challan was generated. Also the status of the order whether Fully Processed (FP), In Process (IP) or Not Processed (NP) needs to be updated in the sales_order table.

a) **Table Name**: product_master
   Description: Used to store product information.

Column Name	Data Type	Size	Attributes
product_no	varchar2	6	Primary Key / first letter must start with 'P'
description	varchar2	15	Not Null
profit_percent	number	4,2	Not Null
unit_measure	varchar2	10	Not Null
qty_on_hand	number	8	Not Null
reorder_lvl	number	8	Not Null
sell_price	number	8,2	Not Null, cannot be 0.
cost_price	number	8,2	Not Null, cannot be 0.

b) **Table Name**: sales_order
Description: Used to store client's orders

Column Name	Data Type	Size	Attributes
order_no	varchar2	6	Primary Key / first letter must start with 'O'
order_date	date		
client_no	varchar2	6	Foreign Key references client_no of client_master table
dely_Addr	varchar2	25	
salesman_no	Varchar2	6	Foreign Key references salesman_no of salesman_master table
dely_type	char	1	Delivery : part(P) / full (F), Default 'F'
billed_yn	char	1	
dely_date	date		cannot be less than order_date
order_status	varchar2	10	Values ('In Process', 'Fulfilled', 'BackOrder', 'Cancelled')

c) **Table Name**: sales_order_details
Description: Used to store client's orders with details of each product ordered.

Column Name	Data Type	Size	Attributes
detlorder_no	varchar2	6	Primary Key / Foreign Key references order_no of the sales_order table
product_no	varchar2	6	Primary Key / Foreign Key references product_no of the product_master table.
qty_ordered	number	8	
qty_disp	number	8	
product_rate	number	10,2	

d) **Table Name**: Challan_Header
Description: Use to store information about challans made for the orders.

Column Name	Data Type	Size	Attributes
challan_no	varchar2	6	Primary Key / first two letters must start with 'CH'.
order_no	varchar2	6	Foreign Key references s_order_no of sales_order table
challan_date	date		Not Null
billed_yn	char	1	values('Y', 'N'). Default 'N'.

e) **Table Name**: Challan_Details
Description: Use to store information about challan details.

Column Name	Data Type	Size	Attributes
challan_no	varchar2	6	Primary Key / Foreign Key references challan_no of challan_header table
product_no	varchar2	6	Primary Key / Foreign Key references product_no of product_master table
qty_disp	number	8	Not Null

In order to simplify the job of updating the two related tables (sales_order and product_master) each time an insert is made in the challan_details table a procedure is created. This procedure is then called in the PL/SQL block while inserting a record in the challan_details table.

Creating Procedure for use:

A procedure called *proc_update* is created and stored in the database. This procedure when called in a PL/SQL block updates the qty_on_hand in the product_master table. It also updates the order_status in the sales_order table.

CREATE OR REPLACE PROCEDURE *proc_update (vproductno IN char,*
                              vsorderno IN char, quantity IN number) **IS**
/ Variable declarations */*
        total_qty_ordered   number(8);
        total_qty_disp   number(8);

BEGIN

/ Updating the qty_on_hand in the product_master table*/*
        UPDATE *product_master*
                SET *qty_on_hand = qty_on_hand - quantity*
                WHERE *product_no = vproductno;*

/ Checking in the sales_order_details table the total quantity ordered and the total quantity dispatched for a certain sales_order and stuffing the values into memory variables*/*
        SELECT *sum(qty_ordered), sum(qty_disp)*
                INTO *total_qty_ordered, total_qty_disp*
                FROM *sales_order_details*
                WHERE *detlorder_no = vsorderno;*

/*Comparing the total quantity ordered with the total quantity dispatched and updating the order_status in the sales_order table*/

```
IF total_qty_ordered = total_qty_disp THEN
        UPDATE sales_order
                SET order_status = 'Fulfilled'
                WHERE order_no = vsorderno;

ELSIF total_qty_disp = 0 THEN
        UPDATE sales_order
                SET order_status = 'Backorder'
                WHERE order_no = vsorderno;
ELSE
        UPDATE sales_order
                SET order_status = 'In Process'
                WHERE order_no = vsorderno;
END IF;

END;
```

Calling the Procedure in a PL/SQL code block:

```
DECLARE

        /* Cursor c_mast_check retrieves all the records of table Challan_header */

        CURSOR c_mast_check IS
                SELECT challan_no. order_no FROM challan_header;

        /* Declaration of memory variables that will hold values */

        vproductno varchar2 (6);
        vsorderno   varchar2(6);
        quantity number (3);
        vmastchallan varchar2(6);
        vdetlchallan   varchar2(6);

BEGIN

        /*Accepting values for product_no, quantity_dispatched and challan_no from the
        user and stuffing them in memory variables*/
        vproductno := '&vproductno';
        quantity     := &quantity;
        vdetlchallan :='&vdetlchallan';
        OPEN c_mast_check;
```

```
        LOOP
                FETCH c_mast_check INTO vmastchallan, vsorderno;
                EXIT WHEN c_mast_check %NOTFOUND;
                IF vdetlchallan =vmastchallan THEN
                        INSERT INTO challan_details
                                VALUES ( vdetlchallan,vproductno,quantity);
                        /* Call procedure proc_update to update sales_order and
                        product_master tables. */

                        proc_update (vproductno, vsorderno, quantity);
                        EXIT;
                END IF;
        END LOOP;
        IF c_mast_check %NOTFOUND THEN
                DBMS_OUTPUT.PUT_LINE ('The given
                        challan_no does not have a master record');
        END IF;
        CLOSE c_mast_check;
        COMMIT;
END;
```

The functionality of the PL/SQL block of code will be as follows:

The above PL/SQL when fired will open a cursor called *c_mast_check* that shall fetch the challan_no and s_order_no from the challan_header table. The *challan_no* fetched is then compared to *the challan_no* entered by the user. This is done to check for a corresponding master record in the challan_header table so that a detail record can be inserted in the challan_details table.

Only when these two challan_no's match, is an *insert* operation performed in the *challan_details* table. Also, a call is made to the procedure ***proc_update*** and the values for product_no, s_order_no and quantity are passed as an IN value to the procedure.

The procedure is then executed and updates the product_master and the sales_order table. In case the challan_no entered by the user does not match the one fetched by the cursor a message is displayed to the user and there is an exit from the PL/SQL block.

Deleting a Stored Procedure or Function

A procedure or function can be deleted by using the following syntax:

<u>Syntax for Deleting a Procedure:</u>
 DROP PROCEDURE <*procedurename*>;

<u>Example:</u>
 DROP PROCEDURE *proc_update;*

<u>Syntax for Deleting a Function:</u>
 DROP FUNCTION <*functionname*>;

<u>Example:</u>
 DROP FUNCTION *f_itemidchk;*

ORACLE PACKAGES

What is a Package?

A package is an Oracle object, which holds other objects within it. Objects commonly held within a package are procedures, functions, variables, constants, cursors and exceptions. The tool used to create a package is SQL*Plus. It is a way of creating generic, encapsulated, re-useable code.

A package once written and debugged is compiled and stored in Oracle's system tables held in an Oracle Database. All users who have execute permissions on the Oracle Database can use the package.

Packages can contain PL/SQL blocks of code, which have been written to perform some process entirely on their own. These PL/SQL blocks of code do not require any kind of input from other PL/SQL blocks of code. These are the package's standalone subprograms.

Alternatively a package can contain a subprogram that requires input from another PL/SQL block to perform its programmed processes successfully. These are also subprograms of the package but these subprograms are not standalone.

Subprograms held within a package can be called from other stored programs, like triggers, precompilers, or any other Interactive Oracle program like SQL*Plus.

Unlike the stored programs, the package itself cannot be called, passed parameters to, or nested.

Components of an Oracle Package:

A package has usually two components, *a specification* and *a body*. A package's *specification* declares the types (variables of the *Record* type), memory variables, constants, exceptions, cursors, and subprograms that are available for use.

A package's *body* fully defines cursors, functions, and procedures and thus implements the specification.

Why use Packages?

Packages offer the following advantages:
1. Packages enable the organization of commercial applications into efficient modules. Each package is easily understood, and the interfaces between packages are simple, clear, and well defined.

2. Packages allow granting of privileges efficiently.

3. A package's public variables and cursors persist for the duration of the session. Therefore all cursors and procedures that execute in this environment can share them.

4. Packages enable the overloading of procedures and functions when required.

5. Packages improve performance by loading multiple objects into memory at once. Therefore, subsequent calls to related subprograms in the package require no I/O.

6. Packages promote code reuse through the use of libraries that contain stored procedures and functions, thereby reducing redundant coding.

Components of a Package:

Package Specification:
The package specification contains:
➤ Name of the package
➤ Names of the datatypes of any arguments
➤ This declaration is local to the database and global to the package

This means that procedures, functions, variables, constants, cursors and exceptions and other objects, declared in a package are accessible from anywhere in the package. Therefore, all the information a package needs, to execute a stored subprogram, is contained in the package specifications itself.

The following is an example of the creation of a package specification. In this example, the specification declares a function and a procedure:

Syntax:
    CREATE PACKAGE *inv_pck_spec* **AS**
       FUNCTION *inv_count(qty number, part_nbr varchar2)*
         RETURN *number*;
       PROCEDURE *inv_adjust(qty number)*;
    END *inv_pck_spec*;

Sometimes a specification only declares variables, constants, and exceptions, and therefore a package body is not necessary. The following example is a package specification for a package that does not have a package body:

Syntax:
> **CREATE PACKAGE** *inv_costings* **IS**
> **TYPE** *inv_rec* **IS RECORD**
> *(part_name varchar2(30), part_price number, part_cost number);*
> *price number;*
> *qty number;*
> *no_cost exception;*
> *cost_or exception;*

The Package Body:
The body of a package contains the definition of public objects that are declared in the specification. The body can also contain other object declarations that are private to the package. The objects declared privately in the package body are not accessible to other objects outside the package. *Unlike package specification, the package body can contain subprogram bodies.*

After the package is written, debugged, compiled and stored in the database applications can reference the package's types, call its subprograms, use its cursors, or raise its exceptions.

Creating Packages:

The first step to creating a package is to create its specification. The specification declares the objects that are contained in the body of the package. A package is created using Oracle's SQL*Plus interactive tool. A package can include Functions and Procedures. The variables declared within the package can be accessed by any Function or Procedure within the Package. To create *a specification*, issue the CREATE PACKAGE command:

Syntax:
> **CREATE OR REPLACE PACKAGE** *salesman_mgmt* **AS**
> **PROCEDURE** *hire (name varchar2, Address1 varchar2, sal number,*
> *tgt_to_get number, ytd_sales number, rate_of_commission number);*
> **PROCEDURE** *increase_sal (sman_no varchar2, sal_incr number);*
> **END** *salesman_mgmt* ;

The **OR REPLACE** clause was used to recreate the package specification without loosing any grants that already exist.

After the specification is created, the body of the package needs to be created. The body of the package is a collection of detailed definitions of the objects that were declared in the specification.

These objects, or package subprograms, are accessible outside the package only if their specifications are included in the package specifications.

In addition to the object definitions for the declaration, the package body can also contain private declarations. These private objects are for the internal workings of the package and are local in scope. External PL/SQL blocks cannot reference or call internal declarations of the package.

If any initialization is done in the package body, it is executed once when the package is initially referenced. The following is an example of the body of the package that was specified in the previous example's specification:

Syntax:

```
CREATE OR REPLACE PACKAGE BODY salesman_mgmt AS
    PROCEDURE hire (name varchar2, address1 varchar2, sal number,
        tgt_to_get number, ytd_sales number,rate_of_commission number) IS
            new_sman_no varchar2(6);
    BEGIN
        SELECT salesmanseq.nextval INTO new_sman_no
            FROM DUAL;
        INSERT INTO salesman_master  (salesman_no, salesman_name,
            address1, tgt_to_get, ytd_sales, sal_amt,
            rate_of_commission)
            VALUES (new_sman_no, name, address1, sal,
                tgt_to_get, ytd_sales, rate_of_commission);
    END;

    PROCEDURE increase_sal (sman_no varchar2, sal_incr number) IS
            curr_sal number(8,2);
    BEGIN
        SELECT sal_amt into curr_sal FROM salesman_master
            WHERE salesman_master.salesman_no = sman_no;
        UPDATE salesman_master
            SET sal_amt = (curr_sal + ( sal_incr * curr_sal / 100))
            WHERE salesman_master.salesman_no = sman_no;
        INSERT INTO emp_raise VALUES
            (sman_no, sysdate, (sal_incr * curr_sal / 100));
    END;
END salesman_mgmt ;
```

The final part of the procedure body in the preceding example is the package initialization. By definition, this runs only once when the procedure's is referenced the first time.

Invoking a Package & the Oracle Engine:

When a package is invoked, the Oracle engine performs three steps to execute it.
1. Verify user access:
   Confirms that the user has 'EXECUTE' system privilege granted for the subprogram.

2. Verify procedure validity:
   Checks with the data dictionary to determine whether the subprogram is valid or not. If the subprogram is invalid, it is automatically recompiled before being executed.

3. Execute:
   The package subprogram is executed.

To reference a package's subprograms and objects, you must use *dot* notation.

The Syntax for Dot Notation:

- Package_name.type_name
- Package_name.object_name
- Package_name.subprogram_name

In this syntax,
- *Package_name* is the name of the declared package.
- *Type_name* is the name of the type that is user defined, such as record.
- *Object_name* is the name of the constant or variable that is declare by the user.
- *Sub_program* is the name of the procedure or function contained in the package body.

Example:
To reference the variable max-balance in the package named inventory, the referencing statement would be

> DECLARE
>   Max_balance number;
> BEGIN
>   ...
>   IF inventory.maxbalance < curr_balance THEN
>   ...
>   END IF;

The procedures defined in the above package can be executed as follows:

Syntax:
      EXECUTE *salesman_mgmt.increase_sal ('S00001',5);*

Output:

      PL/SQL procedure successfully completed.

When the Oracle engine executes a package subprogram, an implicit save point will be created. If the subprogram fails with an unhandled exception, before returning to the host environment, the Oracle engine will rollback to the save point, thereby undoing any changes made by the package subprogram.

Alterations to an Existing Package:

To recompile a package, use the **ALTER PACKAGE** command with the compile keyword. This explicit recompilation eliminates the need for any implicit run time recompilation and prevents any associated runtime compilation errors and performance overhead. It is common to explicitly compile a package after modifications to the package.

Recompiling a package recompiles all objects defined within the package. Recompiling does not change the definition of the package or any of its objects.

This statement recompiles the package specification.

Syntax:
      ALTER PACKAGE *salesman_mgmt* **COMPILE PACKAGE**

The following examples recompile just the body of a package.

Syntax:
      ALTER PACKAGE *salesman_mgmt* **COMPILE BODY**

Note

      All packages can be recompiled by using an Oracle utility called dbms_utility

Syntax:
      EXECUTE DBMS_UTILITY.COMPILE_ALL

Package Objects --Private v/s Public:

Within the body of a package, the definition of subprograms, cursors, and private declarations for types and objects is permitted. For objects that are declared inside the package body, their use is restricted to within that package only. Therefore, PL/SQL code outside the package cannot reference any of the variables *that were privately declared* within the package.

Any items declared within the package's *specification* are visible outside the package. This enables PL/SQL code outside the package to reference objects from within the package using dot notation. These objects declared in the package specifications are called *Public*.

Variables, Cursors and Constants:

Variables, Cursors, and Constants can change their value over time and have a specific life span. This life duration can vary depending on where the declaration is located. For standalone procedures, variables, cursors, and constants persist only for the duration of the procedure call and are lost when the procedure execution terminates.

If the variable, constant, or cursor was declared in a package specification or body, their values persist for the duration of the user's session. The values are lost when the current user's session terminates or the package is recompiled.

Package State:

A package is either valid or invalid. A package is considered valid if none of the source code or objects it references have been dropped, replaced or altered since the package specifications were last compiled.

The package is considered invalid if the source code or any object that it references has been dropped, altered, or replaced since the package specification was last compiled. When a package becomes invalid, the Oracle engine will also make invalid any object that references the package.

Package Dependency:

During the recompiling of a package, the Oracle engine invalidates all objects dependent on the package. These objects include standalone package subprograms that call or reference objects declared in the package's section that is being recompiled.

If another user's program calls or references a package's object before it is recompiled, the Oracle engine automatically recompiles it at run time.

During package recompilation, the Oracle engine determines whether objects on which the package depends are valid. If any of these objects are invalid, the Oracle engine will recompile them before recompiling the package body.

If recompilation is successful then the package body becomes valid. If any errors are detected, the appropriate error messages are generated and the package body remains invalid.

Example for using a package:

Table name: Item_master

Column Name	Data Type	Size	Column Description
itemid	number	4	Primary Key via which we shall seek data in the table
description	varchar	20	The item description
bal_stock	number	3	The balance stock for an item.

Table Name: Item_transaction

Column Name	Data Type	Size	Column Description
itemid	number	4	which we shall seek data in the table.
description	varchar	20	item description
qty	number	3	The Qty sold

Focus:

Based on the itemid in the item_transaction table a check is made in the item_master table to see if the itemid exists in the item_master table or not.

1. If the itemid does not exist then an **Insert** operation is performed and the **itemid** along with **description** and **qty** is inserted into the required columns of the **item_master** table.

2. If the itemid then a modify operation is perfomed and the **qty** is updated with the **bal_stock** column of the table **item_master** where itemid of table **item_master** is same as that of **item_transaction**.

To achieve this, a package composing of:

1. A function, which will check, for the existence of *itemid* in the table *item_master*. The function must have one argument which receives a value for which a matching pattern for *itemid* in the table *item_master*. The function will return value '1' indicating that a match is found and a value '0' indicating that no match is found. This value returned by the function can be used to perform the above operation.

2. A procedure that shall insert values in the item_master table in case the itemid does not exist in the item_master table.

3. A procedure that shall update values in the item_master table in case the itemid already exists in the item_master table.

Syntax: Package specification:
CREATE OR REPLACE PACKAGE check_data AS
       FUNCTION *f_itemidchk(vitemidno IN number)* **RETURN** *number*;
       PROCEDURE *proc_update (vitemidno in number,*
                quantity in number);
       PROCEDURE *proc_insert (vitemidno in number,*
                quantity in number, descrip varchar2);
END check_data;

Syntax: Package Body
CREATE OR REPLACE PACKAGE BODY *check_data* **IS**
       FUNCTION *f_itemidchk (vitemidno IN number)* **RETURN** *number* **IS**
           dummyitem number(4);
       BEGIN
           SELECT *itemid* **INTO** *dummyitem*
             FROM *item_master* **WHERE** *itemid* = *vitemidno*;
           RETURN 1;
       EXCEPTION
           WHEN *no_data_found* **THEN**
           RETURN 0;
      END;

       PROCEDURE *proc_insert (vitemidno IN number, quantity IN*
                number, descrip IN varchar2) **IS**
       BEGIN
           INSERT INTO *item_master (itemid, bal_stock, description)*
               VALUES *(vitemidno, quantity, descrip);*
      END;

```
    PROCEDURE proc_update (vitemidno IN number,quantity IN number) IS
    BEGIN
            UPDATE item_master SET item_master.bal_stock = quantity
                    WHERE itemid = vitemidno;
    END;
    END check_data;
```

Syntax: Calling the package in the PL/SQL code block

```
DECLARE
    CURSOR scantable IS
            SELECT itemid, quantity, description
                    FROM item_transaction;
    vitemidno number(4);
    descrip varchar2(30);
    quantity number(3);
    valexists number(1);
BEGIN
    OPEN scantable;
    LOOP
            FETCH scantable INTO vitemidno, quantity, descrip;
            EXIT WHEN scantable%NOTFOUND;
            valexists := check_data.f_itemidchk(vitemidno);
            dbms_output.put_line(to_char(valexists));
            IF valexists = 0 THEN
                    check_data.proc_insert (vitemidno,quantity,descrip);
            ELSE
                    check_data.proc_update (vitemidno,quantity);
            END IF;
    END LOOP;
    CLOSE scantable;
    COMMIT;
END;
```

OVERLOADING PROCEDURES AND FUNCTIONS

A package is an Oracle object that can hold a number of other objects like procedures and functions. More than one procedure or function _with the same name but with different parameters_ can be defined within a package or within a PL/SQL declaration block.

Multiple procedures that are declared with the same name are called **Overloaded Procedures**. Similarly, multiple Functions that are declared with the same name are called **Overloaded Functions**.

The code in the overloaded functions or overloaded procedures can be same or completely different.

Example:
Create a package to check that a numeric value is greater than zero, and a date is less than or equal to sysdate.

```
CREATE OR REPLACE PACKAGE check_data IS
        FUNCTION value_ok (date_in IN date) RETURN BOOLEAN;
        FUNCTION value_ok (number_in IN number) RETURN BOOLEAN;
END;


CREATE OR REPLACE PACKAGE BODY check_data IS
        FUNCTION value_ok (date_in IN date) RETURN BOOLEAN IS
        BEGIN
                RETURN date_in <= sysdate;
        END;
        FUNCTION value_ok (number_in IN number) RETURN BOOLEAN IS
        BEGIN
                RETURN number_in > 0;
        END;
END;
```

Overloading can greatly simplify procedures and functions. The Overloading technique consolidates the call interface for many similar programs into a single procedure or function. When executing the procedure or function the Oracle engines chooses the procedure or function whose number of parameters and their data type match the values passed by the caller.

As seen in the example, a function with the name _'value_ok'_ is created in the package _'check_data'_. The first function accepts a single parameter of type _date_. The second function also accepts a single parameter of type _number_.

Thus when the _'value_ok'_ function is called and passed a date value, as in

IF *check_data.value_ok ('12-Dec-97')* **THEN**
....
END IF;

the Oracle engine compares the data type of the values passed by the caller against the different parameter lists in the package '*check_data*'. The Oracle engine then executes the code for first function that accepts date as in

FUNCTION *value_ok (date_in* **IN** *date)* **RETURN** *BOOLEAN* **IS**
    BEGIN
               RETURN *date_in <= sysdate;*
    END;

Similarly, when the *'value_ok'* function is called and a numeric value is passed by the caller, as in

    IF *check_data.value_ok (23)* **THEN**
    ....
    END IF;

the Oracle engine executes the second function that accepts numeric value as in

FUNCTION *value_ok (number_in* **IN** *number)* **RETURN** *BOOLEAN* **IS**
    BEGIN
               RETURN *number_in > 0;*
    END;

Overloading Built-in PL/SQL Functions and Procedures:

PL/SQL itself makes extensive use of overloading. An Example of an overloaded function in PL/SQL is the TO_CHAR function. Function overloading allows developers to use a single function to convert both numbers and dates to character format.

Example:
    Date_string := TO_CHAR(sysdate, 'DD/MM/YY');
    Number_string := TO_CHAR(10000, '$099,999');

In this example, the PL/SQL interpreter examines the value passed to the TO_CHAR function. Based on the data type of this value, it executes the appropriate TO_CHAR function.

Benefits of Overloading:

The benefits of overloading are:
1. Overloading can greatly simplify the processing logic of a program by eliminating multiple IF constructs or case constructs that would check the parameters passed and perform appropriate operations.

2. The overloading technique transfers the burden of knowledge from the developer to the software. For example if multiple procedures with different names are written, the programmer will have to remember the names of each of the procedures along with the parameters of each functions.

If procedures or functions are overloaded, the programmer needs to remember a single procedure or function name and pass values as required.

Where to Overload Functions and Procedures:

There are only two places in PL/SQL programs where the procedures and functions can be overloaded.
- Inside the declaration section of a PL/SQL block.
- Inside a package

Standalone programs cannot be overloaded nor can two independent modules be created with the same name but different parameter lists.

Example:

If an attempt is made to "create or replace" the following procedures of "revise estimates", the second attempt will fail.

```
CREATE PROCEDURE revise_estimates (date_in IN date) IS
BEGIN ........
        ........
END;
```

Procedure created.

```
CREATE PROCEDURE revise_estimates (dollars_in IN number) IS
BEGIN ........
        ........
END;
```

ORA-0955: name is already used by an existing object.

Because a procedure with the name used is present, PL/SQL rejected the attempt to replace it with the procedure created in the second attempt.

Restrictions on Overloading:

There are several restrictions on how the procedures and functions can be overloaded. The following restrictions apply since the PL/SQL engine compares overloaded modules (functions or procedure) before executing the appropriate module.

1. *The data subtype of at least one of the parameters of the overloaded function or procedure must differ.*

   For example an overloaded procedure distinguished by parameters of different types of numeric data types is not allowed. Similarly, an overloaded procedure distinguished by parameters with varchar2 and char data types is not allowed.

Example:
```
CREATE OR REPLACE PACKAGE BODY string_fns IS
        PROCEDURE trim_and_center (string_in IN char, string_out OUT char)
        BEGIN .......
              .......
        END;

        PROCEDURE trim_and_center (string_in IN varchar2, string_out OUT varchar2)
        BEGIN .......
              .......
        END;
END;
```
   Such procedure overloading is not allowed.

2. *The parameter list of overloaded functions must differ by more than name or parameter mode.*

   The parameter name is replaced by the values sent to the objects when the package is called, so differences in name do not offer a guide to the overloaded objects that must be used.

Example:
A procedure definition will be as
```
CREATE OR REPLACE PACKAGE BODY check_date IS
        FUNCTION value_ok (date_in IN date) RETURN BOOLEAN IS
            BEGIN
                    RETURN date_in <= sysdate ;
            END;

        FUNCTION value_ok (date_out IN date) RETURN BOOLEAN IS
            BEGIN
                    RETURN date_out >= sysdate;
            END;
END;
```

The call to the function will either be:
```
        Is_date_ok := check_data.value_ok ('12-Dec-97')
```

The name of the parameter is not available in the module call and thus PL/SQL interpreter cannot distinguish objects by name.

Similarly, even if a parameter in the first module is IN and the same parameter is IN OUT in another module, PL/SQL interpreter cannot distinguish using the package call.

The overloading attempts will result in the following error messages:

PLS-00307: too many declarations of 'value_check' match this call.

3. *Overloaded functions must differ by more than their return data type.*

At the time that the overloaded function is called, the PL/SQL interpreter does not know what type of data that function will return. The interpreter therefore cannot distinguish between different overloaded functions based on the return data type.

```
CREATE OR REPLACE PACKAGE BODY check_return IS
     FUNCTION value_ok (date_in IN date) RETURN BOOLEAN IS
         BEGIN
                  RETURN date_in <= sysdate ;
         END;
     FUNCTION value_ok (date_out IN date ) RETURN NUMBER IS
         BEGIN
             IF date_out >= sysdate THEN
                  RETURN 1;
             ELSE
                  RETURN 0;
             END IF ;
         END;
END;
```

4. *All the overloaded modules must be defined within the same PL/SQL scope or block (PL/SQL block or package).*

Two modules cannot be overloaded across two PL/SQL blocks or across two packages.

Example:
```
         PROCEDURE develop_analysis (quarter_end_in IN date, sales_in IN number) IS
             PROCEDURE revise_estimate (date_in IN date) IS
         BEGIN

             PROCEDURE revise_estimate (dollar_in IN number) IS
                  BEGIN
                      ......
                  END;
```

```
            BEGIN
                    revise_estimate(quarter_end_in);
                    revise_estimate(dollars_in);
            END;
        END;
```

When the above code is interpreted, the PL/SQL interpreter displays the following error message.

Error in Line 12 / Column 3:
PLS-00306: wrong number or type of arguments in call to 'REVISE_ESTIMATE'

PL/SQL displays the error message because the scope and visiblity of both the procedures is different. The scope of the *date revise_estimates* is the entire scope of the body *develop_analysis*. The scope of the *numeric revise_estimates* is the inner block only and it takes precedence over the *date revise_estimates*.

Function or Procedure Overloading an example:

Focus:
A HRD manager generally gives raise of 0.05 in salary for the employees in a specific department. The HRD manager can enter the department number or the department so that the new salary is reflected in the employee table. Whenever any such raise is given to the employees, an audit trail of the same is maintained in the *emp_raise* table. The *emp_raise* table holds the employee number, the date when the raise was given and the raise amount. Write a PL/SQL block to update the salary of each employee of dept_no 20 appropriately and insert a record in the *emp_raise* table as well.

Table name: dept

Column name	Data Type	Size	Attributes
Dept_no	number	5	Primary Key, via which we shall seek data in the table
Dname	varchar2	20	The Name of the department.

Table name: employee

Column name	Data Type	Size	Attributes
emp_code	varchar2	6	Primary Key, via which we shall seek data in the table
Ename	varchar2	20	The first name of the candidate.
Dept_no	number	5	The department number.
Job	varchar2	20	Employee job details.
Salary	number	8,2	The current salary of the employee.

Table name: emp_raise

Column name	Data Type	Size	Attributes
emp_code	varchar	6	is the part of a composite key via which we shall seek data in the table
raise_date	date		The date on which the raise was given
raise_amt	number	8,2	The raise given to the employee.

- Emp_code and raise_date together form a composite primary key.

Solution:

Create a package spec and package body named employee_incentives that includes two procedures of the same name. The procedure name is give_emp_raise. The first procedure accepts department number and the second procedure accepts department name.

Syntax: Package Specification:
```
        CREATE OR REPLACE PACKAGE employee_incentives IS
              PROCEDURE give_emp_raise(dept_no IN number);
              PROCEDURE give_emp_raise(dept_name IN varchar2);
        END;
```

Syntax: Package Body:
```
        CREATE OR REPLACE PACKAGE BODY employee_incentives IS
             PROCEDURE give_emp_raise(dept_no IN number) IS
                    CURSOR c_emp(c_dept_no number) IS
                          SELECT emp_code, salary FROM employee
                                 WHERE dept_no = c_dept_no;
                    str_emp_code employee.emp_code%type;
                    num_salary employee.salary%type;
          BEGIN
             OPEN c_emp (dept_no);
             IF c_emp%ISOPEN THEN
                LOOP
                      FETCH c_emp INTO str_emp_code, num_salary;
                      EXIT WHEN c_emp%NOTFOUND ;
                      UPDATE employee SET salary = num_salary + (num_salary * .05)
                            WHERE emp_code = str_emp_code;
                      INSERT INTO emp_raise VALUES (str_emp_code, sysdate,
                            num_salary * 0.05);
                END LOOP;
             COMMIT ;
             CLOSE c_emp;
             ELSE
                    DBMS_OUTPUT.PUT_LINE ('Unable to open Cursor ');
             END IF;
        END;
```

```
PROCEDURE give_emp_raise(dept_name IN varchar2) IS
CURSOR c_emp(c_dept_name varchar2) IS
    SELECT emp_code, salary FROM employee, dept
        WHERE employee.dept_no = dept.dept_no and
                dname = c_dept_name;
str_emp_code employee.emp_code%type;
num_salary employee.salary%type;
BEGIN
        OPEN c_emp(dept_name);
        IF c_emp%ISOPEN THEN
            LOOP
                FETCH c_emp INTO str_emp_code, num_salary;
                EXIT WHEN c_emp%NOTFOUND ;
                UPDATE employee
                    SET salary = num_salary + (num_salary * .05)
                        WHERE emp_code = str_emp_code;
                INSERT INTO emp_raise
                    VALUES (str_emp_code, sysdate, num_salary * 0.05);
            END LOOP;
        COMMIT;
        CLOSE c_emp;
        ELSE
            DBMS_OUTPUT.PUT_LINE ('Unable to open Cursor ');
        END IF;
    END;
END employee_incentives;
```

DATABASE TRIGGERS

Database triggers are database objects created via the SQL*PLUS tool on the client and stored on the Server in the Oracle engine's system table. These database objects consists of the following distinct sections.

❑ A named database event and

❑ A PL/SQL block that will execute when the event occurs.

The occurring of the database event is strongly bound to table data being changed.

Introduction:

The Oracle engine allows the user to define procedures that are implicitly executed (i.e. executed by the Oracle engine itself), when an insert, update or delete is issued against a table from SQL*Plus or through an application. These procedures are called database triggers. The major issue that make these triggers stand-alone is that they are fired implicitly (i.e. internally) by the Oracle engine itself and not explicitly called by the user.

Use of Database Triggers:

Since the Oracle engine supports database triggers it provides a highly customizable database management system. Some of the uses to which the database triggers can be put, to customize management information by the Oracle engine are as follows:

❑ A trigger can permit DML statements against a table only if they are issued, during regular business hours or on predetermined weekdays.

❑ A trigger can also be used to keep an audit trail of a table (i.e. to store the modified and deleted records of the table) along with the operation performed and the time on which the operation was performed.

- It can be used to prevent invalid transactions.
- Enforce complex security authorizations.

Note

When a trigger is fired, an SQL statement inside the trigger's PL/SQL code block can also fire the same or some other trigger. This is called *cascading*, triggers.

Excessive use of triggers for customizing the database can result in complex interdependencies between the triggers, which may be difficult to maintain in a large application.

Database Triggers V/s Procedures:

There are very few differences between these database triggers and procedures. Triggers do not accept parameters whereas procedures can. A trigger is executed implicitly by the Oracle engine itself upon modification of an associated table or its data. To execute a procedure, it has to be explicitly called by the user.

Database Triggers V/s Declarative Integrity Constraints:

Triggers as well as declarative integrity constraints can be used to constrain data input. However both have significant differences as mentioned below:

❑ A declarative integrity constraint is a statement about a database that is always true. A constraint applies to existing data in the table and any statement that manipulates the table.

❑ Triggers constrain what a transaction can do. A trigger does not apply to data loaded before the trigger was created, so it does not guarantee all data in table conforms to the rules established by an associated trigger.

❑ A trigger enforces a transitional constraint, which cannot be enforced by a declarative integrity constraint.

How to Apply Database Triggers:

A trigger has three basic parts:

1. A triggering event or statement
2. A trigger restriction
3. A trigger action

Each part of the trigger is explained below:

1. Triggering Event or Statement:

It is a SQL statement that causes a trigger to be fired. It can be INSERT, UPDATE or DELETE statement for a specific table.

2. Trigger Restriction:

A trigger restriction specifies a Boolean (logical) expression that must be TRUE for the trigger to fire. It is an option available for triggers that are fired for each row. Its function is to conditionally control the execution of a trigger. A trigger restriction is specified using a WHEN clause.

3. **Trigger Action:**

A trigger action is the PL/SQL code to be executed when a triggering statement is encountered and any trigger restriction evaluates to TRUE. The PL/SQL block can contain SQL and PL/SQL statements, can define PL/SQL language constructs and can call stored procedures. Additionally, for row triggers, the statements the PL/SQL block have access to column values (:*new* and :*old*) of the current row being processed.

Types of Triggers:

While defining a trigger, the number of times the trigger action is to be executed can be specified. This can be once for every row affected by the triggering statement (such as might be fired by an UPDATE statement that updates many rows), or once for the triggering statement, no matter how many rows it affects.

Row Triggers:

A row trigger is fired each time a row in the table is affected by the triggering statement. For example, if an UPDATE statement updates multiple rows of a table, a row trigger is fired once for each row affected by the UPDATE statement. If the triggering statement affects no rows, the trigger is not executed at all. Row triggers should be used when some processing is required whenever a triggering statement affects a single row in a table.

Statement Triggers:

A statement trigger is fired once on behalf of the triggering statement, independent of the number of rows the triggering statement affects (even if no rows are affected). Statement triggers should be used when a triggering statement affects rows in a table but the processing required is completely independent of the number of rows affected.

Before V/s After Triggers:

When defining a trigger it is necessary to specify the trigger timing, i.e. specifying when the triggering action is to be executed in relation to the triggering statement. BEFORE and AFTER apply to both row and the statement triggers.

Before Triggers:
BEFORE triggers execute the trigger action before the triggering statement. These types of triggers are commonly used in the following situation:

❑ BEFORE triggers are used when the trigger action should determine whether or not the triggering statement should be allowed to complete. By using a BEFORE trigger, you can eliminate unnecessary processing of the triggering statement.

❑ BEFORE triggers are used to derive specific column values before completing a triggering INSERT or UPDATE statement.

After Triggers:
AFTER trigger executes the trigger action after the triggering statement is executed. These types of triggers are commonly used in the following situation:

❑ AFTER triggers are used when you want the triggering statement to complete *before executing the trigger action*.
❑ If a BEFORE trigger is already present, an AFTER trigger can perform different actions on the same triggering statement.

Combinations Triggers:
Using the options explained above, four types of triggers could be created:

1. ***BEFORE statement trigger*:**
   Before executing the triggering statement, the trigger action is executed.

2. ***BEFORE row trigger:***
   Before modifying each row affected by the triggering statement and before appropriate integrity constraints, the trigger is executed if the trigger restriction either evaluated to TRUE or was not included.

3. ***AFTER statement trigger*** :
   After executing the triggering statement and applying any deferred integrity constraints, the trigger action is executed.

4. ***AFTER row trigger*** :
   After modifying each row affected by the triggering statement and possibly applying appropriate integrity constraints, the trigger action is executed for the current row if the trigger restriction either evaluates to TRUE or was not included. Unlike BEFORE row triggers, AFTER row triggers have rows locked.

Syntax for Creating a Trigger:

CREATE OR REPLACE TRIGGER *[schema.] triggername*
    {BEFORE , AFTER}
    {DELETE, INSERT, UPDATE [OF *column, ...]}*
    ON *[schema.] tablename*
    [REFERENCING { OLD AS *old,* NEW AS *new }]*
    [FOR EACH ROW [WHEN *condition]]*
    DECLARE
      variable declarations ;
      constant declarations ;
    BEGIN
      PL/SQL subprogram body ;
    EXCEPTION
      exception PL/SQL block ;
    END;

Keywords and Parameters:

The keywords and the parameters used for creating database triggers are explained
below:

OR REPLACE	:	recreates the trigger if it already exists. This option can be used to change the definition of an existing trigger without first dropping it.
schema	:	is the schema to contain the trigger. If the schema is omitted, the Oracle engine creates the trigger in the users own schema.
triggername	:	is the name of the trigger to be created.
BEFORE	:	indicates that the Oracle engine fires the trigger before executing the triggering statement.
AFTER	:	indicates that the Oracle engine fires the trigger after executing the triggering statement.
DELETE	:	indicates that the Oracle engine fires the trigger whenever a DELETE statement removes a row from the table.
INSERT	:	indicates that the Oracle engine fires the trigger whenever an INSERT statement adds a row to table.

UPDATE	:	indicates that the Oracle engine fires the trigger whenever an UPDATE statement changes a value in one of the columns specified in the *OF* clause. If the *OF* clause is omitted, the Oracle engine fires the trigger whenever an UPDATE statement changes a value in any column of the table.
ON	:	Specifies the schema and name of the table, which the trigger is to be created. If schema is omitted, the Oracle engine assumes the table is in the users own schema. A trigger cannot be created on a table in the schema SYS.
REFERENCING	:	specifies correlation names. Correlation names can be used in the PL/SQL block and WHEN clause of a row trigger to refer specifically to old and new values of the current row. The default correlation names are **OLD** and **NEW**. *If the row trigger is associated with a table named OLD or NEW, this clause can be used to specify different correlation names to avoid confusion between table name and the correlation name.*
FOR EACH ROW	:	designates the trigger to be a row trigger. The Oracle engine fires a row trigger once for each row that is affected by the triggering statement and meets the optional trigger constraint defined in the when clause. If this clause is omitted the trigger is a statement trigger.
WHEN	:	specifies the trigger restriction. The trigger restriction contains a SQL condition that must be satisfied for the Oracle engine to fire the trigger. This condition must contain correlation names and cannot contain a query. Trigger restriction can be specified only for the row triggers. The Oracle engine evaluates this condition for each row affected by the triggering statement.
PL/SQL block	:	is the PL/SQL block that the Oracle engine executes when the trigger is fired.

Note

The PL/SQL block cannot contain transaction control SQL statements (COMMIT, ROLLBACK, and SAVEPOINT)

Deleting a Trigger

<u>Syntax</u>:

DROP TRIGGER *triggername* ;

Where,

triggername is the name of the trigger to be dropped.

Applications Using Database Triggers:

<u>Focus</u>:

Create a transparent audit system for a table *Client_master*. The system must keep track of the records that are being deleted or updated. The functionality being when a record is deleted or modified the original record details and the date of operation are stored in the audit table, then the delete or update is allowed to go through.

The table definition is given below:

Table Name: Client_master
Description : Use to store information about clients. This is the table for which the auditing must be performed.

Column name	Data type	Size	Attributes
client_no	varchar2	6	Primary Key / first letter must start with 'C'.
name	varchar2	20	Not Null
address1	varchar2	30	
address2	varchar2	30	
city	varchar2	15	
state	varchar2	15	
pincode	number	6	
bal_due	number	10,2	

Table name: auditclient

Description: This is the table, which keeps track of the records deleted or updated when such operations are carried out. Records in this table will be inserted when the database trigger fires due to an update or delete statement fired on the table *client_master*.

Column name	Data Type	Size	Attributes
client_no	varchar	6	
name	varchar2	20	
bal_due	number	10,2	
operation	varchar2	8	
userid	varchar2	20	
odate	date		

Valid **column contents** are explained as follows:
- Operation : The operation performed on the client_master table.
- Odate : The date when the operation was performed.
- Userid : The name of the user performing the operation.

Solution:

This trigger is fired when an update or delete is fired on the table client_master. The trigger first checks for the operation being performed on the table. Then depending on the operation being performed, a variable is assigned the value 'update' or 'delete'. Previous values of the modified record of the table client_master are stored into appropriate variables declared. The contents of these variables are then inserted into the audit table *auditclient.*

```
CREATE TRIGGER audit_trail
        AFTER UPDATE OR DELETE ON client_master
        FOR EACH ROW
    DECLARE
            /* The value in the oper variable will be inserted into the operation field
            in the auditclient table */
            oper  varchar2(8);

            /* These variables will hold the previous values of client_no, name and
            bal_due */
            client_no varchar2(6);
            name varchar2(20);
            bal_due number(10, 2);
    BEGIN
            /* if the records are updated in client_master table then oper is set to
               'update'. */
            IF updating THEN
                    oper := 'update';
            END IF;
```

/* if the records are deleted in client_master table then <u>oper</u> is set to 'delete' */
IF *deleting* **THEN**
      oper := 'delete';
END IF;

/* Store :old.client_no, :old.name, and :old.bal_due into client_no, name and bal_due. These variables can then be used to insert data into the auditclient table */
client_no := :old.client_no ;
name := :old.name ;
bal_due := :old.bal_due ;
INSERT INTO *auditclient*
        VALUES *(client_no, name, bal_due, oper, user, sysdate);*
END;

The creation of the database trigger *audit_trail* results in an auditing system for the table *client_master*. The owner of the table can keep track of time of modification or deletion of a record that was modified or deleted in *client_master* by querying the table *auditclient*.

Observations:
The actual working of the auditing system can be confirmed as below:

This is the data in the table **client_master** before the Database Trigger had been fired.

Syntax:
SQL> **SELECT** *client_no, name, bal_due*
         FROM *client_master;*

Output:

CLIENT_NO	NAME	BAL_DUE
C00001	Rahul	2100
C00003	Joyce	2000
C00004	Varsha	2300
C00005	Donald	2300
C00006	Jayesh	2400
C00007	Anoop	2300
C00008	Sunita	8000
C00009	Arjun	2200

This is the data in the table **auditclient** before the Database Trigger has been fired.

Syntax:
SQL> **SELECT** *client_no, name, bal_due, operation, odate, user*
          FROM *auditclient;*

Output:
          No Rows Selected

Case 1:
When an update statement modifies a record in the table *client_master*.

The following update statement modifies the client_master Arjun's bal_due from 2200 to 2000.

Syntax:
          UPDATE *client_master*
                    SET *bal_due = 2000*
                    WHERE *client_no ='C00009';*

Once the update is complete the contents of the table *client_master* have been modified as shown below. The content of the column *bal_due* in the table *client_master* where the value was 2200 is updated to 2000.

Syntax:
SQL> **SELECT** *client_no, name, bal_due*
          FROM *client_master;*

Output:

Client No	Name	Bal Due
C00001	Rahul	2100
C00003	Joyce	2000
C00004	Varsha	2300
C00005	Donald	2300
C00006	Jayesh	2400
C00007	Anoop	2300
C00008	Sunita	8000
C00009	Arjun	**2000**

The changes made to the table *client_master* must be reflected in the table *auditclient*. table. Auditclient keeps track of the previous contents of client_master whose records were modified as well as the operation and the date when the operation was performed.

Syntax:
SQL> **SELECT** *client_no, name, bal_due, operation, odate, user*
          FROM *auditclient;*

Output:

Client No	Name	Bal_Due	Operation	Odate	User
C00009	Arjun	2200	update	05-JUN-95	vaishali

Case 2:
When a record is deleted from the table *Client_master*.

The following delete statement deletes the records of all client_masters whose names start with 'J' from the table *Client_master*.

Syntax:
SQL> **DELETE FROM** *client_master*
            WHERE *name like 'J%';*
The following select statement confirms that two records have been deleted, that of 'Jayesh' and 'Joyce'.

Syntax:
SQL> **SELECT** *client_no, name, bal_due*
            FROM *client_master;*

Output:

Client No	Name	Bal Due
C00001	Rahul	2100
C00004	Varsha	2300
C00005	Donald	2300
C00007	Anoop	2300
C00008	Sunita	8000
C00009	Arjun	2000

The records deleted from the table *client_master* must be reflected in the table *auditclient*. Records are inserted into this table when an update or delete operation is performed on the table. It can be observed that two more records have been inserted into the table *auditclient*.

Syntax:
SQL> **SELECT** *client_no, name, bal_due, operation, odate*
            FROM *auditclient_master;*

Output:

Client No	Name	Bal_Due	Operation	Odate	User
C00009	Arjun	2200	update	05-JUN-95	Vaishali
C00003	Joyce	2000	delete	05-JUN-95	Lakshmi
C00006	Jayesh	2400	delete	05-JUN-95	Lakshmi

Note

> If the user performs a ROLLBACK after this, then the records, which were modified and deleted from the table *Client_master* are restored to their original status. Since all these changes are being done via the SQL*PLUS tool at the SQL> prompt, a single ROLLBACK will also cause the records inserted into auditclient to be rolled back as well.
>
> If a PL/SQL code block is doing this type of table operations, the same table behavior will result.

RAISE_APPLICATION_ERROR PROCEDURE

The Oracle engine provides a procedure named *raise_application_error* that allows programmers to issue user-defined error messages.

<u>Syntax</u>:

RAISE_APPLICATION_ERROR *(error_number, message)*;

Where,

error_number : is a negative integer in the range **-20000 to -20999**

message : is a character string up to 2048 bytes in length.

An application can call "raise_application_error" only while executing a stored subprogram like stored procedures, functions and database triggers. Typically, "raise_application_error" is used in database triggers.

Raise_application_error ends the subprogram, rolls back any database changes it made, and returns a user-defined error number and message to the application.

<u>Example</u>:

Write database triggers that checks the following:

❑ The quantity to be dispatched is available in the *product_master* table.
❑ The quantity being dispatched, is not equal to zero and
❑ The quantity being dispatched is less than or equal to the *sales_order*.

Table Name: product_master
Description: Used to store product information.

Column Name	Data Type	Size	Attributes
product_no	varchar2	6	Primary Key / first letter must start with 'P'
description	varchar2	30	Not Null
profit_percent	number	4,2	Not Null
unit_measure	varchar2	10	Not Null
qty_on_hand	number	8	Not Null
reorder_lvl	number	8	Not Null
sell_price	number	8,2	Not Null, cannot be 0.
cost_price	number	8,2	Not Null, cannot be 0.

Table Name: sales_order
Description: Used to store client's orders

Column Name	Data Type	Size	Attributes
order_no	varchar2	6	Primary Key / first letter must start with 'O'
order_date	date		
client_no	varchar2	6	Foreign Key references client_no of client_master table
dely_Addr	varchar2	25	
salesman_no	varchar2	6	Foreign Key references salesman_no of salesman_master table
dely_type	char	1	Delivery : part(P) / full (F), Default 'F'
billed_yn	char	1	
dely_date	date		cannot be less than order_date
order_status	varchar2	10	Values ('In Process', 'Fulfilled', 'BackOrder', 'Cancelled')

Table Name: sales_order_details
Description: Used to store client's orders with details of each product ordered.

Column Name	Data Type	Size	Attributes
detlorder_no	varchar2	6	Primary Key / Foreign Key references order_no of the sales_order table
product_no	varchar2	6	Primary Key / Foreign Key references product_no of the product_master table.
qty_ordered	number	8	
qty_disp	number	8	
product_rate	number	10,2	

Table Name : Challan_Header
Description : Use to store information about challans made for the orders.

Column Name	Data Type	Size	Attributes
challan_no	varchar2	6	Primary Key / first two letters must start with 'CH'
order_no	varchar2	6	Foreign Key references s_order_no of sales_order table
challan_date	date		Not Null
billed_yn	char	1	values('Y','N'). Default 'N'.

Table Name : Challan_Details
Description : Use to store information about challan details.

Column Name	Data Type	Size	Attributes
challan_no	varchar2	6	Primary Key / Foreign Key references challan_no of challan_header table.
product_no	varchar2	6	Primary Key / Foreign Key references product_no of product_master table
qty_disp	number	8	Not Null

```
CREATE OR REPLACE TRIGGER qty_check
BEFORE INSERT
ON challan_details
FOR EACH ROW
DECLARE
/* Declaring memory variables that hold values from the product_master,
sales_order, sales_order_details, challan_header, challan_details tables. */
        v_new_qty number(8);
        v_qty_on_hand number(8);
        v_qty_ordered number(8);
        v_qty_disp number(8);
        v_product_no varchar2(6);
        v_challan_no varchar2(6);
BEGIN
        v_new_qty := :new.qty_disp;
/* checking that the quantity to be dispatched is greater than zero and raising an
error condition in case the quantity dispatched is zero. */
        IF v_new_qty <= 0 THEN
                RAISE_APPLICATION_ERROR(-20001,'Quantity Dispatched
                                        cannot be 0');
        ELSE
```

/* storing the values of quantity_ordered and qty_dispatched into memory variables. */

```
SELECT qty_ordered, qty_disp INTO v_qty_ordered, v_qty_disp
FROM sales_order_details, challan_header
WHERE product_no = :new.product_no and
      challan_header.challan_no = :new.challan_no and
      sales_order_details.detlorder_no =
          challan_header.order_no and
      sales_order_details.product_no =
          :new.product_no;
```

/* checking that the v_new_qty + the total quantity dispatched is not greater than the quantity ordered and if found so raising an error condition*/

```
IF (v_new_qty + v_qty_disp) > v_qty_ordered THEN
    RAISE_APPLICATION_ERROR (-20001,
            'Quantity Dispatched is more than what
                        was ordered by the client');
ELSE
```

/* checking that the v_new_qty to be dispatched is not greater than the qty_on_hand in the product_master table and if found so raising an error condition*/

```
    SELECT qty_on_hand INTO v_qty_on_hand
    FROM product_master
    WHERE product_no = :new.product_no;
IF v_new_qty > v_qty_on_hand THEN
    RAISE_APPLICATION_ERROR(-20001,
            'Not enough stock in the inventory');
    END IF;
END IF;
        END IF;
END;
```

GENERATION OF A PRIMARY KEY USING A DATABASE TRIGGER

Introduction:

In a multi-user environment, to allow data entry operators to create and enter a primary key to uniquely identify a record, will always result in a large number of records being rejected due to duplicate values being keyed in. This will result in a time delay between the record being keyed and the record being accepted for storage.

Automatic Primary Key Generation:

If the data entry operator is not allowed to enter the primary key value and the primary key value is generated by the system, it would be possible to conserve on time and resources.

Simple but effective approaches that can be used to generate a primary key are:
1. Use a lookup table that stores the last primary key value. The new primary key value must be generated from the value stored in the lookup table.
2. Use MAX function.
3. Use a Sequence.

As soon as the Oracle engine receives data to be inserted into tables, the Oracle engine must invoke a program that generates the primary key value. The primary key value so generated is merged with the data that has to be inserted into the table. This entire record, now consisting of the primary key as well as the data is then posted into the table.

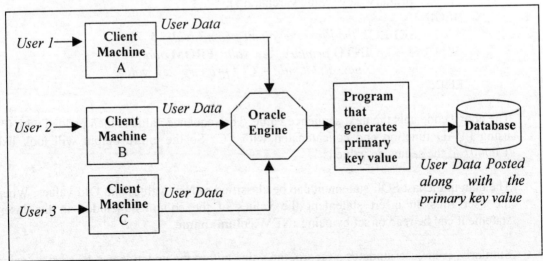

Diagram 9.3 : Automatic Primary Key Generation

The program unit that fires automatically before or after any write operation is performed on the table is called **Database Trigger**. Thus a database trigger can be used to generate a primary key value. The primary key value must be generated before the data is posted into the table. Thus the database trigger must be written such that it executes before the data is posted into the table i.e. a BEFORE INSERT database trigger.

1. Generating Primary Key using Sequences:

The Oracle engine provides an object called a sequence that generates numeric values starting with a given value and with an increment as specified by the user. Thus a sequence must first be created using SQL*Plus. Once the sequence is created a database trigger can be written such that it retrieves the next number from the sequence and uses the same as the primary key value.

Syntax for Sequence Creation:

```
        CREATE SEQUENCE client_seq
            INCREMENT BY 1
            START WITH 1;
```

Syntax for Database trigger creation:

```
        CREATE OR REPLACE TRIGGER client_no_generation
            BEFORE INSERT
            ON client_master
            FOR EACH ROW
        DECLARE
            primary_key_value varchar2(5);
        BEGIN
            SELECT lpad(to_char(client_seq.nextval) , 5 , '0')
                INTO primary_key_value FROM dual;
                :new.client_no := 'C' || primary_key_value;
        END;
```

The above code gets the next sequence value. The sequence value is then padded with 0's using LPAD function and concatenated with 'C'. So the entire output will look like 'C00001' if the sequence value is 1.

The data in the last SQL statement can be classified as **New** values and **Old** values. When the user fires an insert statement the values of the columns included in the insert statement can be read or set by using **:NEW.columnname**.

Similarly, if the user updates a record, the value before the updation can be read by using **:OLD.columnname**. The new values set using an update statement will be referenced by using **:NEW.columnname**.

In the current example, we need to set the value of *client_no*, which will be inserted into the table. Thus we need to set the value of *:new.client_no*.

The sequence number value is then assigned to the column client_no by using :new.client_no.

Since the client_no is generated automatically, the user must insert values in all columns except the client_no column.

<u>Syntax:</u>
      INSERT INTO *client_master*
          (name, address1, address2, city, state, pincode, bal_due)
      VALUES
          ('Ivan Bayross', 'A/5 Jay Apartments',
          'Service Road', 'Mumbai', 'Maharashtra', 400057, 0);

2. Generating Primary Key using MAX Function:

The Oracle engine provides a built-in function that returns the maximum value in a data set. Thus the maximum value retrieved from the table is incremented by 1 to generate a new primary key value.

Syntax:

```
CREATE OR REPLACE TRIGGER product_no_generation
          BEFORE INSERT
          ON product_master
          FOR EACH ROW
DECLARE
          max_pkey_value varchar2(5);
          new_pkey_value varchar2(5);
BEGIN
   SELECT nvl(substr(max(product_no),2,5), 0)
          INTO max_pkey_value FROM product_master;
          new_pkey_value := lpad(to_char(
          (to_number(max_pkey_value) + 1)) , 5 , '0');
          :new.product_no := 'P' || new_pkey_value;
END;
```

Since the product_no is generated automatically, the user must insert values in all columns except the product_no column.

Syntax:

```
INSERT INTO product_master
          (description, profit_percent, unit_measure, qty_on_hand, reorder_lvl,
          cost_price, sell_price)
VALUES
          ('Seagate 2GB HDD', 2, 'Piece', 5, 2, 8000.00, 8500.00);
```

3. **Generating Primary Key using a Lookup table**:

A lookup table with one column that holds the next primary key value can be created and a database trigger can be written to retrieve value from lookup table. The value so retrieved can be inserted into table and the lookup table can be updated such that it holds the next primary key value.

<u>Syntax for Creating Lookup table:</u>
        CREATE TABLE *pkey_lookup (pkey_value varchar2(6));*

<u>Syntax for Create Database Trigger:</u>
        CREATE OR REPLACE TRIGGER *salesman_no_generation*
                BEFORE INSERT
                ON *salesman_master*
                FOR EACH ROW
        DECLARE
                lookup_pkey_value varchar2(6);
                new_pkey_value varchar2(6);
        BEGIN
            BEGIN
                SELECT *pkey_value* **INTO** *lookup_pkey_value*
                    FROM *pkey_lookup;*
            EXCEPTION
                WHEN no_data_found **THEN**
                    lookup_pkey_value := 'S00001';
            END;
            :new.salesman_no := lookup_pkey_value;
            new_pkey_value := to_number(substr(lookup_pkey_value,2,5)) + 1;
            lookup_pkey_value := 'S' || lpad(new_pkey_value, 5, '0');
            IF lookup_pkey_value = 'S00002' **THEN**
                INSERT INTO *pkey_lookup* **VALUES** *(lookup_pkey_value);*
            ELSE
                UPDATE *pkey_lookup* **SET** *pkey_value* = lookup_pkey_value ;
            END IF;
        END;

Since the *salesman_no* is generated automatically, the user must insert values in all columns except the *salesman_no* column.

<u>Syntax:</u>
        INSERT INTO *salesman_master*
            (salesman_name, address1, address2, city, state, pincode,
            sal_amt, tgt_to_get, ytd_sales)
        VALUES *('Ivan Bayross', 'A/5 Jay Apartments', 'Service Road',*
            'Mumbai', 'Maharashtra', 400057, 3000,100, 150);

DBMS_SQL

Processing of an SQL sentence in the Oracle Engine:

When an SQL sentence is fired from the SQL prompt of a client machine, it travels down the network and reaches the Oracle Server. The SQL statement received by the Oracle engine is treated as a string, which is broken up into words that can be categorized as:
- Oracle verbs like SELECT, INSERT, UPDATE and DELETE.
- Oracle objects like user name, table names, column names, etc.

What is Parsing?

Oracle verbs used in the SQL statement are compared with the verbs in the Oracle Parse Tree and checked for syntax. This is done to ensure that the verbs used in the SQL sentence are not only appropriate, but are also placed at correct positions.

Once the SQL verbs and their positions is found correct, the Oracle engine then checks whether the Oracle objects are available in the database and the user who has fired the SQL sentence has valid permissions to use them. In order to perform this check, the Oracle engine references its appropriate Data Dictionary.

DBA can locate data dictionary information through System Views, which are held within the Oracle database. These views maintain reference to the Data Dictionary. A user can view the data in the Data Dictionary by executing a select statement on various Oracle system views.

*These tables can be described only if the connection is made using user name as **SYS** and password as set by the administrator.*

The following is an example of a system table held in the Oracle database.

Syntax:

        SQL> DESC all_users;

Output:

Name	Null?	Type
USERNAME	NOT NULL	VARCHAR2 (30)
USER_ID	NOT NULL	NUMBER
CREATED	NOT NULL	DATE

If an error is encountered in Oracle verbs or Oracle objects, the Oracle engine raises an exception handler. The exception handler is a block of code that locates the error number and its corresponding error description from the Data Dictionary and sends the appropriate error no and message to the client.

Example for wrong syntax - Error encountered in Oracle verbs:
SQL> SELECT * *client_master*;

Output:
select * client_master
       *

ERROR at line 1:
ORA-00923: FROM keyword not found where expected

Example for column name is invalid - Error encountered in Oracle Data Directory:
SQL> SELECT *client_no, client_name* FROM *client_master*;

Output:
select client_no, client_name from client_master
                        *

ERROR at line 1:
ORA-00904: invalid column name

The process of breaking the SQL sentence into words and then checking them for syntax and object privileges is called *Parsing*.

Opening a Cursor:

If no errors are encountered, the Oracle engine must first reserve space in the Shared Global Area to store data sent by the client if the statement is an INSERT, UPDATE or a DELETE. In case the SQL sentence sent by the client is a SELECT statement then the Oracle engine needs to reserve space for storing data retrieved from the table into memory.

In either of the cases, the area that is allocated is called a *Cursor*. The Oracle engine maintains a pointer to this memory location so that the pointer can be used for further manipulation. The cursor pointer that is maintained by the Oracle engine is called the *'Cursor Handle'*.

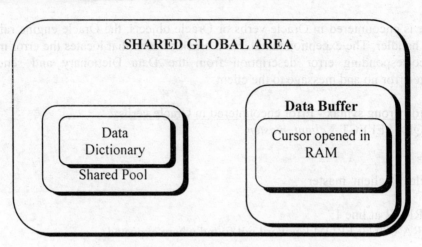

Diagram 9.4 : Opening of Cursor in SGA

What is Data Binding?

Based on the SQL statement the cursor is divided into rows and columns, each cursor column is mapped to the Select list specified in the SQL statement for one or more tables. The process of dividing the cursor into appropriate columns as per the SELECT list is called as '*Binding*'.

Server RAM

Active Data Set

Emp_no	name	salary

Diagram 9.5 : Data Binding

Defining a Column:

If a select statement is curu rently being executed from the SQL prompt, the Oracle engine must retrieve data from table on the hard disk and store it in the opened cursor on the server. The Oracle engine then retrieves one row at a time from the cursor and sends the same to the client machine where each row is printed on the VDU screen.

Thus a set of variables must be defined and mapped to the cursor columns before data is fetched from the cursor. The mapping of variables with the cursor columns is termed as 'Defining a column'.

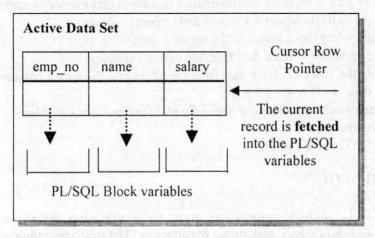

Diagram 9.6 : Assigning cursor values to PL/SQL variables

Executing a Query and Fetching Data from the underlying tables into the Cursor:

Once the required column and cursor settings are made, data is retrieved from the underlying tables. The process of retrieving data into the cursor is done is called *Query Execution*

Positioning the cursor on a Specific row:

Once data is retrieved and held in the cursor, the row focus must be set to a specific row starting with row 1. The process of row positioning is called *Row Fetching*.

Getting values from the specified row:

Once the row pointer is positioned as desired the cursor column values must be assigned to memory variables.

Processing of data:

Once cursor column values are assigned to memory variables, they can be used for further data processing.

Closing the cursor:

Once the required processing on data retrieved from the table is completed, the cursor memory area must be freed. This is achieved by closing the cursor.

Thus for any SQL statement Oracle must perform following steps:
* Open an area in memory and maintain a pointer to that memory location.
* Parse the SQL statement for syntax and Object privileges
* Bind the select list columns to the cursor columns.
* Define variables to fetch data from the cursor variables
* Execute the query i.e. fetch data from the tables into the cursor columns.
* Fetch data one row at a time
* Get cursor column values for a specific row into memory variables
* Perform required processing
* Close the Opened cursor.

DYNAMIC SQL

Since the SQL statement is treated as string, the Oracle users can also apply the above technique to generate SQL statements dynamically. The functions required for generating dynamic SQL are stored in a package named DBMS_SQL.

This package allows PL/SQL to execute SQL data definition language (DDL) and data manipulation language (DML) statements dynamically at run time within a PL/SQL block.

Dynamic SQL allows the user to perform actions such as:

❑ Executing DDL statements such as DROP TABLE, CREATE INDEX etc that are not legal in native PL/SQL.
❑ Executing a query based on column and table information specified by the user at runtime.

Note

To use the DBMS_SQL package, the user will require appropriate database privileges.

General Flow of Dynamic SQL:

In order to execute any dynamic SQL with DBMS_SQL package, the following steps must be followed:

1. <u>Opening a cursor</u>: When a cursor is opened, the Oracle engine sets aside a valid cursor structure for use with future DBMS_SQL calls. The Oracle engine returns an *integer* cursor handle to this cursor. This handle is used for all future calls to the DMBS_SQL modules for this dynamic SQL statement. This is done using the **OPEN_CURSOR** function.

Note

This cursor is completely distinct from normal, native PL/SQL cursors.

The specification for the function is
FUNCTION **OPEN_CURSOR** RETURN *integer*;

Example:
PROCEDURE *raise* (*dept_in* IN *integer*, *raise_in* IN *number*) IS
     Cursor_handle integer;
     Emps_updated integer;
BEGIN
     Cursor_handle := **DBMS_SQL.OPEN_CURSOR**;
     ....*processing*......
END;

2. <u>Parse the SQL statement</u>: The Oracle engine must parse the SQL statement before bind variable values and column structures are specified for the SQL statement. The parse phase verifies that the SQL sentence is properly constructed. It then associates the SQL statement with the cursor handle. This is done using the **PARSE** procedure

The specification for this procedure is:
PROCEDURE **PARSE**
     (*cursor_handle* IN *integer*,
      SQL_sentence IN *varchar2*,
      language_flag IN *integer*);

where,

    cursor_handle is the handle or pointer to the cursor originally returned by a call to the OPEN_CURSOR,

    SQL sentence is the statement to be parsed and

    language_flag is a flag that determines how the Oracle 7 server will handle the statement.

There are *three* valid options for the language flag. These are:

❑ *DBMS_SQL.V6*: Use the Version 6 behavior when processing the statement.

❑ *DBMS_SQL.V7*: Use the Version 7 behavior.

❑ *DBMS_SQL.NATIVE*: Use the normal behavior for the database to which the program is connected.

Example:
CREATE PROCEDURE *raise* (*dept_in* IN *integer*, *raise_in* IN *number*) IS
    Cursor_handle integer;
    Emps_updated integer;
BEGIN
    Cursor_handle := **DBMS_SQL.OPEN_CURSOR**;
    DBMS_SQL.PARSE (*cursor_handle*, **'UPDATE** *employee* **SET** *salary = salary*
                 + *:raise_amount* ' ‖ **'WHERE** *dept_no = :dept'*,
                 DBMS_SQL.V7);
    --- processing -----
END;

3. <u>Bind all host variables</u>: If the SQL statement contains references to host PL/SQL variables, placeholders for those variables must be included in the SQL statement by prefacing their names with a colon. For example, :salary. The actual value for that variable must then be bound into the SQL sentence. This is done using the **BIND_VARIABLE** procedure.

The overload specification supports four data types as follows:

PROCEDURE **BIND_VARIABLE**
    (*cursor_handle* IN *integer*,
    variable_name IN *varchar2*,
    value IN *integer*);

PROCEDURE **BIND_VARIABLE**
    (*cursor_handle* IN *integer*,
    variable_name IN *varchar2*,
    value IN *date*);

PROCEDURE **BIND_VARIABLE**
     (*cursor_handle* IN *integer*,
     variable_name IN *varchar2*,
     value IN *varchar2*);

where,
    cursor_handle is the handle or pointer to the cursor originally returned by a call
                   to the OPEN_CURSOR,
    variable_name is the name of the host variable included in the SQL statement
                   passed to PARSE
    value is the value to be bound to that variable.

Example:
    PROCEDURE *raise* (*dept_in* IN *integer*, *raise_in* IN *number*) IS
        Cursor_handle integer;
        Emps_updated integer;
    BEGIN
        Cursor_handle := **DBMS_SQL.OPEN_CURSOR**;
        DBMS_SQL.PARSE (*cursor_handle*, '**UPDATE** *employee* **SET** *salary*
                 = *salary* + :*raise_amount* ' || '**WHERE**
                 dept_no = :*dept*', *DBMS_SQL.V7*);
        DBMS_SQL.BIND_VARIABLE (*cursor_handle*, ':*raise_amount*',
                        raise_in);
        DBMS_SQL.BIND_VARIABLE (*cursor_handle*, ':*dept*', *dept_in*);

        --- processing -----

    END;

4. Define columns in the SELECT statement: Each column in the SELECT statement must be defined. This step sets up a correspondence between the expressions in the list of the SQL statement and local PL/SQL variables receiving the values when a row is fetched. This step is roughly equivalent to the INTO clause of an implicit SELECT statement in PL/SQL. This is done using the **COLUMN_VALUE** procedure. The overloaded specification for the procedure is:

PROCEDURE **COLUMN_VALUE**
     (*cursor_handle* IN *integer*,
     position IN *integer*,
     value OUT *date*,
     [, column_error OUT *number]*
     [, actual_length OUT *integer]*);

PROCEDURE **COLUMN_VALUE**
        (cursor_handle IN *integer,*
        position IN *integer,*
        value OUT *number,*
        [, column_error OUT *number]*
        [, actual_length OUT *integer]);*

PROCEDURE **COLUMN_VALUE**
        (cursor_handle IN *integer,*
        position IN *integer,*
        value OUT *varchar2,*
        [, column_error OUT *number]*
        [, actual_length OUT *integer]);*

PROCEDURE **COLUMN_VALUE**
        (cursor_handle IN *integer,*
        position IN *integer,*
        value OUT *raw,*
        [, column_error OUT *number]*
        [, actual_length OUT *integer]);*

PROCEDURE **COLUMN_VALUE**
        (cursor_handle IN *integer,*
        position IN *integer,*
        value OUT *rowid,*
        [, column_error OUT *number]*
        [, actual_length OUT *integer]);*

where,

cursor_handle :	is the handle or pointer to the cursor originally returned by a call to OPEN_CURSOR.
position :	is the relative position of the column in the SELECT list
value :	is a local variable that will receive the outgoing value.

There are two *optional* parameters:

column_error :	returns an error code for the specified value (the value might be too large for the variable, for instance)
actual_length :	returns the actual length of the returned value before any truncation takes place. This could be due to difference in the size between the retrieved value in the cursor and the variable.

A COLUMN_VALUE procedure is called after a row has been fetched to transfer the value from the SELECT list of the cursor into a local variable.

Note

> The column must be defined using the DEFINE_COLUMN procedure. The defined column is then passed to the COLUMN_VALUE procedure along with the cursor handle and the cursor column position.

The **DEFINE_COLUMN** procedure:

When a DBMS_SQL.PARSE procedure is used to process a SELECT statement to pass values from the database columns to the local variables, the columns or expressions in the SELECT list must be associated with the local variables. The DEFINE_COLUMN procedure is used for the purpose.

The **DEFINE_COLUMN** procedure is called after the call to **PARSE** is made. After the execution of the SELECT sentence the COLUMN_VALUE procedure is used to grab a column value from the SELECT list and pass it to appropriate local variables.

The overloaded specification for the procedure is:

        PROCEDURE **DEFINE_COLUMN**
            (*cursor_handle* IN *integer*,
            position IN *integer*,
            column IN *date*);

        PROCEDURE **DEFINE_COLUMN**
            (*cursor_handle* IN *integer*,
            position IN *integer*,
            column IN *number*);

        PROCEDURE **DEFINE_COLUMN**
            (*cursor_handle* IN *integer*,
            position IN *varchar2*,
            column IN *integer*
            column_size IN *integer*);

where,

    cursor_handle : is the handle or pointer to the cursor originally returned by a call to OPEN_CURSOR.

    position : is the relative position of the column in the SELECT list

    column : is a local variable or expression whose data type determines the data type of the column being defined.

Note

When the column is defined as a *varchar2* column, the maximum expected size of the column value must be specified.

column_size IN integer

5. <u>Execute the SQL statement</u>: The SQL statement associated with the specified cursor is to be executed. The EXECUTE command returns the number of rows processed by the SQL sentence if the statement is an UPDATE, INSERT, or DELETE. In any other case the return value must be ignored. This is done by using the **EXECUTE** function. The specification of the function is:

FUNCTION **EXECUTE** (*cursor_handle* IN *integer*) RETURN *integer;*

6. <u>Fetch rows for Dynamic SQL query</u>: This is similar to the FETCH statement for regular PL/SQL cursors. It fetches the next row from the cursor.

The specification for the function is:

FUNCTION **FETCH_ROWS** (*cursor_handle* IN *integer*) RETURN *number*;

The function returns 0 when there are no more rows to fetch. The FETCH_ROWS function can therefore be used like the %FOUND (or %NOTFOUND) attribute is used in normal cursors.

For example:
<u>In case of a normal or static:</u>

      FETCH *emp_cur* **INTO** *emp_rec*;
      IF *emp_cur* %NOTFOUND **THEN**
          ------*processing*------
      END IF;

<u>In case of DBMS_SQL used to fetch rows:</u>

      IF DBMS_SQL.FETCH_ROWS (*cursor_handle)* > *0* **THEN**
          ------*processing*------
      END IF;

7. <u>Retrieve values from the execution of the Dynamic SQL</u>: If the SQL statement is a QUERY, then the values from the SELECT expression list can be retrieved using **COLUMN_VALUE** procedure. If the call is made to the procedure using a PL/SQL block then the **VARIABLE_VALUE** procedure is used to retrieve the values returned by the procedure.

The overloading specification for this procedure is as follows:

PROCEDURE **VARIABLE_VALUE**
    (*cursor_handle* IN *integer,*
      variable_name IN *varchar2,*
      value OUT *number*);

PROCEDURE **VARIABLE_VALUE**
    (*cursor_handle* IN *integer,*
      variable_name IN *varchar2,*
      value OUT *date*);

PROCEDURE **VARIABLE_VALUE**
    (*cursor_handle* IN *integer,*
      variable_name IN *varchar2,*
      value OUT *varchar2*);

where,

cursor_handle :	is the handle or pointer to the cursor originally returned by a call to OPEN_CURSOR.
variable_name :	is the name of the host variable included in the PL/SQL statement passed to PARSE.
value :	is a local variable that recieves value from the cursor.

8. <u>Close the cursor</u>: Using the **CLOSE_CURSOR** procedure, the specified cursor is closed. All memory associated with the cursor is released. Also the cursor_handle is set to NULL. The cursor_handle is the handle or pointer to the cursor which was originally returned by a call to OPEN_CURSOR.

The specification for the procedure is:

PROCEDURE **CLOSE_CURSOR** (*cursor_handle* IN OUT *integer*);
<u>For example</u>:
    BEGIN
        ....processing.....
        ....processing.....
        DBMS_SQL.CLOSE_CURSOR (*cursor_handle*);
    END;

APPLICATIONS USING DYNAMIC SQL:

The following are the examples of certain areas where Dynamic SQL can be used:

1. Primary Key Validation
2. Data Definition Language programs

Primary Key Validation:

Focus:

Whist developing any commercial application using Oracle, there is one input/output validation that checks that the value entered in the Primary key column of the table is unique. Each time a record is inserted in the table, unique value check is to be made. This means scanning through the Primary Key column and see if the newly inserted value already exists or not. If a corresponding value is found, the entire record needs to be rejected and appropriate message displayed to the user.

This check needs to be carried out irrespective of the table on which data entry is taking place. To avoid redundant code a database function can be created and stored. This function being a generic function will accept the *table name, column name/s* when it is called and will return a numeric value of 0 or 1 depending upon whether a corresponding value exists in the table or not. It will return 1 if a match is found and 0 if no matching row is found.

The function can be called in any PL/SQL block where a primary key check is to be carried out and depending upon the return value of the function further processing can be done. An insert is allowed to go through if the function returns a 0, else the Insert is prevented and an appropriate error message is displayed.

Solution:

```
        CREATE OR REPLACE FUNCTION gen_pkey_chk
            (table_name IN varchar2, col_name IN varchar2, col_value IN varchar2)
                        RETURN number AS


        /*Declaring a handle to the Dynamic SQL cursor*/
        cursor_handle integer;


        /*Variable that holds the return value from the EXECUTE*/
        execute_feedback integer;


    BEGIN
        /* Open new cursor and return cursor ID. */
        cursor_handle := DBMS_SQL.OPEN_CURSOR;


        /*Parse the query with the columns in the SELECT list*/
        DBMS_SQL.PARSE (cursor_handle, 'SELECT ' || col_name || ' FROM '
            || table_name || ' WHERE ' || col_name || ' = "' || col_value || '"',
                            DBMS_SQL.V7);



        /* Execute the SQL statement*/
        execute_feedback := DBMS_SQL.EXECUTE(cursor_handle);

    /*Returning values 0 or 1 depending upon whether the select returned a row or
    not and closing the cursor */

        IF DBMS_SQL.FETCH_ROWS (cursor_handle) = 0 THEN
                DBMS_SQL.CLOSE_CURSOR (cursor_handle);
                RETURN 0;
        ELSE
                DBMS_SQL.CLOSE_CURSOR (cursor_handle);
                RETURN 1;
        END IF;
    END;
```

Calling the above function in a PL/SQL block:

```
DECLARE
        /* Declaring a variable that will hold the return value of the function */
        rows_found number;
BEGIN

        /* Calling the function gen_pkey_chk that takes the table name and column name/s as the IN
        parameter and returns a number */

        rows_found := gen_pkey_chk ('&tablename','&columnname','&columnvalue');

        /* Displaying message to the user */

        IF rows_found = 0 THEN
                DBMS_OUTPUT.PUT_LINE ('The column value is unique');
        ELSE
                DBMS_OUTPUT.PUT_LINE ('The column value is not unique');
        END IF;
END;
```

Data Definition Language programs:

A regular PL/SQL code block cannot includes references to database objects such as tables and stored procedures. If a CREATE TABLE syntax was being executed with a regular PL/SQL code block, the PL/SQL compiler would check the code and try to validate that all the tables are present before executing the PL/SQL code block. Since the table does not exist the compiler will throw an error.

<u>Syntax:</u>
```
        BEGIN
                CREATE TABLE dept (deptno number (2), ...);  -- illegal
                ...
        END;
```

Similarly in the next example, the compiler cannot bind the table reference in the DROP TABLE statement because the table name is unknown until the procedure is executed:

```
        CREATE PROCEDURE drop_table (table_name IN varchar2) AS
        BEGIN
           DROP TABLE table_name;  -- illegal
           ...
        END;
```

This is where Dynamic SQL comes to the rescue.

Focus:
Write a procedure that drops the objects specified by the user. This procedure also takes wildcards for object names. For example, if the user wants to drop all object with name like 'emp_%'. The following procedure uses both static and dynamic SQL.

Solution:

```
CREATE OR REPLACE PROCEDURE drop_object_proc
        (type_in IN varchar2, name_in  IN varchar2) IS

/* The static cursor retrieving the object */


        CURSOR obj_cur IS
                SELECT object_name, object_type
                FROM USER_OBJECTS
                WHERE object_name like upper (name_in) and
                        object_type like upper(type_in)
                ORDER BY object_name;

/*Declaring a handle to the Dynamic SQL cursor*/
        cursor_handle integer;



BEGIN
/* For each matching object */


        FOR obj_rec IN obj_cur
        LOOP
/* Open new cursor and return cursor ID. */
        cursor_handle := DBMS_SQL.OPEN_CURSOR;

/* Construct the SQL statement and parse it in version 7 mode.*/

        DBMS_SQL.PARSE (cursor_handle, 'DROP '||obj_rec.object_type || ' '||
                                obj_rec.object_name,DBMS_SQL.V7);
/* Close the cursor. */

        DBMS_SQL.CLOSE_CURSOR (cursor_handle);
        END LOOP;
END;
```

Calling the above procedure in a PL/SQL block:

```
BEGIN
/* call to the procedure drop_object_proc. The two parameters the procedure
takes is the type of object and the name of the object. */

        drop_object_proc ('SEQUENCE','MSG_SEQ');
        dbms_output.put_line ('Object Dropped Successfully');
END;
```

SELF REVIEW QUESTIONS

1. What statement is used to recompile a procedure?

2. How is a procedure invoked?

3. What data manipulation statement can support triggers?

4. List some uses of database triggers?

5. How is a procedure or function within a package called?

6. Write a database trigger that allows changes to employee table only during the business hours (i.e. from 8 a.m. to 5.00 p.m.) from Monday to Saturday. There is no restriction on viewing data from the table.

FILL IN THE BLANKS

7. _____ are PL/SQL blocks that return values and are stored in the database.

8. _____ are PL/SQL blocks that fire when an Insert, Update or Delete is performed on the table.

9. _____ is a built-in package that allows Dynamic SQL.

10. _____ is a collection of Stored Procedure and Functions.

TRUE OR FALSE

11. A function can return more than one value.

    A) True   B) False

12. Packages allow overloading of Procedures and Functions

    A) True   B) False

A QUICK REVIEW

➤ **Stored Procedures & Functions**
- **Parts of a Procedure / Function**
  - Declarative Part
  - Executable Part
  - Exception Handling Part
- **Creation of Procedures & Functions**
- **Execution of Procedures & Functions**
- **Advantages of using Procedures & Functions**
- **Differences between Procedures & Functions**
- **Deletion of Procedures & Functions**

➤ **Oracle Packages**
- **What is a Package?**
- **Components of a Package**
  - Package Specification
  - Package Body
- **Use of Packages**
- **Creating and Altering a Package**
- **Package objects**
  - Private
  - Public

➤ **Overloading of Procedures and Functions**
- **Benefits of overloading**
- **Where to Overload Functions and Procedures?**
- **Restrictions on Overloading.**

> ## Database Triggers
> - *Use of Database Triggers*
> - *Database Triggers as compared to*
>   - Stored Procedures
>   - SQL * Forms
>   - Declarative Integrity Constants
> - *Parts of a Database Trigger*
>   - Triggering Event or Statement
>   - Trigger Restriction
>   - Trigger Action
> - *Types of Triggers*
>   - Row Triggers
>   - Statement Triggers
>   - Before and After Triggers
> - *Deletion of a Trigger*
> - *Defining User Error Messages*
>   - Raise_Application_Error
> - *Automatic Primary Key Generation*

> ## Dynamic SQL – DBMS_SQL package
> - *Steps in the processing of an SQL sentence*
>   - Open an area in memory and maintain a pointer to that memory location.
>   - Parse the SQL statement for syntax and Object privileges
>   - Bind the select list columns to the cursor columns.
>   - Define variables to fetch data from the cursor variables
>   - Execute the query i.e. fetch data from the tables into the cursor columns.

- Fetch data one row at a time
- Get cursor column values for a specific row into memory variables
- Perform required processing
- Close the Open cursor.

- *Using the DBMS_SQL Package*
- *The various functions / procedures used in the DBMS_SQL Package*

  - The OPEN_CURSOR function
  - The PARSE procedure
  - The BIND_VARIABLE procedure
  - The COLUMN_VALUE procedure
  - The DEFINE_COLUMN procedure
  - The EXECUTE function
  - The FETCH_ROWS function
  - The VARIABLE_VALUE procedure
  - The CLOSE_CURSOR procedure

REFERENCE BOOKS

	TITLE	AUTHOR	PUBLISHER
1.	Optimize SQL (W/CD)	Gulufzan	BPB
2.	Understanding SQL	Gruber	BPB
3.	Mastering SQL Server 7 (W/CD)	Rick Pal	BPB
4.	MS SQL Server 7 - In Record Time	Chapman	BPB
5.	MS SQL Server 6.5 Unleashed (W/CD)	Solomon	Techmedia
6.	SYBASE SQL SERVER 11 Unleashed (W/CD)	Rankins	Techmedia
7.	SQL Unleashed (W/CD)	Ladanyi	Techmedia
8.	Teach Yourself SQL in 21 Days	Stephen	Techmedia
9.	Teach Yourself SQL in 24 Hours	Stephens	Techmedia
10.	MS SQL SERVER 6.5 Unleashed (W/CD)	Solomon	Techmedia
11.	Teach Yourself MS-SQL Server 6.5 in 21 Days	Mortensen	Techmedia
12.	SQL Server 7 System Administration	Miller	Techmedia
13.	Tech Yourself MS SQL Server 7 in 21 Days	Sawtell	Techmedia
14.	MS SQL Server 7 DBA Sruvival Guide (W/CD)	Spenik	Techmedia
15.	MS SQL Server 7 Programming Unleashed	Galluci	Techmedia
16.	MS SQL Server 7 Unleashed (W/CD)	Mable	Techmedia
17.	Teach Yourself PL/SQL in 21 Days	Lures	Techmedia
18.	SQL Spoken Here	Sayles	BPB
19.	SQL and Relational Databases	Soren Vang	Galgotia

APPENDIX   A

ANSWERS TO SELF REVIEW QUESTIONS

1. Introduction to Managing Data

Answer 1.
Free Form.

Answer 2.
Database.

Answer 3.
Record

Answer 4.
- SQL*PLUS.
- Oracle Forms.
- Oracle Reports Writer.
- Oracle Graphics.
- SQL Pre compilers for C and COBOL.

Answer 5.
Interactive SQL and PL/SQL.

Answer 6.
Oracle Workgroup Server or Oracle Enterprise Server.

Answer 7.
Tables.

Answer 8.
Oracle Database Administrator.

Answer 9.
False.

Answer 10.
False.

2. Interactive SQL

Answer 1.
a) CREATE TABLE *client_master*
    (*client_no varchar2(6),*
        name varchar2(20),
        address1 varchar2(30),
        address2 varchar2(30),
        city varchar2(15),
        pincode number(8),
        state varchar2(15),
        *bal_due number(10,2)***));**

b) CREATE TABLE *product_master*
    (*product_no varchar2(6),*
        description varchar2(15),
        profit_percent number(4,2),
        unit_measure varchar2(10),
        qty_on_hand number(8),
        reorder_lvl number(8),
        sell_price number(8,2),
        *cost_price number(8,2)***));**

c) CREATE TABLE *salesman_master*
    (*salesman_no varchar2(6),*
        salesman_name varchar2(20),
        address1 varchar2(30),
        address2 varchar2(30),
        city varchar2(20),
        pincode number(8),
        state varchar2(20),
        sal_amt number(8,2),
        tgt_to_get number(6,2),
        ytd_sales number(6,2),
        *remarks varchar2(60)***));**

Answer 2.
a) INSERT INTO *client_master*
        (client_no, name, city, pincode, state, bal_due)
        VALUES *('C00001', 'Ivan Bayross', 'Bombay', 400054,*
            'Maharashtra', 15000);

INSERT INTO *client_master*
(*client_no, name, city, pincode, state, bal_due*)
VALUES (*'C00002', 'Vandana Saitwal', 'Madras', 780001,*
      'Tamil Nadu', 0);

INSERT INTO *client_master*
(*client_no, name, city, pincode, state, bal_due*)
VALUES(*'C00003', 'Pramada Jaguste', 'Bombay', 400057,*
      'Maharashtra', 5000);

INSERT INTO *client_master*
(*client_no, name, city, pincode, state, bal_due*)
VALUES (*'C00004', 'Basu Navindgi', 'Bombay', 400056,*
      'Maharashtra', 0);

INSERT INTO *client_master*
(*client_no, name, city, pincode, state, bal_due*)
VALUES (*'C00005', 'Ravi Sreedharan', 'Delhi', 100001, ' ', 2000*);

INSERT INTO *client_master*
(*client_no, name, city, pincode, state, bal_due*)
VALUES (*'C00006', 'Rukmini', 'Bombay', 400050, 'Maharashtra', 0*);

b) INSERT INTO *product_master*
VALUES(*'P00001', '1.44 Floppies', 5, 'Piece', 100, 20, 525, 500*);

INSERT INTO *product_master*
VALUES(*'P03453', 'Monitors', 6, 'Piece', 10, 3, 12000, 11280*);

INSERT INTO *product_master*
VALUES(*'P06734', 'Mouse', 5, 'Piece', 20, 5, 1050, 1000*);

INSERT INTO *product_master*
VALUES(*'P07865', '1.22 Floppies', 5, 'Piece', 100, 20, 525, 500*);

INSERT INTO *product_master*
VALUES(*'P07868', 'Keyboards', 2, 'Piece', 10, 3, 3150, 3050*);

INSERT INTO *product_master*
VALUES(*'P07885', 'CD Drive', 2.5, 'Piece', 10, 3, 5250, 5100*);

INSERT INTO *product_master*
VALUES(*'P07965'*, *'540 HDD'*, *4*, *'Piece'*, *10*, *3*, *8400*, *8000*);

INSERT INTO *product_master*
VALUES(*'P07975'*, *'1.44 Drive'*, *5*, *'Piece'*, *10*, *3*, *1050*, *1000*);

INSERT INTO *product_master*
VALUES(*'P08865'*, *'1.22 Drive'*, *5*, *'Piece'*, *2*, *3*, *1050*, *1000*);

c) INSERT INTO *salesman_master*
VALUES (*'S00001'*, *'Kiran'*, *'A/14'*, *'Worli'*, *'Bombay'*, *400002*,
'Maharashtra', *3000*, *100*, *50*, *'Good'*);

INSERT INTO *salesman_master*
VALUES(*'S00002'*, *'Manish'*, *'65'*, *'Nariman'*, *'Bombay'*, *400001*,
'Maharashtra', *3000*, *200*, *100*, *'Good'*);

INSERT INTO *salesman_master*
VALUES (*'S00003'*, *'Ravi'*, *'P-7'*, *'Bandra'*, *'Bombay'*, *400032*,
'Maharashtra', *3000*, *200*, *100*, *'Good'*);

INSERT INTO *salesman_master*
VALUES(*'S00004'*, *'Ashish'*, *'A/5'*, *'Juhu'*, *'Bombay'*, *400044*,
'Maharashtra', *3500*, *200*, *150*, *'Good'*);

Answer 3.
a) SELECT *name*
FROM *client_master*;

b) SELECT *
FROM *client_master*;

c) SELECT *name, city*
FROM *client_master*;

d) SELECT *description*
FROM *product_master*;

e) SELECT *
FROM *client_master*
WHERE city = 'Bombay';

f) SELECT *salesman_name*
  FROM *salesman_master*
  WHERE sal_amt = 3000;

Answer 4.
a) UPDATE *client_master*
  SET *city* = 'Bombay'
  WHERE *client_no* = 'C00005';
b) UPDATE *client_master*
  SET *bal_due* = 1000
  WHERE *client_no* = 'C00001';

c) UPDATE *product_master*
  SET *cost_price* = 950.00
  WHERE *description* = '1.22 Floppies';

d) UPDATE *client_master*
  SET *city* = 'Mumbai';

Answer 5.
a) DELETE FROM *salesman_master*
  WHERE sal_amt = 3500;

b) DELETE FROM *product_master*
  WHERE *qty_on_hand* = 100;

c) DELETE FROM *client_master*
  WHERE *state* = 'Tamil Nadu';

Answer 6.
a) ALTER TABLE *client_master*
  ADD (telephone number(10));

b) ALTER TABLE *product_master*
  MODIFY (sell_price number(10,2));

Answer 7.
a) DROP TABLE *client_master*;

Answer 8.
a) RENAME *salesman_master* TO *sman_mast*;

3. More on SQL

Answer 1.
a) **CREATE TABLE** *client_master*
    (*client_no varchar2(6)* **PRIMARY KEY**,
    name varchar2(20) **NOT NULL**,
    address1 varchar2(30),
    address2 varchar2(30),
    city varchar2(15),
    pincode number(8),
    state varchar2(15),
    bal_due number(10,2),
    CONSTRAINT *ck_client* **CHECK** *(client_no like 'C%')*);

b) **CREATE TABLE** *product_master*
    (*product_no varchar2(6)* **PRIMARY KEY**,
    description varchar2(15) **NOT NULL**,
    profit_percent number(4,2) **NOT NULL**,
    unit_measure varchar2(10) **NOT NULL**,
    qty_on_hand number(8) **NOT NULL**,
    reorder_lvl number(8) **NOT NULL**,
    sell_price number(8,2) **NOT NULL**,
    cost_price number(8,2) **NOT NULL**,
    CONSTRAINT *ck_product* **CHECK** *(product_no like 'P%')*,
    CONSTRAINT *ck_sell* **CHECK** *(sell_price <> 0)*,
    CONSTRAINT *ck_cost* **CHECK** *(cost_price <> 0)*);

c) **CREATE TABLE** *salesman_master*
    (*salesman_no varchar2(6)* **PRIMARY KEY**,
    salesman_name varchar2(20) **NOT NULL**,
    address1 varchar2(30) **NOT NULL**,
    address2 varchar2(30),
    city varchar2(20),
    pincode number(8),
    state varchar2(20),
    sal_amt number(8,2) **NOT NULL**,
    tgt_to_get number(6,2) **NOT NULL**,
    ytd_sales number(6,2) **NOT NULL**,
    remarks varchar2(60),
    CONSTRAINT *ck_salesman* **CHECK** *(salesman_no like 'S%')*,
    CONSTRAINT *ck_sal* **CHECK** *(sal_amt <> 0)*,
    CONSTRAINT *ck_target* **CHECK** *(tgt_to_get <> 0)*);

355

d) CREATE TABLE *sales_order*
    (*order_no varchar2(6)* **PRIMARY KEY**,
    order_date date,
    client_no varchar2(6) **REFERENCES** *client_master,*
    dely_Addr varchar2(25),
    *salesman_no varchar2(6)***REFERENCES** *salesman_master,*
    dely_type char(1) **DEFAULT 'F',**
    billed_yn char(1),
    dely_date date,
    order_status varchar2(10),
    CONSTRAINT *ck_order* **CHECK** *(order_no like 'O%'),*
    CONSTRAINT *ck_dely_type* **CHECK** *(dely_type IN ('P','F')),*
    CONSTRAINT *ck_ord_status* **CHECK***(order_status IN*
            ('In Process','Fulfilled','BackOrder','Cancelled')),
    CONSTRAINT *ck_date* **CHECK***(dely_date > order_date)) ;*

e) CREATE TABLE *sales_order_details*
    (*order_no varchar2(6)* **REFERENCES** *sales_order,*
    product_no varchar2(6) **REFERENCES** *product_master,*
    qty_ordered number(8), qty_disp number(8),
    product_rate number(10,2),
    PRIMARY KEY *(order_no, product_no));*

Answer 2.
a) INSERT INTO *client_master*
    (*client_no, name, city, pincode, state, bal_due*)
    VALUES *('C00001', 'Ivan Bayross', 'Bombay', 400054,*
        'Maharashtra', 15000);

    INSERT INTO *client_master*
    (*client_no, name, city, pincode, state, bal_due*)
    VALUES *('C00002', 'Vandana Saitwal', 'Madras', 780001,*
        'Tamil Nadu', 0);

    INSERT INTO *client_master*
    (*client_no, name, city, pincode, state, bal_due*)
    VALUES*('C00003', 'Pramada Jaguste', 'Bombay', 400057,*
        'Maharashtra', 5000);

    INSERT INTO *client_master*
    (*client_no, name, city, pincode, state, bal_due*)
    VALUES *('C00004', 'Basu Navindgi', 'Bombay', 400056,*
        'Maharashtra', 0);

INSERT INTO *client_master*
   (client_no, name, city, pincode, state, bal_due)
VALUES (*'C00005', 'Ravi Sreedharan', 'Delhi', 100001, 'Delhi',
   2000*);

INSERT INTO *client_master*
   (client_no, name, city, pincode, state, bal_due)
VALUES (*'C00006','Rukmini', 'Bombay',400050, 'Maharashtra', 0*);

b) INSERT INTO *product_master*
VALUES(*'P00001', '1.44 Floppies', 5, 'Piece', 100, 20, 525, 500*);

INSERT INTO *product_master*
VALUES(*'P03453', 'Monitors', 6, 'Piece', 10, 3, 12000. 11280*);

INSERT INTO *product_master*
VALUES(*'P06734', 'Mouse', 5, 'Piece', 20, 5, 1050, 1000*);

INSERT INTO *product_master*
VALUES(*'P07865', '1.22 Floppies', 5, 'Piece', 100, 20, 525, 500*);

INSERT INTO *product_master*
VALUES(*'P07868', 'Keyboards', 2, 'Piece', 10, 3, 3150, 3050*);

INSERT INTO *product_master*
VALUES(*'P07885', 'CD Drive', 2.5, 'Piece', 10, 3, 5250, 5100*);

INSERT INTO *product_master*
VALUES(*'P07965', '540 HDD', 4, 'Piece', 10, 3, 8400, 8000*);

INSERT INTO *product_master*
VALUES(*'P07975', '1.44 Drive', 5, 'Piece', 10, 3, 1050, 1000*);

INSERT INTO *product_master*
VALUES(*'P08865', '1.22 Drive', 5, 'Piece', 2, 3, 1050, 1000*);

c) INSERT INTO *salesman_master*
VALUES(*'S00001', 'Kiran', 'A/14', 'Worli', 'Bombay', 400002,
   'Maharashta', 3000, 100, 50, 'Good'*);

INSERT INTO *salesman_master*
VALUES (*'S00002', 'Manish', '65', 'Nariman', 'Bombay', 400001,
   'Maharashtra', 3000, 200, 100, 'Good'*);

INSERT INTO *salesman_master*
VALUES(*'S00003', 'Ravi', 'P-7', 'Bandra', 'Bombay'*, 400032,
     'Maharashta',3000, 200, 100, *'Good'*);

INSERT INTO *salesman_master*
VALUES(*'S00004', 'Ashish', 'A/5', 'Juhu', 'Bombay'*, 400044,
     'Maharashtra', 3500, 200, 150, *'Good'*);

d) INSERT INTO sales_order
    (order_no,order_date,client_no,dely_type,billed_yn,
       salesman_no, *dely_date,order_status*)
VALUES(*'O19001', '12-jan-96', 'C00001', 'F', 'N', 'S00001',*
    '20-jan-96', 'In Process');

INSERT INTO sales_order
    (order_no,order_date,client_no,dely_type,billed_yn,
       salesman_no, *dely_date,order_status*)
VALUES(*'O19002', '25-jan-96', 'C00002', 'P', 'N', 'S00002',*
    '27-jan-96', 'Cancelled');

INSERT INTO sales_order
    (order_no,order_date,client_no,dely_type,billed_yn,
       salesman_no, *dely_date,order_status*)
VALUES(*'O46865', '18-feb-96', 'C00003', 'F', 'Y', 'S00003',*
    '20-feb-96', 'Fulfilled');

INSERT INTO sales_order
    (order_no,order_date,client_no,dely_type,billed_yn,
       salesman_no, *dely_date,order_status*)
VALUES(*'O19003', '03-apr-96', 'C00001', 'F', 'Y', 'S00001',*
    '07-apr-96', 'Fulfilled');

INSERT INTO sales_order
       (order_no,order_date,client_no,dely_type,billed_yn,
       salesman_no, *dely_date,order_status*)
VALUES(*'O46866', '20-may-96', 'C00004', 'P', 'N', 'S00002',*
    '22-may-96', 'Cancelled');

INSERT INTO sales_order
       (order_no,order_date,client_no,dely_type,billed_yn,
       salesman_no, *dely_date,order_status*)
VALUES(*'O19008', '24-may-96', 'C00005', 'F', 'N', 'S00004',*
    '26-may-96', 'In Process');

e) INSERT INTO sales_order_details
    (order_no,product_no,qty_ordered,qty_disp,product_rate)
VALUES('*O19001*', '*P00001*', *4, 4, 525*);

INSERT INTO sales_order_details
    (order_no,product_no,qty_ordered,qty_disp,product_rate)
VALUES('*O19001*', '*P07965*', *2, 1, 8400*);

INSERT INTO sales_order_details
    (order_no,product_no,qty_ordered,qty_disp,product_rate)
VALUES('*O19001*', '*P07885*', *2, 1, 5250*);

INSERT INTO sales_order_details
    (order_no,product_no,qty_ordered,qty_disp,product_rate)
VALUES('*O19002*', '*P00001*', *10, 0, 525*);

INSERT INTO sales_order_details
    (order_no,product_no,qty_ordered,qty_disp,product_rate)
VALUES('*O46865*', '*P07868*', *3, 3, 3150*);

INSERT INTO sales_order_details
    (order_no,product_no,qty_ordered,qty_disp,product_rate)
VALUES('*O46865*', '*P07885*', *3, 1, 5250*);

INSERT INTO sales_order_details
    (order_no,product_no,qty_ordered,qty_disp,product_rate)
VALUES('*O46865*', '*P00001*', *10, 10, 525*);

INSERT INTO sales_order_details
    (order_no,product_no,qty_ordered,qty_disp,product_rate)
VALUES('*O46865*', '*P03453*', *4, 4, 1050*);

INSERT INTO sales_order_details
    (order_no,product_no,qty_ordered,qty_disp,product_rate)
VALUES('*O19003*', '*P03453*', *2, 2, 1050*);

INSERT INTO sales_order_details
    (order_no,product_no,qty_ordered,qty_disp,product_rate)
    VALUES('*O19003*', '*P06734*', *1, 1, 12000*);

INSERT INTO sales_order_details
    (order_no,product_no,qty_ordered,qty_disp,product_rate)
VALUES('*O46866*', '*P07965*', *1, 0, 8400*);

```
    INSERT INTO sales_order_details
            (order_no,product_no,qty_ordered,qty_disp,product_rate)
     VALUES('O46866', 'P07975', 1, 0, 1050);

    INSERT INTO sales_order_details
            (order_no,product_no,qty_ordered,qty_disp,product_rate)
     VALUES('O19008', 'P00001', 10, 5, 525);

    INSERT INTO sales_order_details
            (order_no,product_no,qty_ordered,qty_disp,product_rate)
     VALUES('O19008', 'P07975', 5, 3, 1050);
```

Answer 3.

a) SELECT name
   FROM client_master
   WHERE name like '_a%';

b) SELECT client_no, name
   FROM client_master
   WHERE city = '_a%';

c) SELECT client_no, name
   FROM client_master
   WHERE city in ('Bombay', 'Delhi');

d) SELECT client_no, name
   FROM client_master
   WHERE bal_due > 10000;

e) SELECT *
   FROM sales_order
   WHERE to_char(order_date, 'MON') = 'JAN';

f) SELECT *
   FROM sales_order
   WHERE client_no = 'C00001' or client_no = 'C00002';

g) SELECT product_no, description
   FROM product_master
   WHERE sell_price > 2000 and sell_price < 5000;

h) SELECT product_no,description,sell_price,sell_price*15 new_price
   FROM product_master;

i) **SELECT** *name, city, state*
   FROM *client_master*
   WHERE *state NOT IN('Maharashtra');*

j) **SELECT COUNT**(*mastorder_no*)
   FROM *sales_order;*

k) **SELECT AVG**(*sell_price*)
   FROM *product_master;*

l) **SELECT MAX**(*sell_price*) *max_price,* **MIN**(*sell_price*) *min_price*
   FROM *product_master;*

m) **SELECT COUNT**(*product_no*)
   FROM *product_master*
   WHERE *sell_price >= 1500;*

n) **SELECT** *product_no, description*
   FROM *product_master*
   WHERE *qty_on_hand < reorder_lvl;*

Answer 4.
a) **SELECT** *order_no, to_char(order_date, 'day')*
   FROM *sales_order;*

b) **SELECT** *to_char(dely_date, 'month'), dely_date*
   FROM *sales_order*
   ORDER BY *to_char(dely_date, 'month');*

c) **SELECT** *to_char(order_date, 'DD-Month-YY')*
   FROM *sales_order;*

d) **SELECT** *sysdate+15*
   FROM *dual;*

e) **SELECT** *dely_date-sysdate*
   FROM *sales_order;*

Answer 5.
a) **SELECT** *description,* **SUM**(*qty_disp*)
   FROM *product_master, sales_order_details*
   WHERE *product_master.product_no = sales_order_details.product_no*
   GROUP BY *description;*

b) **SELECT** *sales_order_details.product_no, description,*
        SUM*(qty_disp*product_rate)*
   FROM *sales_order_details, product_master*
   WHERE *product_master.product_no = sales_order_details.product_no*
   GROUP BY *sales_order_details.product_no, description;*

c) **SELECT** *client_master.client_no, name,* **AVG** *(qty_disp)*
   FROM   *sales_order_details, sales_order, client_master*
   WHERE *client_master.client_no = sales_order.client_no*
          and sales_order.order_no =sales_order_details.order_no
   GROUP BY *client_master.client_no, name*
   HAVING **MAX***(qty_ordered*product_rate) > 15000;*

d) **SELECT** *sales_order.order_no,***SUM***(qty_ordered*product_rate)*
   FROM   *sales_order, sales_order_details*
   WHERE *sales_order_details.order_no = sales_order.order_no*
          and billed_yn='Y'
          and to_char(order_date, 'MON') = 'JAN'
   GROUP BY *sales_order.order_no;*

Answer 6.
a) **SELECT** *sales_order_details.product_no, description*
   FROM *sales_order_details, sales_order, product_master,client_master*
   WHERE *product_master.product_no= sales_order_details.product_no*
          and sales_order.order_no= sales_order_details.order_no
          and client_master.client_no = sales_order.client_no
          and client_master.name = 'Ivan Bayross';

b) **SELECT** *sales_order_details.product_no, description,*
        SUM*(qty_ordered)*
   FROM *sales_order_details, sales_order, product_master*
   WHERE *product_master.product_no = sales_order_details.product_no*
          and sales_order.order_no = sales_order_details.order_no
          and to_char(order_date,'MON-YY') = 'DEC-97'
   GROUP BY *sales_order_details.product_no, description;*

c) **SELECT DISTINCT** *product_master.product_no, description*
   FROM *sales_order_details, product_master*
   WHERE *product_master.product_no =sales_order_details.product_no;*

d) **SELECT DISTINCT** *sales_order.client_no, name*
   FROM *sales_order_details,sales_order, product_master,client_master*
   WHERE *product_master.product_no = sales_order_details.product_no*
   and sales_order.order_no = sales_order_details.order_no
   and client_master.client_no = sales_order.client_no
   and description = 'CD Drive';

e) **SELECT** *sales_order_details.product_no,sales_order_details.order_no*
   FROM *sales_order_details, sales_order, product_master*
   WHERE *sales_order.order_no = sales_order_details.order_no*
   and product_master.product_no=sales_order_details.product_no
   and qty_ordered < 5
   and description = '1.44 Floppies';

f) **SELECT** *sales_order_details.product_no, description,*
         SUM(*qty_ordered*)
   FROM *sales_order_details,sales_order, product_master, client_master*
   WHERE *sales_order.order_no = sales_order_details.order_no*
   and product_master.product_no=sales_order_details.product_no
   and client_master.client_no = sales_order.client_no
   and name = 'Ivan Bayross' and name = 'Vandana Saitwal'
   GROUP BY *sales_order_details.product_no, description;*

g) **SELECT** *sales_order_details.product_no, description,*
         SUM(*qty_ordered*)
   FROM *sales_order,sales_order_details, product_master,client_master*
   WHERE *sales_order.order_no = sales_order_details.order_no*
   and sales_order_details.product_no = product_master.product_no
   and sales_order.client_no = client_master.client_no
   GROUP BY *sales_order.client_no,sales_order_details.product_no,*
         description
   HAVING *sales_order.client_no = 'C00001' **OR***
         sales_order.client_no='C00002';

Answer 7.
a) **SELECT** *product_no, description*
   FROM *product_master*
   WHERE *product_no NOT IN (**SELECT** product_no*
                   FROM *sales_order_details);*

b) **SELECT** *name ,address1, address2, city, pincode*
   FROM *client_master*
   WHERE *client_no IN (***SELECT** *client_no* **FROM** *sales_order*
                        WHERE *order_no = 'O19001');*

c) **SELECT** *name*
   FROM *client_master*
   WHERE *client_no IN (***SELECT** *client_no* **FROM** *sales_order*
                        WHERE *to_char(order_date, 'MON,YY') =*
                                        'MAY,96');

d) **SELECT** *client_no,name* **FROM** *client_master*
   WHERE *client_no IN (***SELECT** *client_no* **FROM** *sales_order*
                        WHERE *order_no IN (***SELECT** *order_no*
                                        FROM *sales_order_details*
                                        WHERE *product_no IN*
                                        (***SELECT** *product_no*
                                        FROM *product_master*
                                        WHERE *description =*
                                        '1.44 Drive')));

e) **SELECT** *name* **FROM** *client_master*
   WHERE *client_no IN (***SELECT** *client_no* **FROM** *sales_order*
                        WHERE *order_no IN*
                                (***SELECT** *order_no*
                                FROM *sales_order_details*
                                WHERE *qty_ordered*product_rate >=*
                                                10000));

Answer 8.
a) **SELECT** *description||'worth Rs.'||***SUM***(qty_disp*product_rate)||'sold.'*
   FROM *sales_order_details, product_master*
   WHERE *sales_order_details.product_no = product_master.product_no*
   GROUP BY *description;*

b) **SELECT** *description||'worth Rs.'||***SUM***(qty_disp*product_rate)|| 'was*
   ordered in the month of '||to_char(order_date,'MON')
   FROM *sales_order_details,product_master,sales_order*
   WHERE *sales_order_details.product_no = product_master.product_no*
           and sales_order_details.order_no = sales_order.order_no
           and to_char(order_date,'MON') = 'JAN'
   GROUP BY *description,to_char(order_date,'MON');*

c) **SELECT** name||'has placed order'||order_no||'on'||order_date
FROM sales_order,client_master
WHERE sales_order.client_no = client_master.client_no;

4. SQL Performance Tuning

Answer 1.
CREATE SEQUENCE inv_seq
    INCREMENT BY 1
    START WITH 1
    MINVALUE 1
    MAXVALUE 9999
    CYCLE;

Answer 2.
INSERT INTO invoice_hdr
    VALUES (*'I'* || **to_char (inv_seq.nextval)**, sysdate, 'ABC Consultants');

Answer 3.
a) **CREATE VIEW** vw_prod **AS**
    SELECT product_no, description, qty_on_hand, cost_price
    FROM product_master;

b) **INSERT INTO** vw_prod
    VALUES ('P00001','HDD',10, 5000);

c) **UPDATE** vw_prod **SET** qty_on_hand = 50
    WHERE product_no ='P00001';

d) **DELETE FROM** vw_prod **WHERE** product_no ='P00001';

Answer 4.
1. Views

2. Unique Index

3. Read Only Views and Updateable Views.

4. START WITH

5. 20

6. INSERT

7. Detail

8.
   - The use of aggregate functions.
   - The use of DISTINCT, GROUP BY or HAVING clause.
   - The use of Sub-queries.

9. Composite Index

10. ORDER BY.

5. *Security Management using SQL*

Answer 1.
a) GRANT *SELECT*
    ON *challan_header*
    TO *sanjay*
    WITH GRANT OPTION;

b) GRANT *SELECT*
    ON *challan_details*
    TO *sanjay*
    WITH GRANT OPTION;

Answer 2.
GRANT *ALL*
    ON *client_master*
    TO *ashish;*

Answer 3.
SELECT *product_no, description*
    FROM *ajay.product_master;*

Answer 4.
GRANT *SELECT*
    ON *mita.salesman_master*
    TO *cedric*
    WITH GRANT OPTION;

Answer 5.
REVOKE *ALL*
    ON *client_master*
    FROM *ashish;*

Answer 6.
REVOKE *DELETE*
    ON *melba.employee*
    FROM *sanjay;*

6. Introduction to PL/SQL

Answer 1.
Declare, Begin, Exception and End.

Answer 2.
A declaration of NUMBER (6,2) allows to store a maximum value of 9999.99.

Answer 3.
The % TYPE variable attribute enables to base a variable on a table column.

Answer 4.
The above declaration is not a valid as a proper declaration would contain the table name and the column name.

    Declare
    Emp_last_name   emp.last_name%type;

Answer 5.
The EXIT and EXIT WHEN statement allows to break out of execution of a loop.

Answer 6.
False.

Answer 7.
True.

Answer 8.
True.

Answer 9.
False.

Answer 10.
False.

Answer 11.
False.

Answer 12.
False.

Answer 13.
%type

Answer 14.
/*.....*/ and - -

Answer 15.
TRUE

Answer 16.
FALSE

Answer 17.
NULL

Answer 18.
IS

Answer 19.
Constant

Answer 20.
DBMS_OUTPUT.PUT_LINE

Answer 21.
Procedural Language / Structured Query Language.

7. More on PL/SQL

Answer 1.
A transaction is ended when a commit or rollback is encountered.

Answer 2.
When a cursor is opened, the cursor pointer is at the first record in the Active Data Set.

Answer 3.
Cursors opened and managed by the Oracle engine are called *Implicit Cursors.*

Answer 4.
Explicit Cursors are used when queries return multiple rows and each row needs to be processed individually.

Answer 5.
The basic steps to be followed while using an explicit cursor are:
- Declaring the cursor.
- Opening the cursor.
- Fetching the rows into memory variables for processing.
- Closing the cursor when all processing is over.

Answer 6.
Yes, the steps while using an explicit cursor can be reduced. This is done by the use of *Cursor For Loop* construct. This construct takes care of the task of opening, fetching and closing the cursor.

Answer 7.
```
DECLARE
        c_emp_name emp.emp_name%type;
        c_salary emp.salary%type;
        CURSOR emp_cursor IS
        SELECT emp_name, salary FROM emp desc;
BEGIN
        OPEN emp_cursor;
        FETCH emp_cursor INTO c_emp_name, c_salary;
        WHILE emp_cursor%ROWCOUNT <=3
        LOOP
                dbms_output.put_line(c_emp_name|| '   '|| c_salary);
        END LOOP;
END;
```

Answer 8.
False

Answer 9.
True

Answer 10.
False

Answer 11.
False

Answer 12.
False

Answer 13.
False

Answer 14.
Active Data Set

Answer 15.
Explicit Cursors

Answer 16.
SQL%ISOPEN

Answer 17.
End Loop

Answer 18.
Parameterized cursors

8. Improving on PL/SQL

Answer 1.
Locks are mechanisms used to ensure data integrity while allowing maximum concurrent access to data.

Answer 2.
The technique of lock taken on a table or its resources by a user is called Explicit Locking. The statements that can be used for explicit locking are: Select ...for update and Lock table.

Answer 3.
Client B's SQL DML enters into an indefinite wait state waiting for Client A to release the locked resource by using a 'Commit' or 'Rollback' statement.

Answer 4.
The NOWAIT clause acts as an indication to the Oracle engine that the user immediately be returned with a message, if the resources are on which the user is trying to place a lock are already busy.

Answer 5.

Locks are released under one of the following circumstances:

- The transaction is committed successfully using the '*Commit*' verb.
- A *rollback* is performed.
- A *rollback to a savepoint* will release locks set after the specified *savepoint*.

Answer 6.

The types of locks that can be palced on the table are Shared Locks or Exclusive Locks. The type of lock depends upon the kind of transaction. For example, a *read* operation like a SELECT statement will take a shared lock since no data is being changed while viewing whereas a *write* operation like INSERT or UPDATE will take a exclusive row or table level lock.

Answer 7.

The following are four of the Oracle engines named exceptions:

- Too_many_rows
- Value_error
- No_data_found
- Cursor_already_open

Answer 8.

Exception Section

Answer 9.

No_data_found

Answer 10.

Exception_init ( )

Answer 11.

WHERE

Answer 12.

OTHERS

9. *Database Objects*

Answer 1.

The CREATE OR REPLACE PROCEDURE command is used to recompile a procedure.

Answer 2.
A procedure can be invoked at the SQL prompt by using the execute verb followed by the procedure name. If a procedure is being called within a PL/SQL code block it can be called automatically by simply calling the procedure by name.

Answer 3.
INSERT, UPDATE and DELETE DML's support triggers.

Answer 4.
Database Triggers can be possibly used for either
- Enforcing a business rule,
- Enforcing security,
- Cross table updates, etc.

Answer 5.
A specific procedure or function within a package is called by using the dot notation
    packagename. procedure / function name

Answer 6.
CREATE OR REPLACE TRIGGER *time_check*
    BEFORE INSERT OR UPDATE OR DELETE
    ON *employee*

    BEGIN
        IF to_number (to_char(sysdate, 'hh24'))<8 OR
            to_number (to_char(sysdate, 'hh24'))>=17 OR
            to_char (sysdate , 'day') ='SUN' THEN
            Raise_application_error (-20000, 'Changes to employee table
                                allowed only during business hours');
        END IF;
    END;

Answer 7.
Functions

Answer 8.
Database Triggers

Answer 9.
DBMS_SQL

372

Answer 10.
Package

Answer 11.
FALSE

Answer 12.
TRUE

Index

C

D

R

S

W

EXPLORE

the W🌍RLD

of
COMPUTERS

with
BPB

COMPUTER BOOKS

ISBN	TITLE	PRICE

◆ 80386/80486 & HARDWARE

ISBN	TITLE	PRICE
81-7656-185-1	Microprocessor Data Handbook - Revised Edition	270/-
81-7029-808-3	Modern All About Hard Disk drive.	150/-
81-7029-657-9	Modern All About Floppy Disk & Drives	120/-
81-7029-700-1	Modern All About Mother Board	150/-
81-7029-719-2	Modern All About Keyboard & Mouse .	120/-

◆ 3D STUDIO MAX

81-7656-253-X	Mastering 3D Studio MAX3 (W/CD)	297/-
81-7656-312-9	Mastering MAXScript and the SDK for 3D Studio MAX (W/CD)	225/-
81-7656-267-X	Learning 3D Studio MAX/Viz 3.0 - A tutorial Approach (W/CD)	180/-
81-7656-462-1	Mastering 3D Studio MAX 4 (W/CD)	450/-

◆ A+ CERTIFICATION PROGRAMME

81-7656-039-1	A+ Study Guide: Core Module (W/CD)	299/-
81-7656-038-3	A+ Study Guide: DOS / Windows (W/CD)	299/-
81-7656-023-5	A+ Exam Notes: Core Module	99/-
81-7656-025-1	A+ Exam Notes: DOS / Windows	99/-
81-7656-429-X	A+ Complete Exam Notes	120/-

◆ ACCESS 7.0 / WIN 95

| 81-7029-698-6 | Teach Yourself ACCESS for Windows 95 | 165/- |
| 81-7029-708-7 | Learn MS ACCESS 7.0 for Windows 95 in a day | 45/- |

◆ ACCESS 97

81-7029-829-6	ACCESS 97 Developers HandBook (W/CD)	499/-
81-7029-928-4	ACCESS 97 - No Experience Required .	150/-
81-7656-010-3	ACCESS 97 - TRAINING GUIDE	60/-
81-7029-819-9	Mastering ACCESS 97 for Win 95 / NT (W/CD).	450/-
81-7029-866-0	Teach Yourself Access 97 For Windows	180/-

◆ ACCESS 2000

81-7656-084-7	Access 2000 - No Experience Required ..	150/-
81-7656-093-6	Mastering Access 2000 (W/CD)	399/-
81-7656-463-X	Access/Outlook 2000 - An Introduction .	60/-
81-7656-165-7	Access 2000 Fast & Easy	150/-
81-7656-200-9	MS Access 2000 Training Guide	60/-
81-7656-212-2	Access 2000 Developer's Handbook - Vol. I: Desktop Edition (W/CD)	399/-
81-7656-213-0	Access 2000 Developer's Handbook - Vol. II: Enterprise Edition (W/CD)	399/-

◆ ACCESS 2002

| 81-7656-527-X | Access 2002 VBA HandBook (W/CD) | 399/- |

◆ ACTIVE SERVER PAGE 3

81-7656-259-9	Mastering Active Server Pages 3 (W/CD).	360/-
81-7656-292-0	ASP 3.0 Instant Reference	90/-
81-7656-310-2	Practical ASP (W/CD)	225/-
81-7656-428-1	ASP.Net Made Simple	240/-
81-7656-480-X	ASP, ADO and XML Complete	199/-

◆ ACTIVE X

| 81-7029-894-6 | Active X - No Experience Required | 180/- |

◆ ACTIVE DIRECTORY

| 81-7656-260-2 | Mastering Active Directory | 225/- |

◆ ANIMATION

| 81-7029-511-4 | Graphics Programming & Animation | 180/- |

◆ ACCOUNTING

BPB 424	Computerized ACCOUNTING	135/-
81-7029-779-6	Financial Management and Accounting System (W/D)	300/-
81-7656-299-8	Real Accounting Software (W/D)	450/-

◆ MAIN - AS/400

| 81-7029-838-5 | Navigating the AS/400 A Hands on Guide | 180/- |
| 81-7656-066-9 | Secrets of RPG/400 | 270/- |

◆ ASSEMBLER

| 81-7029-470-3 | Teach Yourself ASSEMBLER (W/D) | 180/- |

◆ ASSEMBLY LANGUAGE

| 81-7029-001-5 | ASSEMBLY LANGUAGE Techniques IBM for PC | 150/- |

◆ ASTROLOGY

| 81-7029-375-8 | Computer ASTROLOGY (W/D) | 345/- |

◆ AUTOCAD

| BPB 612 | Encyclopedia AutoCAD | 450/- |

◆ AUTOCAD 11

81-7029-005-8	AutoCAD 11 Instant Reference	54/-
81-7029-006-6	Illustrated AutoCAD (Release 11)	195/-
BPB 3005	Mastering AutoCAD (Release 11)	300/-

◆ AUTOCAD 12

BPB 10012	ABCs of AutoCAD (Release 12)	150/-
BPB 201	Advanced AutoCAD (Release 12)	195/-
81-7029-254-9	Mastering AutoCAD Release 12 (W/D)	350/-
81-7029-501-7	AutoCAD 12 Instant Reference	60/-
81-7029-265-4	Learn AutoCAD 12 in a Day	45/-

◆ AUTOCAD 13

| 81-7029-517-3 | AutoCAD 13 for DOS & WINDOWS Instant Reference | 66/- |
| 81-7029-785-0 | Mastering AutoCAD 13 /WIN /WIN 95 /NT (W/CD) | 450/- |

◆ AUTOCAD 14

81-7029-909-8	AutoCAD 14 Instant Reference	54/-
81-7029-913-6	Mastering AutoCAD 14 (W/CD)	450/-
81-7029-969-1	AutoCAD 14 - No Experience Required	180/-

➢ AUTOCAD 2000

| 81-7656-081-2 | AutoCAD 2000 Instant Reference | 54/- |

ISBN	TITLE	PRICE

◆ CISCO

| 81-7656-277-7 | Cisco Routers 24Seven | 399/- |
| 81-7656-525-9 | Cisco UnAuthorized | 195/- |

◆ CISCO — CCNA 2.0

81-7656-142-8	CCNA Jumpstart : Networking & Internetworking Basics	150/-
81-7656-057-X	CCNP: Advanced Cisco Router Configuration Study Guide (W/CD)	399/-
81-7656-377-3	CCNA Exam Notes: CCNA Cisco Certified Network Associate (Exam 640-507)	120/-
81-7656-290-4	CCNA: Cisco Certified Network Associate Study Guide (W/CD) 2nd Edn. (Exam 640-507)	699/-
81-7656-394-3	CCNA 2.0 : Quick Review (W/CD) (Exam 640-507)	150/-

◆ CISCO — CCNP

81-7656-171-1	CCNP: Cisco LAN Switching Configuration Study Guide (W/CD)	399/-
81-7656-133-9	CCNP: Cisco Internetwork Troubleshooting Study Guide (W/CD)	399/-
81-7656-173-8	CCNP Exam Notes: Cisco Internetwork Troubleshooting	150/-
81-7656-325-0	CCNP Remote Access Study Guide (W/CD) (Exam 640-505)	499/-
81-7656-344-7	CCNP Switching Study Guide (W/CD) (Exam 640-504)	699/-
81-7656-373-0	CCNP Routing Study Guide (W/CD) (Exam 640-503)	699/-
81-7656-376-5	CCNP Support Study Guide (W/CD) (Exam 640-506)	799/-
81-7656-172-X	CCNP Exam Notes: Advanced Cisco Router Configuration	150/-

◆ CISCO — CCDA

| 81-7656-386-2 | CCDA Exam Notes: CCDA Cisco Certified Design Associate (Exam 640-441) | 120/- |

◆ CISCO — CCDP

| 81-7656-387-0 | CCDP Exam Notes: CCDP Cisco Internetwork Design (Exam 640-025) | 120/- |

◆ CISCO - CCIE

| 81-7656-365-X | CCIE: Cisco Certified Internetwork Expert Study Guide (W/CD) | 999/- |

◆ COLDFUSION

81-7656-266-1	Mastering ColdFusion 4.5 (W/CD)	399/-
81-7656-528-8	Mastering ColdFusion 5 (W/CD)	499/-
81-7656-294-7	ColdFusion Fast & Easy Web Development (W/CD)	180/-

◆ CLIENT/SERVER

81-7029-462-2	Client/Server Computing Sybase SQL Server	225/-
81-7029-385-5	Client/Server Computing with ORACLE	225/-
81-7029-488-6	Novell's Client/Server Applications & Architecture	350/-

◆ CNE

| 81-7029-791-5 | CNE - 4 Study Guide for NetWare 4.1 Certification (W/CD) | 495/- |

◆ COBOL

| BPB 412 | COBOL: Language of Business | 75/- |
| 81-7656-061-8 | Mastering COBOL (W/CD) | 399/- |

◆ COMPUTER COURSE

| 81-765-464-8 | BPB Computer Course (W/CD) | 120/- |

◆ COMPUTER - TEXTBOOKS

81-7029-775-3	A First Course in Computer SCIENCE (ICSE class IX TO XII)	120/-
81-7029-814-8	Computers Don't Byte: A Beginners Guide to Understanding Computers	45/-
81-7656-422-2	Computer - An Introduction	99/-
81-7029-813-X	Computer Basics	30/-
81-7029-486-X	Computer Concepts & Facts	36/-
81-7029-151-7	Computer Lab Manual	99/-
81-7656-360-9	Computer Fundamentals	99/-
BPB 303	Basic Computing - Book A	33/-
BPB 304	Basic Computing - Book B	33/-
BPB 305	Basic Computing - Book C	33/-
BPB 306	Basic Computing - Book D	33/-
BPB 307	Basic Computing - Book E	33/-
BPB 308	Basic Computing - Book F	33/-
BPB 309	Basic Computing Principles	54/-
81-7029-626-9	Build Your Own Computer	54/-
81-7029-767-2	Computer Fundamentals and C++ Programming VOL. I (CBSE-XI)	81/-
81-7029-844-X	Computer Fundamentals and C++ Programming VOL. II (CBSE-XII)	150/-
81-7029-754-0	Fun with Computers Vol. I	36/-
81-7029-756-7	Fun with Computers Vol. II	36/-
81-7029-755-9	Fun with Computers Vol. III	36/-
81-7029-757-5	Fun with Computers Vol. IV	36/-
81-7029-758-3	Fun with Computers Vol. V	36/-
81-7029-759-1	Fun with Computers Vol. VI	36/-
81-7656-047-2	Informatics Practices Vol. I (CBSE - CLASS XI CODE 065)	150/-
81-7656-110-X	Informatics Practices Vol. II (CBSE - CLASS XII CODE 065)	150/-
BPB 1019	Introducing Computers - Part - I Rev.	39/-
BPB 1020	Introducing Computers - Part - II Rev.	39/-
BPB 1021	Introducing Computers - Part - III Rev.	39/-
81-7029-189-5	Introduction to Computer Science Vol. II	99/-
BPB 2006	Let us Learn Computers (Rev. Edn.)	45/-
81-7029-497-5	Programming in PASCAL -Vol. I	75/-
81-7029-498-3	Programming in PASCAL -Volume II	60/-
BPB 20005	Understanding Computer System Architecture	150/-
81-7029-521-1	We can use the COMPUTERS - A	33/-
81-7029-522-X	We can use the COMPUTERS - B	33/-
81-7029-523-8	We can use the COMPUTERS - C	33/-

ISBN	TITLE	PRICE

◆ COMPUTER - TEXTBOOKS
81-7029-524-6	We can use the COMPUTERS - D	33/-
81-7029-525-4	We can use the COMPUTERS - E	33/-
81-7029-526-2	We can use the COMPUTERS - F	33/-
81-7656-454-0	Information Technology for Everybody Vol. I	99/-
81-7656-455-9	Information Technology for Everybody Vol. II	99/-
81-7656-399-4	Successful Projects in Word	75/-
81-7656-400-1	Successful Projects in Excel	75/-
81-7656-402-8	Successful Projects in Access	75/-
81-7656-401-X	Successful Projects in Visual Basic	90/-
81-7656-403-6	Successful Computer Projects in Access with Visual Basic for Applications	75/-
81-7656-406-0	Successful Projects in FrontPage 2000	75/-

◆ COREL DRAW - 4 - 5 - 6 - 7 - 8 - 9
BPB 2002	Learn COREL DRAW In a Day	45/-
81-7029-634-X	Looking Good with Corel DRAW (4&5)	150/-
81-7029-505-X	Teach Yourself COREL DRAW 5.0	120/-
81-7029-696-X	Teach Yourself COREL DRAW 6.0	135/-
81-7029-857-1	Mastering COREL DRAW 7 (W/CD)	450/-
81-7656-123-1	Mastering COREL DRAW 9	360/-
81-7656-497-4	COREL DRAW 9 (H)	66/-

◆ CORBA
81-7656-302-1	CORBA Networking with Java (W/CD)	180/-

◆ CD RECORDABLE
81-7029-874-1	CD Recordable Hand Book (W/CD)	399/-
81-7029-889-X	Complete Recordable CD Guide (W/CD)	390/-

◆ COM & COM+
81-7656-181-9	Mastering COM & COM+	270/-
81-7656-183-5	Visual Basic Developer's Guide to COM & COM+	180/-

◆ COM PROGRAMMING
81-7656-263-7	Developer's Workshop to Com & ATL 3.0 (W/CD)	270/-

◆ CRYSTAL REPORTS 8
81-7656-281-5	Prima's Guide to Seagate Crystal Reports 8	360/-

◆ DREAMWEAVER 3
81-7656-242-4	Mastering Macromedia Dreamweaver 3 (W/CD)	299/-

◆ DATABASE
BPB 8001	Relational DATABASE - Theory & Practice	99/-
81-7656-551-2	Teach Yourself Database Technologies	240/-

◆ DBASE III PLUS
81-7029-035-X	Advanced Techniques in dBase III PLUS	180/-
BPB 509	dBase Workbook	36/-
BPB 504	dBase III PLUS: A Comprehensive Users Manual	90/-
BPB 505	dBase III PLUS Instant Reference	60/-
81-7029-031-7	dBase III PLUS Programmers Reference Guide	275/-

◆ DBASE III PLUS
BPB 502	dBase III PLUS Programming Tips & Techniques	180/-
BPB 503	dBase III PLUS Students & Instructor Work Book	99/-
BPB 10024	Illustrated dBase III PLUS Book	99/-
BPB 3001	Mailing List Using dBase	45/-
81-7029-029-5	Understanding dBase III PLUS	99/-

◆ DBASE IV
81-7029-506-8	Teach Yourself dBase V for Windows	120/-
81-7029-207-7	Understanding dBase IV 1.5	275/-

◆ DATA PROCESSING
81-7029-994-2	DATA Processing and Information Technology	135/-

◆ DCOM
81-7656-301-3	DCOM Networking with Visual J++ 6.0 (W/CD)	180/-

◆ DELPHI 5
81-7656-215-7	Mastering DELPHI 5	450/-

◆ DICTIONARY
BPB 419	Computer DICTIONARY	36/-
81-7029-730-3	The PC User's Pocket DICTIONARY	66/-
81-7029-665-X	DICTIONARY of Networking	75/-
81-7656-174-4	Dictionary of Computing & Digital Media	150/-

◆ DIRECTOR 6
81-7029-895-4	Mastering Macromedia Director 6 (W/CD)	450/-

◆ DTP
81-7029-873-3	DeskTop Publishing on PC	99/-

◆ EXCEL
81-7029-230-1	Mastering EXCEL - 4 for Windows	195/-
81-7656-424-9	Microsoft Excel - An Introduction	60/-

◆ EXCEL 5 / WIN
81-7029-478-9	EXCEL 5 for Windows Instant Reference	45/-
81-7029-464-9	Learn EXCEL 5.0 For Windows In a Day	45/-
81-7029-479-7	MS EXCEL 5.0 For Windows at a Glance	60/-
81-7029-476-2	Mastering EXCEL - 5 for Windows	225/-
81-7029-596-3	PCLL-Teaches EXCEL 5.0 for Windows (W/D)	150/-

◆ EXCEL 7 / WIN 95
81-7029-705-2	Learn MS EXCEL 7.0 for Windows 95 in a day	45/-
81-7029-682-X	PCLL-Teaches EXCEL 7.0 for Windows 95 (W/D)	165/-
81-7029-677-3	Teach Yourself EXCEL 7.0 for Windows 95 (W/D)	150/-

◆ EXCEL 97
81-7029-806-7	Abcs of EXCEL 97	120/-
81-7029-810-5	Mastering EXCEL 97	399/-
81-7656-016-2	Excel 97 - Training Guide	60/-

ISBN	TITLE	PRICE

◆ INTERNET

ISBN	TITLE	PRICE
81-7656-329-3	Hacker Attack! (W/CD)	195/-
81-7656-389-7	Surf's Up - The Ultimate Guide to The Internet	99/-
81-7656-488-5	Seurity Complete	199/-

◆ INTERNET EXPLORER

| 81-7029-764-8 | ABC of MS Internet Explorer 3 | 99/- |
| 81-7029-929-2 | ABC of MS Internet Explorer 4 (With Free MS-I.E.4.0 CD) | 150/- |

◆ IIS

81-7029-790-7	Mastering MS Internet Information Server	399/-
81-7029-903-9	MCSE: Internet Info. Server 3 Study Guide (W/CD)	450/-
81-7656-141-X	IIS 4 and Proxy Server 2 24seven	180/-

◆ INTRANETS

81-7029-875-X	ABCs of INTRANETS	120/-
81-7029-837-7	Building INTRANETS on NT, Netware and Solaris	399/-
81-7029-830-X	Mastering INTRANETS for WIN 95 /NT (W/CD)	450/-
81-7029-936-5	Practical Guide to INTRANETS Client Server Applications Using the Web (W/CD)	225/-

◆ JAVA

81-7656-302-1	CORBA Networking with Java (W/CD)	180/-
81-7029-834-2	JAVA 1.1 Developers Handbook (W/CD)	450/-
81-7029-854-7	JAVA 1.1 : No Experience Required (W/CD)	225/-
81-7656-362-5	Java Developer's Guide to E-Commerce with XML & JSP (W/CD)	240/-
81-7029-877-6	Mastering JAVA 1.1 (W/CD) - 2nd Rev. Edn.	450/-
81-7656-391-9	Practical XML with Java (W/CD)	270/-
81-7656-475-3	Learning Java (W/CD)	210/-
81-7656-456-7	Complete Java Book	225/-

◆ JAVASCRIPT

81-7029-826-1	ABCs of JAVA Script	150/-
81-7029-937-3	Learn Advance JAVA script Programming (W/CD)	399/-
81-7656-075-8	Mastering JavaScript and JScript	399/-

◆ JAVA 2

81-7656-337-4	Java 2 Exam Notes	99/-
81-7656-077-4	Java 2 - Complete	199/-
81-7029-786-9	Java Workshop Programming (W/D)	150/-
81-7656-156-8	Mastering Java 2 (W/CD)	499/-
81-7656-155-X	Java 2 Developer's Handbook (W/CD)	450/-
81-7656-035-9	JAVA 2 - In Record Time (W/CD)	180/-
81-7656-356-0	Web Enabled Commercial Applications Development using Java 2 (W/CD) - 2nd Edn.	240/-
81-7656-320-X	Complete JAVA 2 Certification Study Guide (W/CD) 2nd Edition	399/-

◆ JAVA SERVLETS & JSP

| 81-7656-335-8 | Java Developer's Guide to Servlets & JSP (W/CD) | 360/- |
| 81-7656-359-5 | Java Servlets JSP | 150/- |

◆ JAVA BEANS

| 81-7029-881-4 | Mastering Java Beans (W/CD) | 399/- |
| 81-7656-280-7 | Hands on Java Beans (W/CD) | 225/- |

◆ LINUX

81-7029-685-4	Complete LINUX Kit (W/CD)	450/-
81-7029-906-3	LINUX Configuration & Installation (Including Slackware) (W/2CD's)	300/-
81-7656-219-X	Mastering GNOME (W/CD)	297/-
81-7656-170-3	LINUX Complete	199/-
81-7656-131-2	Mastering LINUX Premium Edition (W/2 CDs)	450/-
81-7656-147-9	LINUX Network Server 24seven	195/-
81-7656-236-X	Learn Red Hat Linux Server Tips (W/CD)	150/-
81-7656-160-6	Red Hat Linux 6 Fast & Easy	150/-
81-7656-319-6	Linux Command - Instant Reference	99/-
81-7656-327-7	RHCE: Red Hat Certified Engineer Study Guide (W/CD) (Exam RH302)	399/-
81-7656-382-X	RCHC Exam Notes: Red Hat Certified Engineer (Exam RH 302)	120/-
81-7656-293-9	Linux DNS Server Administration	225/-
81-7656-303-X	Learn Red Hat Linux OS Tips (W/CD)	180/-
81-7656-328-5	Linux for Windows NT/2000 Administration (W/CD)	270/-
81-7656-332-3	Learn Red Hat Linux Security (W/CD)	240/-
81-7656-343-9	Linux SAMBA Server Administration	270/-
81-7656-342-0	Linux Apache Web Server Administration	270/-
81-7656-372-2	Linux System Administration	350/-
81-7656-457-5	Linux Security	225/-
81-7656-487-7	Mastering Red Hat Linux 7.1 (W/CD)	450/-

◆ LOGO

BPB 2010	LOGO Work Book	36/-
81-7029-487-8	The School LOGO Book	45/-
81-7029-483-5	Working with LOGO	36/-

◆ LOTUS 1-2-3

BPB 10010	ABCs of 1-2-3 (Release 2.2)	90/-
BPB 10011	ABCs of 1-2-3 (Release 3)	90/-
BPB 1006	Illustrated LOTUS 1-2-3 (Release 3)	135/-
81-7029-078-3	Illustrated LOTUS 1-2-3 Book	120/-
81-7029-466-5	Learn LOTUS 1-2-3 in a Day (Revised Edition)	45/-
81-7029-587-4	Learn LOTUS 1-2-3 Rel. 4 for Windows In a day	45/-
81-7029-704-4	Learn LOTUS 1-2-3 Rel. 5 for Windows in a day	54/-
981-214-314-9	LOTUS 1-2-3 Release 5 Quick & Easy	360/-
81-7029-496-7	LOTUS 1-2-3 Release 5 For WINDOWS Instant Ref.	54/-

ISBN	TITLE	PRICE

◆ LOTUS 1-2-3

81-7029-248-4	LOTUS 1-2-3 For Windows at a Glance	75/-
BPB 10027	Manual LOTUS 1-2-3	54/-
981-3005-46-3	Up & Running with LOTUS 1-2-3 (Release 2.3)	180/-
981-214-697-0	Understanding 1-2-3 Release 4.0 for Windows	540/-

◆ LOTUS SMARTSUITE MILLENNIUM

| 81-7656-207-6 | Mastering Lotus SmartSuite Millennium Edn. Rel. 9.5 | 399/- |

◆ LOTUS-NOTES 4.5 & DOMINO

81-7029-876-8	ABCs of LOTUS NOTES 4.5	120/-
81-7029-870-9	Learn LOTUS DOMINO (W/D)	99/-
81-7029-882-2	LOTUS NOTES 4.5 Administrator Guide	300/-
81-7029-869-5	LOTUS NOTES Developer's Guide for Users Rel 4.0-4.5 (W/CD-ROM)	275/-
81-7029-659-5	LOTUS NOTES Plain & Simple	180/-
81-7029-835-0	Mastering LOTUS NOTES 4.5 & DOMINO (W/CD)	450/-
81-7029-865-2	Teach Yourself LOTUS NOTES 4.5 (W/D)	225/-

◆ LOTUS-NOTES 5

| 81-7656-109-6 | Mastering LOTUS NOTES R5 (W/CD) | 399/- |

◆ MIS

| 81-7029-999-3 | Management Information System (8th Edition) | 99/- |

◆ MATHS

| BPB 422 | Computer Related MATHEMATICS | 120/- |
| 81-7029-280-8 | MATHEMATICS for Computer Students | 120/- |

◆ MEMORY

| BPB 10030 | The One Minute MEMORY MANAGER | 180/- |

◆ MICROPROCESSORS

81-7029-458-4	MICROPROCESSORS X86 Programming	180/-
81-7029-278-6	Microprocessor & Microcomputers Technology	120/-
81-7656-185-1	Microprocessor Data Handbook (Rev. Edn.)	270/-

◆ MCSD - 1999

81-7656-087-1	MCSD Test Success: Analyzing Requirements and Defining Solution Architecture	150/-
81-7656-090-1	MCSD Test Success : Visual Basic 6 Desktop Applications	150/-
81-7656-161-X	MCSD Test Success : Visual Basic 6 Distributed Applications	150/-
81-7656-062-6	MCSD : Visual Basic 6 Distributed Applications Study Guide (W/CD)	360/-
81-7656-058-8	MCSD : Visual Basic 6 Desktop Applications Study Guide (W/CD)	360/-

➤ MCSE

81-7029-981-0	Workstation Study Guide 4 2nd Ed. (W/2CDs)	450/-
81-7656-056-1	MCSE JumpStart: Computer & Network Basic	150/-
81-7656-134-7	MCSE COMPLETE : CORE REQUIREMENTS	199/-

➤ MCSE - ELECTIVE STUDY GUIDES

81-7029-898-9	MCSE: Windows 95 Study Guide (W/CD)	450/-
81-7656-135-5	MCSE Complete : Elective Study Guide	199/-
81-7029-903-9	MCSE: Internet Information Server 3 Study Guide (W/CD)	450/-
81-7029-700-2	MCSE: Exchange 5 Study Guide (W/CD)	450/-
81-7656-003-0	MCSE: Exchange Server 5.5 Study Guide (W/CD)	450/-
81-7656-048-0	MCSE: Windows 98 Study Guide (W/CD)	450/-

➤ MCSE - EXAM NOTES

81-7656-028-6	MCSE Exam Notes: TCP/IP For NT Server 4	99/-
81-7029-996-9	MCSE Exam Notes: NT Server 4	99/-
81-7029-997-7	MCSE Exam Notes: NT Server 4 In The Enterprise	99/-
81-7656-005-7	MCSE Exam Notes: NT Workstation 4	99/-
81-7656-024-3	MCSE Exam Notes: SQL Server 6.5 Administration	99/-
81-7656-119-3	MCSE Exam Notes: SQL Server 7.0 Administration	99/-
81-7656-029-4	MCSE Exam Notes: Exchange Server 5.5	99/-
81-7656-049-9	MCSE Exam Notes: Windows 98	99/-
81-7656-013-8	MCSE Exam Notes: Networking Essential	99/-
81-7656-511-3	MCSE Windows 2000 4 in 1 Core Requirement Exam Notes	399/-

➤ MCSE - TEST SUCCESSS-CORE REQUIREMENT

81-7029-968-3	MCSE Test Success: NT Server 4	150/-
81-7029-974-8	MCSE Test Success: Networking Essentials	150/-
81-7029-973-X	MCSE Test Success: NT Server 4 in the Enterprise	150/-
81-7029-976-4	MCSE Test Success: NT Workstation 4	150/-

➤ MCSE - TEST SUCCESSS - ELECTIVE

81-7029-998-5	MCSE Test Success: TCP/IP for NT 4	150/-
81-7656-007-3	MCSE Test Success: Exchange Server 5.5	150/-
81-7029-979-9	MCSE Test Success: WINDOWS 95	150/-
81-7656-042-1	MCSE Test Success: WINDOWS 98	150/-
81-7656-214-9	MCSE Test Success System Management Server 2	150/-
81-7656-248-3	MCSE 2000 JumpStart	150/-

◆ MCSE 2000 — ELECTIVE STUDY GUIDE

| 81-7656-417-6 | MCSE: Exchange Server 2000 Administration Study Guide (W/CD) (Exam 70-224) | 450/- |
| 81-7656-416-8 | MCSE: Exchange Server 2000 Design Study Guide (W/CD) (Exam 70-225) | 450/- |

ISBN	TITLE	PRICE

◆ MCSE 2000 — ELECTIVE STUDY GUIDE

81-7656-418-4 MCSE: SQL Server 2000 Administration Study Guide (W/CD) (Exam 70-228) 450/-

81-7656-510-5 MCSE: SQL Server 2000 Design Study Guide (W/CD) (Exam 70-229) 450/-

◆ MCSE 2000 — STUDY GUIDE

81-7656-291-2 MCSE: Windows 2000 Professional Study Guide (W/CD) (Exam #70-210) .. 450/-

81-7656-311-0 MCSE: Windows 2000 Network Infrastructure Administration Study Guide (W/CD) (Exam 70-216) 450/-

81-7656-316-1 MCSE: Windows 2000 Directory Services Design Study Guide (W/CD) (Exam 70-219) 450/-

81-7656-297-1 MCSE: Windows 2000 Directory Service Administration Study Guide (W/CD) (Exam 70-217) 450/-

81-7656-315-3 MCSE: Windows 2000 Network Infrastructure Design Study Guide (W/CD) (Exam 70-221) 450/-

81-7656-298-X MCSE: Windows 2000 Server Study Guide (W/CD) (Exam 70-215) 450/-

81-7656-326-9 MCSE: Windows 2000 Network Security Design Study Guide (W/CD) (Exam 70-220) 450/-

81-7656-323-4 MCSE: Accelerated Windows 2000 Study Guide(W/CD) (Exam 70-240) 450/-

81-7656-314-5 MCSE: Windows 2000 Professional Manual (W/CD) 399/-

81-7656-371-4 MCSE: Windows 2000 Migration Study Guide (W/CD) (Exam 70-222) 450/-

◆ MCSE 2000 — EXAM NOTES

81-7656-388-9 MCSE Exam Notes: Windows 2000 Netwrok Infrastructure Administration (Exam 70-216) 120/-

81-7656-385-4 MCSE Exam Notes: Windows 2000 Professional (Exam 70-210) 120/-

81-7656-384-6 MCSE Exam Notes: Windows 2000 Network Security Design (Exam 70-220) 120/-

81-7656-383-8 MCSE Exam Notes: Windows 2000 Accelerated (Exam 70-240) 199/-

81-7656-381-1 MCSE Exam Notes: Windows 2000 Server (Exam 70-215) 120/-

81-7656-380-3 MCSE Exam Notes: Windows 2000 DirectoryService Design (Exam 70-219) 120/-

81-7656-379-X MCSE Exam Notes: Windows 2000 Directory Services Administration (Exam 70-217) 120/-

81-7656-378-1 MCSE Exam Notes: Windows 2000 Network Infrastructure Design (Exam 70-221) . 120/-

◆ MP3

81-7656-154-1 MP3! I Didn't Know You Could Do That (W/CD) 150/-

81-7656-341-2 MP3 Complete 199/-

◆ MAYA

81-7656-227-0 Mastering Maya Complete 2 (W/CD) .. 450/-

81-7656-486-9 Mastering Maya 3 (W/CD) 499/-

◆ MEDICAL TRANSCRIPTION

81-7656-465-6 Learning Medical Transcription Word Processing, Projects & Exercises 180/-

◆ MS-DOS

BPB 10015 ABCs of DOS 5 .... 90/-

81-7029-485-1 Advanced MS DOS Programming 275/-

81-7029-239-5 DOS (3.3 & 5) Instant Reference 45/-

BPB 514 DOS 3.3 & 5.0 Test 45/-

81-7029-231-X DOS 6 Running Start 75/-

81-7029-374-X DOS 6.0 & 6.22 Companion 99/-

81-7029-296-4 DOS 6.0 & 6.2 Instant Reference 54/-

81-7029-289-1 DOS Quick Reference Manual -Vol. (upto ver.-5) 45/-

81-7029-290-5 DOS Quick Reference Manual -Vol. II (upto ver.-6.2) 45/-

81-7029-554-8 Illustrated MS DOS 6.22 .... 99/-

81-7029-310-3 Learn DOS in a Day (Upto 6.2) 45/-

81-7029-512-9 PCLL Teaches DOS 6 & 6.2 .... 150/-

81-7029-516-5 MS-DOS System Programming (W/D) 225/-

81-7029-313-8 Mastering DOS 6 & 6.2 - Special Edition .. 325/-

BPB 3071 Murphy's Laws of DOS-6 .... 99/-

BPB 10001 Teach Yourself - DOS 90/-

81-7656-495-8 DOS 6 & 6.22 - An Introduction 60/-

◆ MULTIMEDIA / SOUND BLASTER / CD-ROM

981-214-218-5 Choosing & Using Your First CD-ROM Drive -(W/CD) 350/-

81-7029-441-X Multimedia on the PC (W/D) 120/-

81-7029-972-1 Multimedia Magic (W/CD) 270/-

81-7029-372-3 Sound Blaster Book 300/-

◆ NORTON UTILITIES

81-7029-274-3 Learn NORTON UTILITIES in a Day 45/-

981-214-600-8 NORTON Desktop for Windows Instant Reference 240/-

◆ NETWORKING

BPB 10037 ABCs of LOCAL AREA NETWORKS 99/-

81-7029-665-X Dictionary of NETWORKING 75/-

81-7029-962-4 Introduction to Local Area Network (Rev. Edn.) 150/-

81-7656-060-X Mastering Local Area Networks 360/-

81-7029-229-8 LAN Troubleshooting Handbook (W/D) 240/-

81-7656-018-9 Local Area Networks - 3rd Rev. Edn. 120/-

81-7029-920-9 Multiprotocol Network Design & Troubleshooting 450/-

81-7029-553-X PC Magazine - Guide to Connectivity . 225/-

81-7029-952-7 The Network Technical Guide (W/CD) . 450/-

81-7656-491-5 Networking Complete - 2nd Edn. 199/-

81-7656-197-5 Network + LAB Manual 99/-

81-7656-225-4 Frame Relay Internetworking 150/-

ISBN	TITLE	PRICE

◆ PERL / CGI

| 81-7029-934-9 | PERL/CGI : No Experience Required .. | 150/- |
| 81-7656-296-3 | Perl, CGI and JavaScript Complete ..... | 199/- |

◆ PHOTOSHOP

81-7656-217-3	Mastering Photoshop 5.5 for the Web .	297/-
81-7656-350-1	Photoshop 6 for Windows - fast&easy ..	195/-
81-7656-364-1	Mastering Photoshop 6 (W/CD)	399/-
81-7656-374-9	Photoshop 6 : Visual Jumpstart	150/-
81-7656-531-8	Photoshop 6 Complete	199/-

◆ PHOTO DRAW 2000

| 81-7656-109-2 | Mastering MS PhotoDRAW 2000 .... | 270/- |
| 81-7656-192-4 | MS PhotoDRAW 2000 Fast & Easy ..... | 150/- |

◆ POWER BUILDER

| 81-7029-629-3 | Commercial Applications in POWER BUILDER .... | 225/- |

◆ POWER BUILDER 6 & 7

| 81-7656-195-9 | PowerBuilder Vedas (W/CD) -Rev. Edn. (Covers version 7) .... | 450/- |

◆ POWER POINT

| 81-7029-718-4 | Learn MS POWER POINT 7.0 for Win 95 in a day .... | 45/- |

◆ POWER POINT 2000

81-7656-113-4	MS POWERPOINT 2000 Training Guide ...	60/-
81-7656-132-0	Mastering POWERPOINT 2000	195/-
81-7656-163-0	PowerPoint 2000 Fast & Easy	150/-
81-7656-430-3	MS PowerPoint 2000 - An Introduction ..	60/-

◆ PUBLISHER

| 81-7656-161-4 | Publisher 2000 Fast & Easy .... | 150/- |

◆ PRINTSHOP

| 81-7029-664-1 | The Official PRINTSHOP Deluxe H/B . | 180/- |

◆ PRINTER

| 81-7029-751-6 | Modern all about PRINTER .... | 99/- |
| 81-7029-699-4 | Winn L. Rosch's PRINTER Bible (W/CD) . | 450/- |

◆ PROGRAMMING

81-7029-495-9	Mixed Language Programming (W/D) .	225/-
81-7029-444-4	PROGRAMMING Techniques for PC's .	66/-
81-7029-762-1	Structured Programming: Go To Controversy To Object Oriented Programming	120/-
81-7029-380-4	Welcome to PROGRAMMING (W/D) ..	180/-

◆ PHP 4

| 81-7656-273-4 | PHP 4 Essentials .... | 180/- |

◆ PROJECT

| 81-7029-597-1 | PCLL-Teaches MS PROJECT 4.0 for Windows (W/D) .... | 150/- |
| 81-7029-715-X | Teach Yourself MS PROJECT for Windows 95 (W/D) .... | 180/- |

◆ PROJECT 2000

| 81-7656-244-0 | Mastering Microsoft Project 2000 .... | 299/- |

◆ RS-232

| BPB 10032 | The RS-232 Solution .... | 150/- |

◆ REMOTE ACCESS

| 81-7656-153-3 | Remote Access - 24seven .... | 165/- |

◆ STAROFFICE

| 81-7656-553-9 | Mastering StarOffice 5.2 for Linux .... | 399/- |

◆ SAP's

81-7029-800-8	Developing SAP's R/3 Applications with ABAP/4 (W/CD-ROM)	499/-
81-7656-046-4	SAP R/3 System Administration: The Official SAP Guide (W/CD)	399/-
81-7656-059-6	SAP R/3 Implementation with ASAP (W/CD) The Official SAP guide	399/-
81-7656-146-0	SAP R/3 Performance Optimization : The Official SAP Guides	399/-
81-7656-220-3	SAP R/3 Change and Transport Management: The Official SAP Guide	450/-

◆ SGML FILTERS

| 81-7029-938-1 | Practical Guide To SGML Filters (W/2 DISKS) .... | 180/- |

◆ SOFTWARE

| BPB 208 | ALMOST PERFECT : How a Bunch of Regular Guys Built WORDPERFECT Corporation .... | 150/- |
| 81-7029-283-2 | SOFTWARE FACTORY : Managing SOFTWARE Development & Maintenance .... | 150/- |

◆ SOLARIS 8

| 81-7656-509-1 | Mastering Solaris 8 .... | 390/- |

◆ SQL

81-7029-644-1	Understanding SQL	225/-
81-7656-230-0	Mastering SQL (W/CD)	349/-
81-7656-235-1	SQL Instant Reference	54/-
81-7656-500-8	**SQL SERVER AND ADO PROGRAMMING COMPLETE**	**199/-**

◆ SQL 7

81-7656-054-5	MS SQL Server 7 - In Record Time	240/-
81-7656-140-1	SQL Server 7 24seven	180/-
81-7656-128-2	SQL Server 7 Administrator's Guide (W/CD)	360/-
81-7656-175-4	Learn MS SQL Server 7 (W/CD)	240/-

◆ SQL SERVER 2000

| 81-7656-321-8 | Mastering SQL Server 2000 .... | 450/- |
| 81-7656-393-5 | Learn SQL Server 2000 Administration ... | 150/- |

◆ SYBASE

| 81-7029-462-2 | Client/Server Computing Sybase SQL Server . | 225/- |

◆ SYSTEM ANALYSIS & DESIGN

| 81-7029-627-7 | Introducing System Analysis - NCC ...... | 90/- |
| BPB 1022 | Introducing System Analysis - NCC ...... | 90/- |

◆ SYSTEM MANAGEMENT SERVER 2

| 81-7656-214-9 | MCSE Test Success: Systems Management Server 2 .... | 150/- |
| 81-7656-216-5 | System Management Server 2-24seven .. | 240/- |

◆ TCP/IP & SNA

81-7029-282-4	Demystifying TCP/IP	90/-
81-7029-472-X	Troubleshooting TCP/IP	399/-
81-7656-148-7	TCP/IP 24seven	180/-
81-7656-228-9	TCP/IP Jumpstart	150/-

ISBN	TITLE	PRICE
	◆ **WINDOWS 2000 - SERVER**	
81-7656-231-9	Mastering Windows 2000 Server	499/-
	◆ **WINDOWS 2000 - REGISTRY**	
81-7656-224-6	Mastering Windows 2000 Registry	297/-
	◆ **WINDOWS ME — MILLENNIUM EDITION**	
81-7656-355-2	Mastering Windows ME	450/-
81-7656-357-9	Windows ME - Instant Reference	60/-
81-7656-363-3	Windows ME - Complete	199/-
81-7656-398-6	Windows ME - Training Guide	75/-
	◆ **WINDOWS XP**	
81-7656-512-1	Mastering Windows XP Home Edn. (W/CD)	399/-
81-7656-515-6	Mastering Windows XP Prof. Edn.	399/-
81-7656-508-3	MS Windows XP H. Ed. Simply Visual	195/-
81-7656-514-8	Windows XP Home & Prof. Edn. Inst. Ref.	75/-
81-7656-530-X	Windows XP Home Edn. Complete	199/-
	◆ **WINDOWS NT**	
81-7029-957-8	NT Network Security (W/CD)	450/-
81-7029-269-7	Learn WINDOWS NT in A Day	54/-
81-7029-735-4	Mastering WINDOWS NT Server 3.51	399/-
81-7656-043-X	Expert Guide to Windows NT Registry	399/-
	◆ **WINDOWS NT 4.0 SERVER**	
81-7029-832-6	NT 4.0 / Windows 95 Developers Handbook (W/CD)	499/-
81-7656-102-7	NT Server 4 - 24seven	195/-
81-7029-816-4	Mastering WINDOWS NT Server 4.0	499/-
81-7029-858-X	Windows NT Server 4 : No Experience Required	150/-
81-7656-105-3	Windows NT 4 Complete	199/-
	◆ **WINDOWS NT 4.0 WORKSATION**	
81-7029-792-3	ABCs of WINDOWS NT 4.0 Workstation	99/-
81-7029-787-7	Mastering Windows NT 4.0 Workstation	399/-
	◆ **WIRLESS APPLICATIONS**	
81-7656-351-X	Wireless Application Programmer's Library (W/CD)	240/-
	◆ **WML & WMLSCRIPT**	
81-7656-390-0	WML and WMLScript	180/-
81-7656-413-3	Getting Started with WAP & WML (W/CD)	210/-
	◆ **WORD 6 / WIN**	
81-7029-465-7	Learn WORD 6.0 for Windows in a Day	45/-
81-7029-595-5	PCLL-Teaches Word 6.0 for WIN (W/D)	150/-
81-7029-679-X	Teach Yourself Word for WIN 95 (W/D)	180/-
81-7029-297-2	WORD 6 For Windows Instant Reference	54/-

ISBN	TITLE	PRICE
	◆ **WORD 7 / WIN 95**	
81-7029-707-9	Learn MS WORD 7.0 for Windows 95 in a day	45/-
81-7029-681-1	PCLL-Teaches Word for WIN 95 (W/D)	165/-
	◆ **WORD 97**	
81-7029-805-9	The ABCs of WORD 97	120/-
81-7029-809-1	Mastering WORD 97	399/-
81-7656-017-0	WORD 97 - Training Guide	60/-
	◆ **WORD 2000**	
81-7656-089-8	Mastering Word 2000 -Premium Edition (W/CD)	399/-
81-7656-101-0	MS Word 2000 - No Experience Required	150/-
81-7656-117-7	Learning MS Word 2000 (W/CD)	195/-
81-7656-130-4	Essential MS Word 2000 (W/CD)	225/-
81-7656-166-5	Word 2000 Fast & Easy	150/-
81-7656-264-5	Word 2000 Training Guide	60/-
81-7656-431-1	MS Word 2000 - An Introduction	60/-
	◆ **WORD 2002**	
81-7656-474-5	MS Word 2002 -Simply Visual	165/-
	◆ **WORDPERFECT**	
BPB 1011	Illustrated WORDPERFECT - 5.1	99/-
	◆ **WORDSTAR**	
BPB 1012	Illustrated WORDSTAR 6.0	99/-
BPB 1025	Introduction to WORDSTAR	90/-
81-7029-116-X	Mastering WORDSTAR (Release 4)	99/-
81-7029-113-5	Manual : WORDSTAR	54/-
BPB 40003	WORDSTAR Instant Reference	54/-
BPB 40006	WORDSTAR Tips & Traps	75/-
81-7029-438-X	Wordstar 7.0 for Everyone Rev. Edn.	150/-
	◆ **XML**	
81-7656-055-3	XML - In Record Time	180/-
81-7656-191-6	Mastering XML (W/CD)	399/-
81-7656-307-2	Learn XML Tips (W/CD)	165/-
81-7656-313-7	XML Developer's Handbook (W/CD)	240/-
81-7656-391-9	Practical XML with Java (W/CD)	270/-
81-7656-300-5	CORBA Developer's Guide with XML (W/CD)	180/-
81-7656-483-4	Mastering XML - Premium Edition (W/CD)	450/-
81-7656-513-X	XML Complete	199/-
81-7656-550-4	XML Web Services and SOAP	150/-
	◆ **XHTML**	
81-7656-271-8	XHTML - Fast & Easy Web Development (W/CD)	180/-
81-7656-482-6	Mastering XHTML	450/-
81-7656-539-3	XHTML Complete	199/-

COMPUTER BOOKS

ISBN	TITLE	PRICE
ISBN No.	◆ **3D STUDIO MAX / ANIMATION**	
81-87105-00-3	Inside 3D STUDIO MAX Vol. II (W/CD)	350/-
81-87105-20-8	Inside 3D STUDIO MAX Vol. III (W/CD)	399/-
81-87105-09-7	3D STUDIO for Beginners (W/CD)	240/-
81-87105-21-6	3D GRAPHICS & ANIMATION From tarting up to Standing Out (W/CD)	399/-
	◆ **3D STUDIO MAX 2**	
81-7635-164-4	3D Studio Max 2 Fundamentals (W/CD)	275/-

ISBN	TITLE	PRICE
	◆ **3D STUDIO MAX 2**	
81-7635-165-2	Inside 3D Studio MAX 2 Vol. 1 (W/CD)	499/-
81-7635-166-0	Inside 3D Studio MAX 2 Vol. 2 (W/CD)	350/-
81-7635-167-9	Inside 3D Studio MAX 2 Vol. 3 (W/CD)	399/-
81-7635-227-6	Inside 3D Studio MAX 2 Resource Kit (W/4CDs)	799/-
81-7635-141-5	Teach Yourself 3D Studio MAX 2 in 14 Days (W/CD)	225/-

◆ 3D STUDIO MAX 3

81-7635-322-1 3D Studio Max 3 Fundamentals (W/CD) .. 275/-
81-7635-348-5 Inside 3D Studio MAX 3 - Modeling,
    Materials & Rendering (W/CD) 270/-
81-7635-409-0 3D Studio MAX 3 Professional
    Animation (W/CD) 240/-
81-7635-440-6 3D Studio MAX 3 Workshop (W/CD) ... 195/-
81-7635-465-1 Teach Yourself 3D Studio MAX 3
    in 24 Hours 225/-

◆ 3D STUDIO MAX 4

81-7635-532-1 3D Sdutio MAX 4 Fundamentals (W/CD) . 300/-
81-7635-540-0 3D Studio MAX 4 Magic (W/CD) 240/-
81-7635-553-4 3D Studio MAX 4 Media Animation
    (W/CD) 270/-

◆ ABAP/4

81-7635-162-8 Teach Yourself ABAP/4 in 21 Days
    (W/CD) 297/-

◆ ACTIVE SERVER PAGES

81-7635-299-3 Teach Yourself Active Server Pages
    In 24 Hours 165/-

◆ ACTIVE SERVER PAGES 2.0

81-7635-198-9 Teach Yourself ACTIVE SERVER
    Pages 2.0 in 21 Days 270/-
81-7635-316-7 Active Server Pages 2.0 Unleashed
    (W/CD) 399/-

◆ ACTIVE SERVER PAGES 3.0

81-7635-401-5 Teach Yourself Active Server Pages 3.0
    in 21 Days 225/-
81-7635-442-2 Teach Yourself Web Development with ASP
    In 24 Hours (2 Books Set) (W/2CD) . 399/-
    • Teach Yourself ASP in 24
    Hours..................165/-
    • Teach Yourself Visual InterDev 6 in 24
    Hours (W/CD).165/-

◆ ACTIVE X

81-87105-88-7 Teach Yourself ACTIVE X Programming
    in 21 Days (W/CD) 270/-
81-7635-031-1 Teach Yourself ACTIVE X Control
    Programming with VISUAL BASIC 5
    in 21 Days (W/CD) 275/-
81-7635-087-7 Developing COM/ActiveX Components
    with Visual Basic 5 (W/CD) 450/-
81-7635-201-2 Developing COM/ActiveX Components
    with Visual Basic 6 (W/CD) 450/-

◆ ACCESS 97

81-87105-32-1 Peter Norton's guide to ACCESS 97
    Programming (W/CD) 399/-
81-7635-065-6 Alison Balter's Mastering ACCESS 97
    Development - 2nd Edn. (W/CD) 399/-
81-7635-005-2 Teach Yourself ACCESS 97 In 24 Hours .. 135/-

◆ ACCESS 2000

81-7635-288-8 Teach Yourself MS ACCESS 2000
    In 24 Hours 165/-
81-7635-300-0 MS ACCESS 2000 Power Programming
    (W/CD) 450/-
81-7635-317-5 Mastering MS ACCESS 2000
    Development (W/CD) 450/-
81-7635-308-6 MS ACCESS 2000 Development
    Unleashed (W/CD) 450/-
81-7635-332-9 Teach Yourself Access 2000
    in 21 Days (W/CD) 240/-
81-7635-385-X Teach Yourself Access 2000 Programming
    in 24 Hours 165/-
81-7635-351-5 Peter Norton's Guide to Access 2000
    programming 297/-

◆ ADOBE

81-7635-111-3 Adobe - FAQ Frequently Asked Question
    Answered (W/CD) 450/-
81-7635-396-5 Adobe InDesign - Classroom in a
    Book (W/CD) 240/-

◆ ADOBE AFTER EFFECTS

81-7635-528-3 Applying Adobe After Effects -
    Studio Techniques (W/ 2 CDs) 240/-

◆ APACHE SERVER

81-7635-419-8 Apache Server Unleashed (W/CD) 299/-

◆ ATL

81-7635-410-4 Teach Yourself ATL Programming
    in 21 Days 195/-

◆ AUTOCAD

81-7635-036-2 AutoCAD 14 Fundamentals 195/-
81-87105-15-1 Inside AutoCAD 14 (W/CD) 450/-

◆ AUTOCAD 2000

81-7635-422-8 Inside AutoCAD 2000 (W/CD) - Limited
    Edition 450/-

◆ AUTOCAD 2002

81-7635-558-5 Inside AutoCAD 2002 (W/CD) 480/-

◆ BACKOFFICE

81-7635-019-2 Microsoft BackOffice Unleashed
    (W/CD) -2nd Edn. 499/-
    (Covers NT Server 4.0, SQL Server 6.5,
    Transaction Server 1.0, Exchange Server
    5.0, IIS 3.0, Proxy Server 1.0)

◆ BizTalk

81-7635-424-4 Understanding BizTalk 240/-

◆ COLDFUSION

81-7635-475-9 Teach Yourself Allaire ColdFusion
    in 21 Days (W/CD) 270/-

◆ C++

81-87105-36-4 C++ Interactive Course (W/CD) 399/-
81-7635-174-1 C++ Primer Plus : MWSS (3rd Revised
    & Updated Edn.) 330/-

ISBN	TITLE	PRICE

◆ CCNA (#640-507)

81-7635-445-7	CCNA Exam Certification Guide (#640-507) (W/CD) Rev. Edn.	499/-
81-7635-446-5	Cisco CCNA Preparation Library - 3 Books Set (W/CD)	1450/-
	• CCNA Exam Certification Guide (W/CD)	499/-
	• Cisco Interconnecting Cisco Network Devices	499/-
	• Internetworking Technologies Handbook-3rd Rev. Edn	750/-

◆ CCDA — (EXAM - 640-441)

81-7635-447-3	Cisco CCDA Preparation Library (3 Books+CD)	1690/-
	• CCDA Exam Certification Guide (W/CD)	599/-
	• Internetworking Technologies Handbook-3rd Rev. Edn.	750/-
	• Designing Cisco Networks	599/-
81-7635-454-6	CCDA Exam Certification Guide (W/CD) New Syllabus	599/-

◆ CCNP / CCDP

81-7635-199-7	Cisco CCNP / CCDP Advanced CISCO ROUTER Configuration	599/-
81-7635-510-0	Cisco CCNP/CCDP Building Cisco Multiplayer Switched Networks	699/-
81-7635-511-9	Cisco CCNP/CCDP Building Cisco Remote Access Networks	699/-
81-7635-512-7	Cisco CCNP/CCDP Building Scalable Cisco Networks	699/-
81-7635-522-4	Cisco CCNP Switching Exam Certification Guide (W/CD) - Exam #640 504	699/-
81-7635-523-2	Cisco CCNP Remote Access Exam Certification Guide (W/CD) - Exam #640-505	699/-
81-7635-525-9	CCNP Routing Exam Certification Guide (exam #640-503) (W/CD)	699/-
81-7635-513-5	CCNP Support Exam Certification Guide (exam #640-506) (W/CD)	699/-

◆ CLIENT / SERVER

81-7635-017-6	Client / Server Unleashed (W/CD)	399/-

◆ COBOL

81-7635-154-7	COBOL Unleashed (W/CD)	450/-
81-87105-35-6	Teach Yourself COBOL in 21 Days	300/-
81-7635-208-X	Teach Yourself COBOL in 24 Hours - Starter Kit (W/CD)	240/-

◆ CORBA

81-7635-127-X	Teach Yourself CORBA in 14 Days	165/-
81-7635-225-X	CORBA Programming Unleashed (W/CD)	297/-

◆ COM / DCOM

81-7635-234-9	COM / DCOM Primer Plus (W/CD)	270/-
81-7635-262-4	COM / DCOM Unleashed (W/CD)	297/-

◆ COM+

81-7635-472-4	COM+ Unleashed (W/CD)	399/-
81-7635-488-0	COM+ Programming with Visual Basic (W/CD)	270/-

◆ CORELDRAW 8

81-7635-092-3	Teach Yourself CorelDraw 8 in 24 Hours	135/-

◆ CORELDRAW 9

81-7635-310-8	Teach Yourself CorelDraw 9 in 24 Hours	150/-

◆ DIGITAL PHOTOGRAPHY

81-87105-97-6	Teach Yourself Digital Photography in 14 Days	180/-

◆ DATA COMMUNICATION

81-7635-319-1	Understanding Data Communications - Sixth Edition (Covers PDA's, ISDN, SNMP, TCP/IP)	180/-

◆ DATABASE DESIGN

81-7635-508-9	Database Design	450/-

◆ DIRECTX 7

81-7635-237-3	Teach Yourself DirectX 7 in 24 Hours (W/CD)	225/-
81-7635-594-1	DirectX 8 and Visual Basic Development	240/-

◆ DATA STRUCTURE & ALGORITHMS

81-7635-293-4	Teach Yourself Data Structure & Algorithms In 24 Hours (W/CD)	195/-

◆ DB2

81-87105-40-2	DB2 Developer's Guide (Also cover V4 and V5) (W/CD) - 3rd Edn.	495/-
81-7635-175-X	Teach yourself DB2 Universal Database in 21 Days (W/CD)	240/-

◆ DOS

81-87105-22-4	Peter Norton's Complete Guide To DOS 6.22	399/-

◆ DIRECTOR 6 - MACROMEDIA

81-87105-11-9	Inside Macromedia Director 6 with Lingo (W/CD)	450/-

◆ DIRECTOR 7 - MACROMEDIA

81-7635-428-7	Macromedia Director Workshop - Covers Version 7.0 (W/CD)	195/-

◆ DREAMWEAVER 3

81-7635-432-5	Teach Yourself Macromedia Dreamweaver 3.0 in 24 Hours	150/-
81-7635-433-3	Short Order Macromedia Dreamweaver 3	99/-

◆ DREAMWEAVER 4

81-7635-516-X	Teach Yourself Macromedia Dreamweaver 4.0 in 24 Hours	180/-

ISBN	TITLE	PRICE
	♦ DREAMWEAVER 4	
81-7635-539-9	Dreamweaver 4 Magic (W/CD)	240/-
81-7635-541-0	Inside Dreamweaver 4 (W/CD)	450/-
	♦ E-COMMERCE	
81-7635-435-X	Teach Yourself E-Commerce Programming with ASP in 21 Days (W/CD)	210/-
81-7635-481-3	Realizing e-Business with applications Service Providers	225/-
	♦ ERwin	
81-7635-451-1	Data Modeling with ERwin	360/-
	♦ EXCHANGE SERVER	
81-87105-34-8	MS Exchange Server 5 Unleashed (W/CD)	450/-
	♦ EXCHANGE SERVER 5.5	
81-7635-266-7	Teach Yourself MS Exchange Server 5.5 In 21 Days (W/2CDs)	399/-
	♦ EMACS	
81-7635-273-X	Teach Yourself EMACS In 24 Hours (W/CD) - Starter Kit	180/-
	♦ EXCEL 97	
81-7635-001-X	Teach Yourself MS Excel 97 in 24 Hours	135/-
	♦ EXCEL 2000	
81-7635-286-1	Teach Yourself MS Excel 2000 In 24 Hours	165/-
81-7635-291-8	Teach Yourself Excel 2000 Programming In 21 Days	300/-
81-7635-329-9	Teach Yourself MS Excel 2000 Programming In 24 Hours	150/-
	♦ FLASH 4	
81-7635-417-1	Flash 4 Magic (W/CD)	180/-
81-7635-427-9	Flash Web Design (The Art of Motion Graphics)	240/-
	♦ FLASH 5	
81-7635-506-2	Teach Yourself Macromedia Flash 5 in 24 Hours	195/-
81-7635-526-7	Flash 5 Magic with ActionScript (W/CD)	240/-
81-7635-531-3	Generator / Flash - Web Development (W/CD)	240/-
81-7635-545-3	ActionScripting in Flash	270/-
81-7635-571-2	Flash Web Design (The Art of Motion Graphics)	180/-
	♦ FRONTPAGE 98	
81-7635-041-9	Teach Yourself MS FrontPage 98 in a week	180/-
	♦ FRONTPAGE 2000	
81-7635-292-6	Teach Yourself MS FrontPage 2000 In 24 Hours	150/-
81-7635-349-3	Short Order MS FrontPage 2000	75/-
81-7635-324-8	Teach Yourself MS FrontPage 2000 In 21 Days (W/CD)	240/-

ISBN	TITLE	PRICE
	♦ FRONTPAGE 2002	
81-7635-550-X	Teach Yourself MS FrontPage 2002 in 24 Hours	165/-
	♦ GENERAL COMPUTING	
81-7635-436-8	How Computers Work - Millennium Revised Edition (W/CD)	540/-
81-7635-395-7	Constructing Superior Software	240/-
81-7635-407-4	Teach Yourself Computer Basics in 24 Hours	120/-
81-7635-423-6	The Object Oriented Thought Process	195/-
81-7635-542-9	Business Process Management	270/-
81-7635-576-3	Teach Yourself Object Oriented Programming in 21 Days	240/-
	♦ GTK+	
81-7635-406-6	Teach Yourself GTK+ Programming in 21 Days	240/-
	♦ HOMEPAGE	
81-87105-68-8	Teach Yourself to create HomePage in 24 Hours (W/CD)	180/-
	♦ HTML	
81-7635-238-1	HTML 4 Unleashed - 2nd Rev. Edn.	450/-
81-7635-054-0	HTML 4 How To (W/CD) - Waite Group	399/-
81-87105-94-1	Teach Yourself Dynamic HTML in a week	195/-
81-7635-434-1	Teach Yourself Web Publishing with HTML in 21 Days - Revised Edition	270/-
81-7635-046-X	Dynamic HTML Unleashed	300/-
81-7635-362-0	Teach Yourself HTML 4 in 24 Hours - 4th Rev. Edn.	150/-
81-7635-350-7	Short Order HTML 4	75/-
81-7635-547-X	Teach Yourself HTML with XHTML in 24 Hours - Fifth Edition	195/-
81-7635-562-3	How To Use HTML and XHTML - Visually	180/-
	♦ XHTML	
81-7635-521-6	XHTML (W/CD)	240/-
	♦ ILLUSTRATOR 8	
81-7635-202-0	Teach Yourself Illustrator 8 In 24 Hours	150/-
81-7635-203-9	Adobe Illustrator 8 - Classroom In a Book (W/CD)	270/-
	♦ ILLUSTRATOR 9	
81-7635-458-9	Teach Yourself Adobe Illustrator 9 In 24 Hours	180/
	♦ INFORMIX	
81-87105-37-2	Informix Unleashed (W/CD)	499/
	♦ INTERNET SECURITY	
81-7635-016-8	Internet Security Professional Reference (W/CD)	499/
81-7635-039-7	Maximum Security: A Hacker's Guide to Protecting Your Internet Site and Network (W/CD)	499/

ISBN	TITLE	PRICE

◆ **INTERNET SECURITY**

| 81-7635-564-X | Maximum Security - 3rd Edition (W/CD) .. | 499/- |
| 81-7635-555-0 | Voice & Data Security .... | 399/- |

◆ **INTRANETS**

| 81-7635-023-0 | Intranets Unleashed (W/CD) .... | 499/- |

◆ **INTERNET**

81-7635-259-4	How Internet Works - Millennium Edition ..	540/-
81-7635-097-4	Teach Yourself The Internet Starter Kit in 24 Hours (W/CD)	180/-
81-7635-563-1	How To Use The Internet -Visually	120/-

◆ **INTERNET EXPLORER 5**

| 81-7635-271-3 | Teach Yourself MS Internet Explorer 5 In 24 Hours (W/CD) - Starter Kit ...... | 180/- |

◆ **INTERNET INFORMATION SERVER 5**

| 81-7635-480-5 | MS IIS 5 Administration .... | 240/- |

◆ **JAVA**

81-7635-186-5	Data Structure & Algorithms in Java (W/CD)	270/-
81-87105-61-5	Peter Norton's Guide to JAVA Programming (W/CD)	450/-
81-7635-082-6	JAVA Industrial Strength (W/CD)	450/-
81-7635-223-3	JAVA Distributed Objects (W/CD)	450/-
81-87105-89-5	Object-Oriented Programming in JAVA (W/CD)	450/-
81-7635-185-7	Object-Oriented Design in Java (W/CD) ...	270/-

◆ **JAVA 1.1**

81-87105-38-0	JAVA 1.1 Interactive Course (W/CD) ...	495/-
81-7635-086-9	Maximum JAVA 1.1-(W/CD)	450/-
81-7635-071-0	Teach Yourself More JAVA 1.1 in 21 Days	165/-
81-7635-079-6	Teach Yourself JAVA 1,1 in 21 Days	225/-

◆ **JAVA 1.2**

81-7635-231-4	JAVA 1.2 - How To (W/CD)	360/-
81-7635-218-7	JAVA 1.2 Class Libraries Unleashed (W/CD)	399/-
81-7635-149-0	Teach Yourself JAVA 1.2 In 24 Hours ...	150/-

◆ **JAVA 2**

81-7635-243-8	Teach Yourself JAVA 2 Platform - Professional Reference Edition In 21 Days (W/CD)	450/-
81-7635-509-7	Teach Yourself Java 2 in 24 Hours (Covers SDK 1.3)	180/-
81-7635-492-9	Teach Yourself Java 2 in 21 Days (Covers SDK 1.3)	300/-
81-7635-318-3	JAVA 2 for Professional Developers	399/-
81-7635-304-3	JAVA 2 Platform Unleashed (W/CD) ...	499/-
81-7635-335-3	Java Thread Programming	180/-
81-7635-379-5	Pure Java 2 - A Code Intensive Premium Reference.	195/-
81-7635-390-6	Java Programming on Linux (W/CD) ...	360/-

ISBN	TITLE	PRICE

◆ **JAVA 2**

| 81-7635-538-0 | Wireless Java Programming with J2ME ... | 360/- |
| 81-7635-551-8 | Teach Yourself Wireless JAVA with J2ME in 21 Days (W/CD) .... | 270/- |

◆ **JAVA ENTERPRISE**

| 81-7635-443-0 | Building Java Enterprise System with J2EE (W/CD) .... | 570/- |

◆ **JAVA SCRIPT**

81-87105-39-9	JavaScript Interactive Course (W/CD) .	450/-
81-7635-327-2	Pure Java Script	270/-
81-7635-460-0	JavaScript Unleashed (W/CD) 3rd Edn.	399/-

◆ **JAVA SCRIPT 1.3**

| 81-7635-294-2 | Teach Yourself Java Script 1.3 In 24 Hours .... | 150/- |

◆ **JAVA SCRIPT 1.5**

| 81-7635-497-X | Teach Yourself JavaScript 1.5 in 24 Hours .... | 165/- |

◆ **JAVA SERVLETS**

| 81-7635-535-6 | Developing Java Servlets - 2nd Edn. .... | 300/- |

◆ **JAVA SECURITY**

| 81-7635-489-9 | Java Security Handbook .... | 270/- |

◆ **JAVA GUI**

| 81-7635-333-7 | JAVA GUI Development .... | 240/- |

◆ **JAVABEANS**

| 81-7635-382-5 | JavaBeans Unleashed .... | 299/- |

◆ **JAVA CERTIFICATION**

| 81-7635-323-X | JAVA 2 Certification Training Guide (W/CD)- (Exam 310 -025, 27) .... | 399/- |

◆ **JDBC**

| 81-7635-015-X | Teach Yourself Database Programming with JDBC in 21 Days (W/CD) .... | 275/- |

◆ **JFC**

81-7635-232-2	JFC Unleashed (W/CD)	495/-
81-7635-249-7	Pure: JFC Swing	240/-
81-7635-365-5	Pure JFC 2D Graphics & Imaging	150/-

◆ **JAVA SERVER PAGES**

81-7635-441-4	Pure JSP	150/-
81-7635-504-6	Java Server Pages Applications Development (W/CD)	240/-
81-7635-517-8	Teach Yourself Java Server Pages in 24 Hours (W/CD) - Starter Kit	180/-

◆ **KDE 1.1**

| 81-7635-274-8 | Teach Yourself KDE 1.1 In 24 Hours (W/CD) -Starter Kit .... | 180/- |

◆ **LINUX**

| 81-7635-256-X | Developing LINUX Applications with GTK+ & GDK .... | 240/- |

ISBN	TITLE	PRICE

◆ LINUX

ISBN	TITLE	PRICE
81-7635-295-0	LINUX Unleashed - The Comprehensive Solution (W/ 2CDs) 3rd Edn.	450/-
81-7635-353-1	Peter Norton's Guide to Linux	240/-
81-7535-326-4	Red Hat LINUX 6 Unleashed (W/ 2 CDS)	450/-
81-7635-459-7	Red Hat Linux System Administration Unleashed (W/CD)	450/-
81-7635-499-6	Teach Yourself LINUX in 24 Hours (W/CD) - Starter Kit - 3rd Edition	225/-
81-7635-378-7	GIMP Essential Reference	150/-
81-7635-376-0	Linux Firewalls	195/-
81-7635-392-2	Linux Networking for your Office (W/CD)	240/-
81-7635-390-6	Java Programming on Linux (W/CD)	360/-
81-7635-375-2	Maximum Linux Security (W/CD)	297/-
81-7635-377-9	Linux System Administration	180/-
81-7635-393-0	Linux System Administrator's Survival Guide - 2nd Edn.	297/-
81-7635-394-9	Teach Yourself C for Linux Programming in 21 Days (W/CD)	270/-
81-7635-464-3	Linux Hardware Handbook	270/-
81-7635-546-1	Teach Yourself Linux Security Basics in 24 Hours	180/-
81-7635-554-2	Advanced Linux Programming	180/-

◆ RED HAT LINUX 7

ISBN	TITLE	PRICE
81-7635-503-8	Red Hat Linux 7 Unleashed (W/ 3 CDs)	499/-
81-7635-514-3	Installing Red Hat Linux 7	90/-
81-7635-518-6	Teach Yourself Red hat Linux in 24 Hours (W/2 CDs) - Starter Kit	195/-

◆ LIVE MOTION - ADOBE

ISBN	TITLE	PRICE
81-7635-450-3	Teach Yourself Adobe LiveMotion in 24 Hours	195/-

◆ LOTUS NOTES

ISBN	TITLE	PRICE
81-87105-41-0	LOTUS NOTES & DOMINO Server 4.5 Unleashed (W/CD)	450/-
81-7635-024-9	Teach Yourself LOTUS NOTES 4.5 in 14 Days	195/-

◆ LOTUS NOTES R5

ISBN	TITLE	PRICE
81-7635-370-1	Lotus Notes & Domino R5 Development Unleashed (W/CD)	399/-
81-7635-371-X	Teach Yourself Lotus Notes & Domino R5 Development in 21 Days	225/-
81-7635-336-1	Teach Yourself Lotus Notes R5 in 24 Hours	150/-

◆ LOTUS SMARTSUITE - MILLENNIUM

ISBN	TITLE	PRICE
81-7635-142-3	Teach Yourself Lotus Smartsuite Millennium in 24 Hours	150/-

◆ LDAP

ISBN	TITLE	PRICE
81-7635-090-7	LDAP Programming Directory-Enabled Applications with Lightweight Directory Access Protocol	499/-

◆ MFC

ISBN	TITLE	PRICE
81-87105-80-7	Microsoft Foundation Class 4 Bible (W/CD)	499/-
81-7635-261-6	Teach Yourself MFC In 24 Hours	180/-

◆ MCSD: MICROSOFT CERTIFIED SOLUTION DEVELOPERS

ISBN	TITLE	PRICE
81-7635-267-5	MCSD: Visual Basic 6 - Training Guide (Exam 70-175 & 70-176) (W/CD)	450/-
81-7635-374-4	MCSD: Solution Architecture - Training Guide (Exam 70-100)	399/-

◆ MCSD FAST TRACK SERIES

ISBN	TITLE	PRICE
81-7635-226-8	MCSD Fast Track: Visual Basic 6 - Designing & Implementing Distributed Applications - Exam 70-175	120/-
81-7635-221-7	MCSD Fast Track: Visual Basic 6 - Designing & Implementing Desktop Applications - Exam 70-176	120/-
81-7635-347-7	MCSD : Solutions Architecture	Matsik 120/-

◆ MCSE: MICROSOFT CERTIFIED SOFTWARE ENGINEERS

ISBN	TITLE	PRICE
81-7635-239-X	Networking Essentials - Training Guide (W/CD) - Next Generation	425/-
81-7635-245-4	Windows NT Server 4 - Training Guide (W/CD) - Next Generation	425/-
81-7635-247-0	Windows NT Server 4 Enterprise - Training Guide (W/CD) Revised Edition - Next Generation	425/-
81-7635-246-2	Windows NT Workstation 4 - Training Guide (W/CD) - Next Generation	425/-
81-7635-296-9	SQL Server 7 Database Design Training Guide (W/CD) (Exam 70-029)	425/-
81-7635-290-X	SQL Server 7 Administration Training Guide (W/CD) (Exam 70-028)	425/-
81-87105-44-5	Windows 95 - Training Guide (W/CD)	425/-

◆ MCSE: WINDOWS 2000

ISBN	TITLE	PRICE
81-7635-466-X	Windows 2000 Professional Training Guide (W/CD)	299/-
81-7635-468-6	Windows 2000 Server Training Guide (W/CD)	299/-
81-7635-469-4	Windows 2000 Network Security Design Training Guide (W/CD)	299/-
81-7635-474-0	Windows 2000 Network Infrastructure Training Guide (W/CD)	299/-
81-7635-479-1	Windows 2000 Network Infrastructure Design Training Guide (W/CD)	299/-
81-7635-478-3	Windows 2000 Directory Service Design Training Guide..	299/-
81-7635-477-5	Windows 2000 Directory Service Infrastructure Training Guide..	299/-
81-7635-494-5	Windows 2000 Accelerated (W/CD) Training Guide (Exam 70-240)..	450/-

ISBN	TITLE	PRICE

◆ OLE DB & ADO
81-7635-012-5 Teach Yourself OLE DB and ADO
in 21 Days (W/CD) 275/-

◆ ORACLE
81-87105-02-X Developing Client/Server Applications with
ORACLE Developer/2000 (W/CD) 423/-
81-7635-048-6 Teach Yourself ORACLE 8 in 21 Days . 195/-
81-7635-171-7 OCP Oracle DBA Training Guide (W/CD) 399/-
81-7635-014-1 Teach Yourself PL/SQL in 21 Days (W/CD) . 270/-
81-87105-33-X Developing Personal ORACLE 7 for
WINDOWS 95 Applications (W/CD) . 360/-
81-87105-49-6 ORACLE 7.3 Developer's Guide (W/CD) . 399/-
81-7635-038-9 ORACLE Unleashed (W/CD) -
(2nd Rev. Edn. also Cover Oracle 8) . 599/-
81-87105-60-7 Teach Yourself ORACLE 8 Database
Development in 21 Days (W/CD) 270/-
81-87105-73-9 ORACLE 8 Data Warehousing Unleashed 450/-
81-87105-07-0 ORACLE DBA Survival Guide (W/CD) . 399/-
81-7635-402-3 ORACLE Developer Forms Techniques ... 150/-
81-7635-315-9 ORACLE Development Unleashed -
3rd Edn. (W/CD) 450/-
81-7635-044-3 ORACLE How - TO (W/CD) 375/-
81-87105-08-9 ORACLE Performance Tuning &
Optimization (W/CD) 450/-
81-7635-037-0 ORACLE Electronic Resource Kit
(W/3 CDs) 799/-
81-7635-126-1 ORACLE 8 Server Unleashed 450/-
81-87105-28-3 ORACLE 8 How To - Waite Group 300/-
81-7635-575-5 Programming with Oracle Developer ... 195/-

◆ ORACLE 8i
81-7635-301-9 Teach Yourself ORACLE 8i on WINDOWS
NT In 24 Hours 180/-
81-7635-352-3 Migrating to Oracle 8i 270/-

◆ PREMIERE 5.0 - ADOBE
81-7635-188-2 Adobe Premiere 5.0 - Class Room in a
Book (W/CD) 270/-

◆ PREMIERE 6.0 - ADOBE
81-7635-599-2 How To Use Adobe Premiere 6.0 - Visually 270/-

◆ PAGEMAKER
81-87105-50-X PAGEMAKER 6.5 Complete 360/-

◆ PROGRAMMING LANGUAGE
The Handbook of Programming Language - HPL
81-7635-122-9 Vol. I - Object-Oriented Programming
Language 399/-
81-7635-123-7 Vol. II - Imperative Programming
Languages 240/-
81-7635-124-5 Vol. III - Little Languages & Tools 300/-
81-7635-125-3 Vol. IV - Functional, and Logic Prog.
Languages 210/-

◆ PC - SERVICING / HARDWARE
81-7635-321-1 Peter Norton's Inside The PC -
8th Edition 270/-
81-7635-055-9 Teach Yourself PCs in 24 Hours 150/-
81-7635-260-8 Peter Norton's Complete Guide to
Upgrading & Repairing PCs (Rev. Edn.) 240/-

◆ PC - SERVICING / HARDWARE
81-87105-23-2 Winn Rosch Hardware Bible (W/CD) ... 450/-
81-7635-152-0 Teach Yourself Upgrading & Fixing
PC's in 24 Hours 135/-

◆ PERL
81-87105-70-4 PERL 5 How - To (W/CD) 399/-
81-87105-51-8 PERL 5 Interactive Course (W/CD) 495/-
81-7635-263-2 Teach Yourself PERL in 21 Days Rev. Edn. 240/-
81-7635-360-4 Teach Yourself Perl in 24 Hours -
Starter Kit (W/CD) 150/-

◆ PHOTO DRAW 2000
81-7635-420-1 Short Order MS PhotoDRAW 2000 .... 75/-

◆ PHOTOSHOP 4 -ADOBE
81-87105-06-2 Adobe PhotoShop 4 Interactive Course
(W/CD) 495/-
81-87105-12-7 Inside Adobe PhotoShop 4 (W/CD) 399/-
81-87105-10-0 PhotoShop 4 Complete (W/CD) 450/-
81-7635-070-2 PhotoShop 4 Studio Skills (W/CD) 195/-
81-87105-69-0 Teach Yourself PhotoShop 4 in 24 Hours .. 120/-
81-7635-069-9 Teach Yourself PhotoShop 4
in 14 Days (W/CD) 180/-

◆ PHOTOSHOP 5 - ADOBE
81-7635-214-4 Adobe PhotoShop 5 - How To (W/CD) 399/-

◆ PHOTOSHOP 5.5 - ADOBE
81-7635-355-8 Short Order Adobe Photoshop 5.5 .... 99/-
81-7635-372-8 Teach Yourself Adobe Photoshop 5.5
in 24 Hours 150/-
81-7635-387-6 Adobe Photoshop 5.5 Fundamentals -
with ImageReady2 (W/CD) 195/-
81-7635-429-5 Adobe Photoshop 5.5 Classroom In a Book
(W/CD) 275/-
81-7635-425-2 Inside Adobe Photoshop 5.5 (W/CD) .. 399/-

◆ PHOTOSHOP 6 - ADOBE
81-7635-502-X Teach Yourself Adobe Photoshop 6
in 24 Hours 195/-
81-7635-519-4 Inside Adobe Photoshop 6 (W/CD) 450/-
81-7635-527-5 Photoshop 6 Web Magic (W/CD) 240/-
81-7635-556-9 Photohop 6 - Down & dirty Tricks 180/-
81-7635-560-7 How To Use Adobe Photoshop 6 - Visually . 165/-
81-7635-570-4 Photoshop 6 Effect Magic (W/CD) 225/-

◆ PHP 4
81-7635-515-1 PHP Developer's Cookbook 240/-
81-7635-456-2 Teach Yourself PHP 4 in 24 Hours 165/-
81-7635-461-9 Web Applications Development
with PHP 4.0 (W/CD) 270/-

◆ POSTFIX
81-7635-537-2 PostFix 450/-

◆ POWERBUILDER 5.0
81-87105-30-5 Power Builder 5 Unleashed (W/CD) 450/-
81-87105-14-3 Power Builder 5 HOW - TO (W/CD) 399/-

◆ POWERBUILDER 6.0
81-7635-049-4 PowerBuilder 6.0 Unleashed (W/CD) .. 450/-

ISBN	TITLE	PRICE
	◆ POWERBUILDER 7.0	
81-7635-381-7	PowerBuilder 7.0 Unleashed (W/CD) ..	499/-
	◆ POWERPOINT 97	
81-7635-004-4	Teach Yourself MS Power Point 97 in 24 Hours	135/-
	◆ POWERPOINT 2000	
81-7635-287-X	Teach Yourself MS Power Point 2000 In 24 Hours	165/-
	◆ PL / SQL	
81-7635-388-4	Teach Yourself PL/SQL in 21 Days - 2nd Edn.	270/-
	◆ PUBLISHER 2000	
81-7635-320-5	Teach Yourself MS Publisher 2000 In 24 Hours	150/-
	◆ PROJECT 98	
81-7635-179-2	Teach Yourself MS Project 98 in 24 Hours	150/-
	◆ PROJECT 2000	
81-7635-439-2	Teach Yourself MS Project 2000 in 24 Hours	225/-
	◆ QUARK XPRESS 4	
81-7635-073-7	Teach Yourself QUARK Express 4 in 14 Days (W/CD)	180/-
	◆ SAMBA	
81-7635-272-1	Teach Yourself SAMBA In 24 Hours (W/CD)-Starter Kit	180/-
	◆ SAP R/3	
81-7635-118-0	SAP R/3 Implementation	360/-
81-7635-311-6	Teach Yourself SAP R/3 In 24 Hours ...	165/-
	◆ SOFTWARE TESTING	
81-7635-507-0	Software Testing	450/-
	◆ SOLARIS 2.6	
81-7635-414-7	Solaris 2.6 Administrator Certification Training Guide Part-I (W/CD)	150/-
81-7635-415-5	Solaris 2.6 Administrator Certification Training Guide Part-II (W/CD)	150/-
	◆ SOLARIS 7	
81-7635-496-1	Solaris 7 Administration Certification Training Guide (Vol. I & II) (W/CD)	360/-
	◆ SOLARIS 8	
81-7635-582-8	Solaris 8 Network Administrator Certification Training Guide (W/CD)	390/-
	◆ SMS	
81-7635-411-2	SMS 2 Administration	150/-
	◆ SYBASE	
81-87105-27-5	Sybase SQL Server 11 Unleashed (W/CD)	499/-
	◆ SOAP	
81-7635-438-4	Understanding SOAP	300/-

ISBN	TITLE	PRICE
	◆ SQL	
81-87105-83-6	SQL Unleashed (W/CD)	499/-
81-7635-364-7	Teach Yourself SQL in 21 Days - Rev. Edn.	195/-
81-7635-098-2	Teach Yourself SQL in 24 Hours	150/-
	◆ SQL SERVER 6.5 - MICROSOFT	
81-87105-52-6	MS SQL Server 6.5 Unleashed (W/CD) ...	450/-
81-7635-101-6	Teach Yourself MS-SQL Server 6.5 in 21 Days	195/-
	◆ SQL SERVER 7 - MICROSOFT	
81-7635-211-X	SQL Server 7 System Administration ..	300/-
81-7635-219-5	Teach Yourself MS SQL Server 7 in 21 Days	225/-
81-7635-373-6	Teach Yourself SQL Server 7 in 24 Hours .	150/-
81-7635-250-0	MS SQL Server 7 DBA Survival Guide (W/CD)	450/-
81-7635-306-X	MS SQL Server 7 Programming Unleashed	399/-
81-7635-297-7	MS SQL Server 7 Unleashed (W/CD) .	360/-
	◆ SQL SERVER 2000 - MICROSOFT	
81-7635-485-6	Writing Stored Procedure for MS SQL Server (Covers SQL Server 7.0 & 2000)	240/-
81-7635-500-3	Teach Yourself SQL Server 2000 in 21 Days (W/CD)	270/-
	◆ TRANSACT - SQL	
81-7635-011-7	Teach Yourself TRANSACT - SQL in 21 Days	225/-
	◆ TCP/IP	
81-7635-060-5	Inside TCP/IP - 3rd Edition	300/-
81-87105-90-9	Networking with Microsoft TCP/IP (W/CD)	450/-
81-7635-040-0	Teach Yourself TCP/IP in 14 Days - 2nd Edition	150/-
81-7635-544-5	Teach Yourself TCP/IP In 24 Hours	165/-
81-7635-077-X	TCP/IP Blueprints (W/CD)	360/-
81-7635-151-2	Teach Yourself TCP/IP Network Administration In 21 Days	195/-
81-7635-386-8	TCP/IP Unleashed	399/-
	◆ TURBO C++	
81-87105-75-5	Teach Yourself TURBO C++ 4.5 for WINDOWS in 21 Days	270/-
	◆ TCL/TK	
81-7635-368-X	Teach Yourself TCL/TK in 24 Hours	180/-
	◆ UNIX	
81-7635-072-9	Exploring The UNIX System - Third Revised Edition	150/-
81-7635-233-0	Teach Yourself UNIX In 24 Hours - Revised Edition	180/-
81-7635-113-X	Teach Yourself UNIX SHELL Programming in 14 Days	165/-
81-7635-303-5	Teach Yourself Shell Programming in 24 Hours	150/-
81-7635-354-X	Teach Yourself UNIX System Administration in 21 Days	297/-

◆ UNIX

ISBN	TITLE	PRICE
81-7635-389-2	Unix Primer Plus - 3rd Edn.	150/-
81-7635-075-3	UNIX System V Primer - Waite Group	150/-
81-7635-236-5	UNIX Unleashed (W/CD) (3rd Edition)	499/-
81-7635-059-1	UNIX Unleashed, Internet Edition (W/CD)	450/-
81-7635-241-1	UNIXWARE 7 - System Administration - SCO	225/-
81-7635-491-0	Advanced UNIX Programming	225/-

◆ UML

ISBN	TITLE	PRICE
81-7635-314-0	Teach Yourself UML In 24 Hours (W/CD)	150/-
81-7635-398-1	Designing Flexible Object-Oriented System with UML	195/-
81-7635-412-0	A UML Pattern Language	150/-

◆ VISUAL BASIC 5

ISBN	TITLE	PRICE
81-7635-085-0	Doing Objects in MS VISUAL BASIC 5 -(W/CD)	360/-
81-87105-25-9	Teach Yourself VISUAL BASIC 5 in 24 Hours (W/CD)	180/-
81-87105-18-6	Teach Yourself VISUAL BASIC 5 in 21 Days	270/-
81-7635-109-1	Teach Yourself VISUAL BASIC 5 in 21 Days (W/CD) Vol. II	210/-
81-87105-26-7	Teach Yourself DATABASE Programming with Visual Basic 5 in 21 Days (W/CD)	330/-
81-7635-105-9	Teach Yourself MORE Visual Basic 5 in 21 Days	195/-
81-7635-022-2	Visual Basic for Applications Unleashed (W/CD)(Covers Office 97, Internet, Active X)	399/-
81-87105-53-4	Visual Basic 5 Interactive Course (W/CD)	495/-
81-87105-54-2	Visual Basic 5 Client/Server How-To (W/CD)	450/-
81-87105-24-0	Visual Basic 5 Developer's Guide (W/CD)	399/-
81-7635-053-2	Visual Basic 5 How-To (W/CD)	375/-
81-7635-052-4	Visual Basic 5 Database How-To (W/CD)	450/-
81-7635-042-7	Visual Basic 5 Development Unleashed (W/CD)	300/-
81-7635-088-5	Visual Basic 5 Programmer's Guide to the WIN 32 API-(W/CD)	599/-
81-87105-72-0	Visual Basic 5 Fundamentals Unleashed (W/CD)	360/-

◆ VISUAL BASIC 6

ISBN	TITLE	PRICE
81-7635-222-5	Database Developer Guide with Visual Basic 6 (W/CD)	495/-
81-7635-228-4	Doing Objects in Visual Basic 6	399/-
81-7635-244-6	Database Access with Visual Basic 6 (W/CD)	399/-
81-7635-487-2	Internationalization with Visual Basic (W/CD)	300/-
81-7635-276-4	MTS Programming with Visual Basic - The Authoritative Solution (W/CD)	299/-
81-7635-145-8	Peter Norton's Guide to Visual Basic 6 (W/CD)	270/-
81-7635-328-0	Pure Visual Basic	135/-

◆ VISUAL BASIC 6

ISBN	TITLE	PRICE
81-7635-173-3	Teach Yourself Database Programming with Visual Basic 6 in 21 Days (W/CD)	270/-
81-7635-207-1	Teach Yourself Database Programming with Visual Basic 6 in 24 hours	165/-
81-7635-229-2	Teach Yourself Internet Programming with Visual Basic 6 in 21 Days	195/-
81-7635-139-3	Teach Yourself More Visual Basic 6 in 21 Days	240/-
81-7635-150-4	Teach Yourself Visual Basic 6 in 21 Days	270/-
81-7635-413-9	Teach Yourself Visual Basic 6 in 24 Hours (W/CD)	180/-
81-7635-190-3	Visual Basic 6 Client Server - How to (W/CD)	399/-
81-7635-177-6	Visual Basic 6 - How To (W/CD)	399/-
81-7635-146-6	Visual Basic 6 - Unleashed (W/CD)	375/-
81-7635-220-9	Visual Basic 6 Source Code Library (W/CD)	399/-
81-7635-269-1	Visual Basic 6 - Super Bible (W/CD)	575/-
81-7635-176-8	Visual Basic 6 Interactive Course (W/CD)	499/-
81-7635-181-4	Visual Basic 6 Database - How to (W/CD)	399/-
81-7635-180-6	Teach Yourself OOP with VB in 21 Days (W/CD)	225/-
81-7635-438-4	Developing Secure Applications with Visual Basic	225/-

◆ VBSCRIPT

ISBN	TITLE	PRICE
81-87105-55-0	VBSCRIPT Interactive Course (W/CD)	495/-

◆ VISUAL C++ 5

ISBN	TITLE	PRICE
81-7635-080-X	Teach Yourself VISUAL C++ 5 in 24 Hours	150/-
81-87105-19-4	Teach Yourself Visual C++ 5 in 21 Days	270/-
81-87105-71-2	VISUAL C++ 5 Developer's Guide	450/-
81-87105-16-X	VISUAL C++ 5 Unleashed (W/CD)	450/-

◆ VISUAL C++ 6

ISBN	TITLE	PRICE
81-7635-196-2	Teach Yourself Database Programming with Visual C++ 6 in 21 Days (W/CD)	270/-
81-7635-135-0	Teach Yourself Visual C++ 6 in 21 Days	270/-
81-7635-136-9	Teach Yourself Visual C++ 6 in 24 Hours	135/-
81-7635-309-4	MFC Programming with Visual C++ 6 Unleashed (W/CD)	450/-
81-7635-467-8	Visual C++ 6 Unleashed (W/CD)	450/-

◆ VISUAL J++ 6

ISBN	TITLE	PRICE
81-7635-213-6	Teach Yourself Visual J++ 6 In 21 Days	195/-

◆ VISUAL INTERDEV 6

ISBN	TITLE	PRICE
81-7635-399-X	Teach Yourself Database Programming with Visual InterDev 6 in 21 Days	270/-
81-7635-143-1	Teach Yourself Visual InterDev 6 In 21 Days	180/-
81-7635-275-6	Visual InterDev 6 Unleashed (W/CD)	399/-
81-7635-334-5	Teach Yourself Visual InterDev 6 In 24 Hours	165/-

ISBN	TITLE	PRICE

◆ WINDOWS NT 4 - SERVER

ISBN	TITLE	PRICE
81-7635-265-9	Teach Yourself WINDOWS NT Server 4 In 21 Days	270/-
81-87105-59-3	Peter Norton's Maximizing Windows NT Server 4	399/-

◆ WINDOWS NT 4 - WORKSTATION

| 81-87105-62-3 | Peter Norton's Complete Guide to Windows NT 4 Workstation | 450/- |
| 81-7635-062-1 | Teach Yourself NT Workstation 4 in 24 Hours | 165/- |

◆ WINDOWS NT / 2000

81-7635-457-0	Windwos NT/2000 The Thin Client Solution	240/-
81-7635-430-9	Windows NT /2000 ADSI Scripting for System Administrations	399/-
81-7635-482-1	Windows NT/2000 Network Secutiry	195/-

◆ WIRELESS NETWORKING

| 81-7635-089-3 | Wireless Networking Handbook | 499/- |

◆ WEB

81-87105-74-7	Teach Yourself How To Become A Webmaster in 14 Days (W/CD)	210/-
81-87105-86-0	Creating Commercial Web Pages (W/CD)	450/-
81-87105-17-8	Adobe WEB Design & Publishing Unleashed (W/CD)	450/-
81-7635-063-X	Designing Interactive Websites (W/CD)	270/-
81-7635-400-7	Teach Yourself To Create Web Pages in 24 Hours - Starter Kit (W/CD)	165/-

◆ WEB

81-7635-026-5	Teach Yourself Active Web Database Programming in 21 Days (W/CD)	399/-
81-87105-68-2	Most Popular Web Sites (W/CD)	480/-
81-87105-91-7	Web Site Construction Kit for WIN 95 (W/CD)	270/-
81-87105-42-9	Macromedia Web Publishing - Unleashed (W/CD)	450/-
81-7635-051-6	Dynamic Web Publishing Unleashed, (HTML, JavaScript, Java, CGI, Style Sheets) Second Edition	300/-
81-7635-534-8	Web Objects, Web Applications Construction Kit	240/-
81-87105-85-2	World Wide WEB Directory (W/CD)	450/-
81-87105-84-4	World Wide WEB Yellow Pages (W/CD)	450/-

◆ WEB AUTHORING

| 81-87105-95-X | Web Authoring Desk Reference | 450/- |

◆ XML

81-7635-549-6	XML-Internationalization and Localization	225/-
81-7635-476-7	Applied XML Solutions (W/CD)	180/-
81-7635-268-3	Teach Yourself XML In 21 Days	165/-
81-7635-380-9	XML Unleashed (W/CD)	399/-
81-7635-471-6	Teach Yourself XML In 24 Hours	165/-
81-7635-501-1	XML Development with Java 2 (W/CD)	270/-
81-7635-590-9	Microsoft .NET XML Web Services	240/-
81-7635-505-4	Inside XML	399/-
81-7635-559-3	XML, XSLT, JAVA, AND JSP	360/-
81-7635-565-8	XML for ASP.net Developers	225/-